PERFORMANCE APPRAISAL IN LIBRARIES

PERFORMANCE APPRAISAL IN LIBRARIES

G. PRABHAKAR
K. SOMESEKHARA RAO

AKANSHA PUBLISHING HOUSE
NEW DELHI • GUWAHATI • VISAKHAPATNAM

AKANSHA PUBLISHING HOUSE
4649-B/21, Ansari Road
Darya Ganj, New Delhi - 110 002
Ph.: 23263193 / 9811582579 / 09435116718
Fax: 011-23263193
Email: ektabooks@yahoo.com
www.akanshapublishinghouse.com

Performance Appraisal in Libraries

First Published 2011
ISBN 978-81-8370-281-2

[The responsibility for the facts stated, conclusions reached etc., is entirely that of the author. The publisher is not responsible for them, whatsoever.]

PRINTED IN INDIA

Published by Akansha Publishing House, New Delhi and Printed at Hermain Offset Press, Delhi.

Acknowledgements

We profusely thank Dr. P. Bhaskara Rao, Associate Professor. I would like to acknowledge with thanks the cooperation extended by Prof. M. Vivekananda Murty, Head, Department of Statistics, Andhra University for his academic support.

We express our sincere thanks and gratitude to Dr. K.S.S. Rama Raju Professor, MVGR College of Engineering, Vizianagaram, for his academic advice support to accomplish this work.

We convey our sincere gratitude towards our beloved Lord Amma and Bhagavan, who helped us in this work. We would like to acknowledge with thanks the co-operation extended by Sri K.V.S.S.N. Murthy, Secretary and Correspondent, Dr. P. Prasad, Principal and Sri. Ch. Suryanarayana, Ex-Principal, and Staff of SDS(A) College of Arts and Applied Sciences, Shreeramnagar, Vizianagaram, for their moral support.

We are highly indebted to the Library professionals of all Universities for their cooperation extended in responding to the questionnaires in a short time. It is not an abatement to furnish all their names, but lack of space. Our thanks are due to professional colleagues of Dr. V.S. Krishna Library, Andhra University for their support.

My (G. Prabhakar) whole hearted gratitude to my parents G. Mohan Rao, G. Surya Kantham and my thanks are due to my sister G. Pragathi and life partner Smt. G. Sridevi for their co-operation and support to complete this task. My special thanks are extended to my family for their cooperation and support to complete this task.

Our thanks are also extended to our friends and research colleagues, Dr. V. Neerkshna Babu, Dr. C. Nageswara Rao, Mr. T. Sai Ramesh, Dr. G.A. Prasad Rao, Mr. K. Durga Prasad, Mr. G. Ayya Babu, Mr. M. Venkata Rao, Mr. L. Satyanarayana, Mr. S. Siva Prasad and other scholars, who have provided valuable suggestions to accomplish this work.

Our final nay, paramount gratitude to Dr. M. Sudhakar Babu, Population Research Centre Visakhapatnam, for his valuable guidance during data entry, tabulation and analysis of my research work, and also our sincere thanks go to Mr. D. Appa Rao, and Mr. P. Prasada Rao for their patience and talent exhibited in typing and printing of this research work neatly.

We are responsible and pardonable for shortcomings and omissions.

G. PRABHAKAR
K. SOMESEKHARA RAO

Contents

Abbreviations

AACR	:	Anglo American Cataloguing Rules
ALA	:	American Library Association
ANGRAU	:	Acharya N.G.Ranga Agricultural University
AP	:	Andhra Pradesh
APPSC	:	Andhra Pradesh Public Service Commission
APSWAN	:	Andhra Pradesh Social Welfare Network
AU	:	Andhra University
BLISc	:	Bachelor of Library and Information Science
CAT	:	Common Admission Test
CCF	:	Common Communication Format
CD-ROM	:	Compact Disk-Read Only Memory
CDS/ISIS	:	Computerized Documentation System/ Integrated Set of Information System
CLISc	:	Certificate of Library and Information Science
CR	:	Confidential Report
CT	:	Central Tendency
DBMS	:	Database Management System
DCA	:	Diploma in Computer Applications
DDC	:	Dewey Decimal Classification
DOS	:	Disk Operating System
Dr.BRAOU	:	Dr. B.R. Ambedkar Open University
DVD	:	Digital Versatile Disk
EIS	:	Electronic Information Services
e-Mail	:	Electronic Mail

e-Valued	:	Electronic Valued
GMAT	:	Graduate Management Admission Test
GRE	:	Graduate Record Examination
IFLA	:	International Federation for Library Association
ILA	:	Indian Library Association
INFLIBNET	:	Information Library and Network
INFONET	:	Information Network
IT	:	Information Technology
JNTU	:	Jawaharlal Nehru Technological University
KU	:	Kakatiya University
LAN	:	Local Area Network
LCD	:	Liquid Crystal Display
LIS	:	Library and Information Science
LISIM	:	The Library and Information Sector Improvement Model
M.Phil	:	Master of Philosophy
MARC	:	Machine Readable Catalogue
MBO	:	Management By Objectives
MEDLINE	:	Medical Library Network
MHRD	:	Ministry of Human Resource Development
MLISc	:	Master of Library and Information Science
NAAC	:	National Assessment and Accreditation Council
NTRHU	:	Nandamuri Taraka Rama Rao Health University
NU	:	Acharya Nagarjuna University
OCLC	:	Online Computer Library Centre
OCLS	:	Online Catalogues Service
OPAC	:	Online Public Access Catalogue
OU	:	Osmania University
PA	:	Performance Appraisal
PDMU	:	Padmavathi Mahila University

PERT	:	Programme Evaluation and Review Technique
PG	:	Post Graduation
PGDCA	:	Post Graduate Diploma in Computer Applications
PGDLAN	:	Post Graduate Diploma in Library Automation and Networking
Ph.D	:	Doctor of Philosophy
PSTU	:	Potti Sreeramulu Telugu University
R&D	:	Research and Development
S&T	:	Science and Technology
SDI	:	Selective Dissemination of Information
SKDU	:	Sree Krishna Devaraya University
SOUL	:	Software for University Libraries
SPSS	:	Statistical Package for Social Sciences
SVU	:	Sree Venkateswara University
T&D	:	Training and Development
TOFEL	:	Test of English as a Foreign Language
TQM	:	Total Quality Management
UG	:	Under Graduate
UGC	:	University Grants Commission
UK	:	United Kingdom
UOH	:	University of Hyderabad
USA	:	United States of America
VCR	:	Video Cassette Recording
VDU	:	Visual Display Unit
VSNL	:	Videsh Sanchar Nigam Limited
WAN	:	Wide Area Network
www	:	World Wide Web

1

Introduction

Human resources constitute an important input for any productivity. Therefore, reasonable emphasis should be given for the development of human resources in order to achieve the defined objectives and goals in industries and organizations. For various reasons, the product is being influenced by several factors such as social, economical, technical, etc. The organizations have to develop the products up to the level of satisfaction of their ultimate customers in order to withstand competition. For this, sufficient application of technology and thorough understanding of customer requirements are to be considered, and studied from time to time. In this context, the employee's attitudes, opinions, acceptability etc., are to be understood as and when the new technologies or new concepts applied in organizations. In order to cope up with the technological changes, the employees need to be sensitized to the required changes through self-renewal methods, otherwise it would be impossible to achieve the goals of the organization. In a sense, personal efficiency of an employee becomes very important. Generally, the factors that contribute to the personal efficiency are motivation, self-awareness, proactiveness and action orientation. The employee needs to change not only benefiting the organization but also to keep up his own interest. The employee should realize that acceptance and adaption to changes is necessary for their development as well as survival. Therefore, self-awareness of an individual is one of the important factors to meet the goals of an organization, and holds good in libraries.

It is not only a self-assessment in their work environment, but also it allows them to express their interests and disinterests, likes and dislikes, personal problems, etc. The satisfaction of the employee in all aspects both in his personal life and work life will lead to the organizational growth otherwise the organization may not get proper results up to it's expatiation.

The strength of any individual lies only in his capabilities. If an individual performs his functions efficiently by recognizing his strength and weaknesses, identifying the hidden talents, and by developing skills and contribute them to the maximum extent possible to his parental organization, he is likely to be dynamic and he will grow fast when compared with his colleagues. Ultimately, the individual can accomplish a variety of tasks for his parental organization's goals in a multi-dimensional way.

It is necessary for any employee in an organization to develop and mould himself / herself in accordance with the latest technological changes occurred in the field of work. The appropriate answer to this issue is, training for employees. Therefore, the organization should take necessary steps to conduct training programmmes for their employees to develop product in such a way to withstand in competitions. Individuals are not static and they will change by acquiring new knowledge, skills, attitudes and beliefs. Once the training is completed, they may also get an opportunity to demonstrate certain hidden skills for which they may not get a proper platform for performing those functions before. The employees can find new capabilities within themselves or learn to interact with each other more productively after they have received for sufficient training. To understand the changes in human behaviour, once effort would not yield perfect results. It would be better to allow the individuals to express their opinions on their behaviour, by giving them a pre-determined set or questionnaire from time to time.

Every human being has a necessity to grow and develop both professionally and personally. Development of individual's capabilities will keep him abreast of the latest technological changes occurred in his field of interest. This development needs to be monitored frequently by the individuals to match with their parental organization's requirements, which will enable the individuals to aware about the right and mis-leaded tracks.

Therefore, the above discussion points out a need for the 'Assessment'. As everybody knows, assessment means assessing or estimating a pre-defined objective, which may include individuals, group of persons, employees, organizations etc. This can be assessed by individuals about themselves or by others. Assessment is a good mechanism to lead individual's performance in a better way. As mentioned in the above stages, individuals need to develop their capabilities by themselves only. For that, they need the present status on their performance, which demands Assessment. Through this Assessment, every individual knows about himself in a better way and can try to accomplish his parental organization's objectives and goals in the best possible way.

For several reasons, assessment in libraries becomes necessary. This assessment activity is more important in such libraries where the number of professionals is more, offers different services, budget limitations, application of information technology etc., the libraries are broadly categorized into – public, academic and special. Since, the present study is aimed to study the university library system and the issues relating to professionals working in these libraries. Therefore, it would be necessary to understand functions and objectives of school, college and University libraries.

ACADEMIC LIBRARIES

Academic Libraries are the libraries established in academic institutions to support teaching and research activities of students, researchers and teachers.

Library occupies an important place in the framework of the academic system and it is a dynamic instrument for education. According to Sahai[1], the prime objectives of the library in an academic system are:

- conservation of knowledge and information;
- expansion of ideals and dissemination, research and publication; and
- dissemination of knowledge through teaching and extension services.

The academic libraries include libraries in schools, colleges and Universities. All these cater to the needs of the academic community for supplementing the study and research programmes of the institutions and help to conserve and disseminate the knowledge.

School Libraries

A school library is a part and parcel of school set-up. It is established to serve the objectives of its parent organization. A school library can play a very important role in helping the educational system to achieve its goals at the gross root level. The aim of a good school library is to supplement the class work and to develop reading habits in the children. In fact, it is the responsibility of school libraries to cultivate the reading habits among the children right from their childhood which will enable the children to compete themselves with the present competitive world.

College Libraries

The objective of a college library is to supplement the instructions imparted in the classroom. It aims to function as an independent teaching agency, encouraging and promoting the use of books in the ways beyond those suggested or required by the classroom.

The college library functions basically to assist and support the study and teaching in the respective college. It helps to meet the reading requirements of the students as well as the teachers of the college.

Randall and Francis[2] stated that, to meet the educational objectives of a college, its library has to perform the following functions:

- Make available to the students, books and allied reading material relevant to the courses offered in the college;
- Make available the books and documents required by faculty members in preparation of their instructional courses;
- Provide supplementary books and reading material to helps in study and teaching at the college;
- Provide comprehensive selection of authoritative books and documents needed by the faculty members to pursue their research programmes;
- Promote the proper use of reading material available in the stock; and
- Train the students in making use of the library properly and derive full advantage of it, by integrating the library with the educational courses.

The objective of college libraries should be emphasized on the provision of latest information to users, support to user studies, etc. In order to cope with these activities, the professionals should be given an opportunity to learn the skills in IT from time to time.

University Libraries

Generally, a University should stands for truth, reason, tolerance and humanism. It helps in the progress of the universe and thereby adds to the well being of a nation and it's people. The task of a university is no longer confined to the traditional functions of teaching and advancement of knowledge.

Objectives of University Libraries

- To support and facilitate the research, learning, teaching and administrative activities of the University; by organizing, maintaining and providing access to appropriate literature and information resources in such a way as to provide optimum benefit for library users;
- To supply services and expertise designed actively to promote the effective exploitation of library and information resources, including the teaching of transferable information handling skills;
- To provide an appropriate and comfortable environment, accommodation and facilities to the user community for the use of library resources and for individual and group study.

Functions of University Libraries[3]

In the contemporary world, the broad functions of the university are, briefly identified as follows[3]:

- To pursue the truth, explore and cultivate new knowledge and interpret the old knowledge and beliefs in the light of the contemporary needs and necessities;

- It should strive to promote equality, liberty, fraternity and justice to the people and reduce the social and cultural gap in the society by disseminating knowledge and information;
- To diffuse and foster the real values and attitudes, amongst the teachers and students necessary for attaining good citizenship, create a happy and assuring life for the people, besides developing the society.
- It should impart knowledge to the students in the fields of science, arts, agriculture, engineering and technology, medicine and various other subjects and give professional and vocational training for the development of the nation and the people.

Modern University Libraries play a pivotal role in the success of higher education not only in India but also in the remaining places of the world. Teaching, research and extension services are the three major aims of a modern university library. Louis and Tauber[4] assigned six functions to the university library. They are:

- Conservation of knowledge and idea;
- Teaching;
- Research;
- Publication;
- Extension services; and
- Interpretation.

Dr. S. Radhakrishnan has rightly said about the importance of University Library in the report of "University Education Commission"[5] as 'the library is the heart of University work directly so as regards its research work and indirectly as regards its educational work, which derives its life from research work. Scientific research needs library as well as its laboratories, which for humanistic research, the library is both library and laboratory in one", Kothari Commission also says that no university, college or department should be set-up without taking into account its library needs in terms of staff, books, journals and building. Nothing could be more damaging to a growing department than to neglect its library or to give it a low priority. On contrary the library should be a centre of attraction on college and university campus.

India Education Commission (1964-66)[6] stressed the need to develop university library system in the country and recommended that, a university library should:

- provide resources necessary for research in field of special interest to the university;
- aid the university faculty in keeping abreast of latest developments in their respective field;
- provide library facilities and services necessary for the success of all formal programmes of instruction;
- open the doors to the wide world of books which would lies beyond the borders of one's own field of specialization;
- bring the books, students and the scholars together under same conditions which should encourage reading for pleasure, self-discovery, personal growth and the sharpening of intellectual curiosity".

The observations about the university library are:

- The library is the heart of education;
- Methods and fashion in education change from generation to generation, but each generation uses the library as a means of realizing its items; hence the library remains the great conservator of learning;
- A quality education is impossible without a well equipped qualitative and quantitative library;

- You can't have a qualitative faculty without a qualitative library;
- The library is vital to proper exploitation of our intellectual resources;
- A library is essential for the maintenance of free access to ideas and to the functioning of a untrammeled mind.

Thus the objective of university libraries demands the continuous improvement of professional skills to attend information requirements of users. Therefore, the professionals should develop a kind of attitude towards the learning of latest developments in IT. A good academic library has its complete identification with its institution. The measure of its excellence is the extent to which its resources and services support the institution's academic pursuits. A well-administered university library should direct its activities towards the fulfilment of these functions. By accumulating and organizing the reading material, a university library should play an important role in the conservation of knowledge.

Growth and Development of University Libraries in India

Cultural advancement and technological development in a society is a continuous process, but cannot take place overnight. Today, tremendous progress has taken place in all sectors of the society. For improvement in a particular sector can be better understood if there is information regarding the situation over a period in the past. The past information in a recorded form facilitates for development in other words. So, the best utilization of this available information for a longer period will only be possible by storing it in a safest place. For which, there must be some storehouses for the information available in the society, which in turn were called as libraries.

Pre-Independence Period

Before getting Independence, India had its first University at Bihar named as 'Nalanda University'. This University had a well-designed library named as 'Dharma-ganja' which has a huge collection and well-equipped staff to cater the needs of their academic community in a best way. This University Library was the oldest and first academic library established in the history of India. After the Nalanda University, many other well-known universities have been established viz., Vikramshila (Bihar), Taxila (Punjab), Vallabhi (in Kathiawar) etc., with beautifully functioned big libraries. Any how, till know the Nalanda University library was the biggest store house of knowledge in Asian Continent. In 1857, on the recommendations made by 'Woods Education Commission' appointed by British Government, three modern Universities have been established in the presidency states viz., Bombay, Calcutta and Madras on par with the model of London University. But their concerned university libraries have been established in the later years. These facts reveal our keen interest on storing the information available on the society and in the society even before getting independence.

Post-Independence Period

After attaining the Independence in 1947, the Government of India recognized the importance of Higher Education and research activities, which contributes a lot for the development of a society. So, to suggest some better changes in the existed educational system, Government of India has appointed a commission for University education (Dec 1948-Aug 1949) under the chairmanship of Dr. S. Radhakrishnan. Based on the recommendations made by this commission, some changes have been taken place in the existed educational system up to some extent by the Government of India in consonance with the changing socio-economic and political conditions of the country. The

Commission recognized the importance of University Libraries and made some recommendations about their betterment in it's report. The Commission emphasized the importance of University Libraries in a way that for scientific research, there is a need of both laboratory and library, where as in case of social sciences and humanities research, library alone will act as both laboratory and library. Though the commission's recommendations were implemented up to some extent, it is not satisfactory in it's practical context.

In order to make the above-mentioned activities as best productive ones, there should be some independent mechanism to look after their functioning. So, the Government of India established an independent statutory authority named as UGC in the year 1956. The main motto behind this establishment is to support the above-mentioned activities in both financial media and some other media if necessary. Since the establishment of UGC, it supports the maximum number of university libraries and some other aided Under-Graduate academic libraries, which come under the higher education in both financial terms and teaching activities. Prior to the establishment of UGC, no recognizable and systematic study was made at the national level to find out whether the functioning of university libraries is in accordance with it's aims and objectives or not. Today there are more than 300 universities and about 50 institutions deemed as universities. Almost all the universities have their libraries with huge collection, well-equipped staff and furniture.

To organize and manage the collections in University Libraries a well-trained professionals are necessary. To offer variety of information services, the staff should be equipped with latest technologies particularly in information processing and handling. The professionals need to be trained from time to time to update their knowledge. The funding agencies of university libraries have expressed their inability to provide all budgetary requirements. At the same time the demands from users are increasing for several reasons, the only option left is to use the services of professionals systematically and scientifically. Therefore, an attempt is made to understand the profession, assessment methods in libraries etc.

REFERENCES

1. Sahai, Shrinath: *Academic Library System*. New Delhi, Allied, 1990, p.1.
2. Randall, W.M. and Francis, Z.G: *Principles of College Library Administration*. Chicago, American Library Association, 1936, p.19.
3. http://www.lboro.ac.uk/library/objectives.html
4. Sahai, Shrinath: *Academic Library System*. New Delhi, Allied, 1990, p.26
5. Wilson, Louis Round and Tauber, Maurice: *The University Library – The Organization, Administration and Functions of Academic Libraries*, 2nd Ed. New York, Columbia University Press, 1958, p.16.
6. Government of India, Ministry of Education, *Report of the University Education Commission*, Vol.1, New Delhi, Dec.1948–Aug.1949.
7. Government of India, Ministry of Education, *Report of the Education Commission 1964-66*, New Delhi, Education and National Development.

2

Assessment of Professionals in University Libraries

The assessment of library services and programmes has become more necessary in recent time for several reasons. The respective management/funding agency is expressing its inability to provide the total budgetary requirements of the library. To seek required funds, the libraries have definable outcomes, which can be readily measured to increase the credibility and put pressure on educational institutions. Therefore, a kind of assessment on inputs and outputs in libraries attained importance. Input is defined as a resource, that goes into an organization and outputs are the services, sharing resources etc.

Another reason that necessitated assessment is the impact of Information Technology on libraries. It is a fact that information services can be offered to the expectations of users by applying information technology efficiently and economically. Therefore, the professionals should be assessed by an appropriate method whether they are capable enough to understand the information technology facilities in processing and disseminating of information.

The aim of assessment is to prepare a plan that discusses the issues and problems of libraries. If these issues and problems are understood and solved, then the libraries will become more efficient, productive and service oriented. The employees of the programmes will develop new skills.

The self-motivation is another advantage of assessment. This situation will help the library professionals to be more creative at their work, take risks by initiating changes, and be more receptive to new ideas and concepts. Through this assessment plan, necessary changes and adjustments can be brought into libraries to meet the challenges appearing in libraries, particularly due to the Information Technology. The library staff should be given an opportunity to assess their services and contributions from time to time, which may help them to engage and accept influence of information technology in the libraries and their services.

A situation has reached that many of the traditional library services are to be withdrawn or modified greatly in which case the attitudes, opinions and adaptability of the employees need to be assessed. The funding agencies of libraries do not come forward to provide funds to meet any additional budgetary requirements. Therefore, the libraries should continue the library services and respond to changes appearing in information technology with the available resources. In such a case, proper use of skills and services of library professionals is inevitable.

The University libraries which are mostly run by public funds needs to be assessed qualitatively and quantitatively. In order to assess the quality of services in these libraries, some pre-set norms, guidelines or standards are necessary. Except the standards laid down in 1960, no systematic efforts have been made to develop standards for university libraries in India. This situation in western countries is a bit better. They often use assessment guide developed by professional experts. It is reported that these guides are of little value to assess the abilities and activities of library personnel. Therefore, these libraries develop their own assessment methods at local and regional level as reported in the study of "Academic libraries in Andalusia[1]". There are some assessment guides developed by various agencies, which may be useful to develop own assessment methods. In this context, the first of these guides was compiled by the "Catalan Agency for quality" in 1999. In 2000, the Andalusian University's quality unit convened a technical committee to draft a new assessment guide for academic libraries.

To understand the existing services, improvement of services and offer new services, a kind of assessment of library professional is necessary in the light of issues discussed.

PROFESSION

The *Oxford Advanced Learner's Dictionary of Current English*[2] defines profession as "occupation, one requiring advanced education and special training".

It is defined as "concerned with the specialized knowledge and skills, and these attitudes, standards and values, which together contribute to competence in the conduct of our vocation".

Willace and Boyce[3] have observed the profession "Information Science" inherently dependent upon technology and must respond to new developments or risk becoming obsolete.

According to Metzer[4] "a profession possesses and draws on a store of knowledge that is more than ordinary; a profession possesses a theoretical and intellectual knowledge to solve human and social problems; a profession strives to add and to provide its body of knowledge through research; a profession passes on the body of knowledge to novice generations for the most part in a university setting; a profession is involved with an altruistic spirit".

A professional, who engages in these goals should have acquired extensive training with a significant intellectual component and should be in a position to provide an important service to the society.

Bayles[5] suggests that there are three features to a profession - (1) extensive training; (2) a significant intellectual component; (3) a trained ability that puts one in a position to provide an important service to society.

Ezekwugo[6] gave the general characteristics of a profession as -

- Long period of specialized preparation;
- Involvement in activities that are mainly intellectual;
- Posing specialized knowledge and skills;
- Relatively high standards of admission policy;
- Ability to regard the job as a life corner;
- Natural love and aptitude for the job;
- Having a disciplinary council to regulate ethical standards to stipulate do's and don'ts and to protect the image and integrity of the profession.

Elements of a Profession

As stated by Emmanuel M.K. Dawha and R. Thambaiah[7], for a profession to grow and succeed, it should have some or all of the following elements:

- It must have systematic theory, that is knowledge organized into a consistent system;
- It must have authority that is, control over its field;
- It must have community sanction that is, the capability of effecting control over its members, and must have a formulated standard for the accreditation of institution(s) that train and produce manpower in its field.

- It must have legally backed-up by ethics and codes that is standardized rules
- It must have culture that is norms, values, symbols, which are career concepts;
- It must have service orientation.

Windal and Corley[8] noted that "all who consider themselves to be professional ethics, responsibility and liability but should make them a matter of on going concern".

For every profession to have its impact on society, it must have an organized body, which has control over its field and clients.

There are many ways to assess the caliber *of* professionals. The main focus on two key areas according to Richard O. Mason[9], are: (1) Professionals possess specialized knowledge; and (2) They use this knowledge in the service of others.

William Barrett[10] says that "professionalism is the price, we pay for the advancement of knowledge".

A profession, therefore, must have a solid foundation consisting of a recognized body essential to the well-being of society. Herben Blumer[11] says "professionalization seeks to clothe a given area with standards of excellence, to established rules of conduct, to develop a sense of responsibility, to set criteria for recruitment and training to ensure a measure of protection of members, to establish collective control over the area and elevate to a position of dignity and social standing in the society".

The concept of a profession is therefore characterized by several commitments, according to Ramansu Lahiri[12]

- Associating with specialized work of noble cause;
- Undergoing through rigorous and specialized preparations;

- Agreeing to work along with the guidelines of 'code of conduct';
- Performing the duties, responsibility and accountability.

KingsleyDaw's[13], a Sociologist, noted two basic criteria for judging professional status as:

- Duration and rigor of training required to acquire the necessary expertise; and
- Utility of the profession for the survival and the development of the society.

The other factors suggested by persons[14] are:

- Life long career commitment
- Social service
- Intellectual techniques
- Mastery of knowledge and the central focus of the professional role lies in "the technical competence of the professional and the recognition of this by the society".

Most of the definitions on profession reveal reasonable importance to specialized knowledge and regular improvement of specialized skills. The professionals in library and information science should therefore inculcate the habit of learning new knowledge and develop skills of IT from time to time.

Professional Behaviour

One of the important elements of profession is 'code of ethics/professional behavior'. It must be guided by a code of professional ethics ordained by the professional group as a body and accepted by the professionals as their guiding principles so far as their professional performance and conduct are concerned.

Varalakshmi[15] stressed that the professional duties encompass a variety of activities in the changing trends of society. The professional should have the following characters to meet the challenges in contemporary information environment:

(a) Be committed, enthusiastic leader, capable of dealing with computer problems on several fronts; some have a thorough knowledge in the new methods and technologies;

(b) Involved in collaborative work with resource sharing among libraries;

(c) Capable of effective exploitation of existing information retrieval services both manual and online; and also carried out the attitudinal changes required –

- specialized professional knowledge and skills,
- the professionals have to incorporate the changes occurring in information environment in their work,
- to develop the positive attitude,
- should cultivate communication skills to interact and maintain good relationships with management and clients.

In any profession the responsibilities are not static, so also in LIS profession. The prime responsibility of any profession is to respond positively to environmental change, which influences the behavior of professionals. The LIS professionals should keep themselves concerned with the on-going developments and changes taking place in the profession.

Besides the aforesaid characters and responsibilities, the following skills are essential for the professionals[16]

- knowledge of specialized reference materials;
- specialized analytical skills and techniques;

- knowledge of collection development theories and practices;
- knowledge of automation theories and practices;
- on-line retrieval skills;
- supervisory skills;
- counseling skills;
- knowledge of policy-making services;
- knowledge of cost-effectiveness;
- knowledge of document reproduction technologies;
- knowledge of binding policies; methods and issues;
- knowledge of conservation methods for library materials;
- knowledge of teaching and research skills;
- knowledge of information consolidation techniques.

According to Dowlin[17], professionals functioning in an electronic age need the following qualities:

1. technical knowledge related to computers and communication devices;
2. readiness to introduce organizational changes necessitated by technological innovations, and
3. ability to deal with a wide range of people outside the Library-People who supply hardware and software.

Professional Attitude

Attitude is the most important factor in human life. It applies to every sphere of life, relating to one's personal or professional life. William James[18] of Harvard University said, 'the greatest discovery of my generation is that human beings can alter their lives by altering their attitudes of mind". The foundation of success is being dependant on the personal attitude of the individual.

According to Mohsin[19], "an attitude is a mental and neural state of readiness organized through experience, exerting a directive or dynamic influence upon the individual's response to all objects and situations with which it is related. Attitude determines as to how we look at a setback. To a positive thinker it can be a stepping-stone to success.

Great organizations are not measured by wages and working conditions, but they are measured by feelings, attitudes and relationships of their personnel.

Factors of Attitudes

There are three major factors, which determine the attitude:

- Environment,
- Experience, and
- Education.

These are called the triple Es of attitude, and each of these factors is divided into some more areas.

Environment

It consists the following:

- Home: Positive and negative influences
- School: Peer pressure
- Work: Supportive or over critical supervisor
- Media: Television, newspapers, magazines, radio, movies
- Cultural background
- Religious background
- Traditions and beliefs

- Social environment
- Political environment

Experience

Behavior changes according to the experiences gained with people and events in the life. The positive experience with a person, made the attitude towards him/her positively and *vice versa*.

Education

Knowledge strategically applied translates into wisdom, ensuring success. Education ought to teach us not only how to make a living but also how to live.

Characteristics of attitude

Some important characteristics of attitude as given by Mohsin[20] are:

- attitudes are not in born; they are learnt through experience.
- like most psychological concepts they can be inferred from the observed antecedent stimulus and consequent behavior pattern. They are thus, of the nature of an intervening variable and a hypothetical construct.
- attitudes have objective reference; one holds an attitude regarding some object, person or issue. In this respect, they differ from motives or personality traits that have subjective reference.
- attitudes differ in valence; having an attitude regarding an object signifies that the person concerned is either favourably or unfavourably disposed towards it. Stated otherwise, attitudes are positive or negative, pro or anti.
- from operational point of view, attitudes are

manifested in the consistency of responses made to a specific object or situation.

Positive Attitude

People with positive attitudes have certain personality traits that are easy to recognize. They are caring, confident, patient and humble. They have high expectations of themselves and others. They anticipate positive outcomes. A person with positive attitude is like a fruit of all seasons.

The following are the benefits of positive attitude:

- increases productivity,
- fosters teamwork,
- solves problems,
- improves quality,
- makes for congenial atmosphere,
- breeds loyalty,
- fosters better relationships with employer and employees,
- reduces stress, and
- makes a pleasing personality.

Hence, the library professionals need to develop a positive attitude to accept the introduction of IT into their profession. They should come forward to equip themselves with the latest technical skills of IT, which enables them to provide better quality of information services in the changing environment.

ASSESSMENT

Assessment is more than just a 'grade'. Assessment means the process by which the grades are assigned to employees or library professionals in Library and Information Centres. Assessment is a mechanism for providing library professionals with data for improving their skills, and to achieve the goals and objectives of the library. In a way the assessment mechanism provides a feed back to both library staff and library administrators. Assessment provides us with crucial information about the services offered in libraries and their match with the set goals. The improvement of library services and facilities is possible by the thorough understanding of the feedback. It also helps to understand the user's capabilities in making use of the available library facilities and services. In this way the library can adopt the changes in information services from time to time. Assessment is a method used to understand the current knowledge on different aspects that a library professional possesses.

Definitions of Assessment

Evaluation (by self or peers) of functioning of an institution from aspects of efficiency and accountability as well as "quality way"[21].

"The process of collecting, synthesizing, and interpreting information to aid in decision making is called Assessment"[22].

"An opinion or a judgment about somebody or something that has been thought about very carefully"[23].

"Any systematic method of obtaining evidence from tests, examinations, questionnaires, surveys and collateral sources used to draw inferences about characteristics of people, objects or programs for a specific purpose"[24].

"Assessment is the process of documenting, often times in measurable terms, knowledge, skills, attitudes and beliefs. Assessment is often used in an educational context but applies to many other areas as well"[25].

Purpose of Assessment

i. to develop standards in libraries;

ii. to focus on goals and objectives of libraries;

iii. to monitor the quality of information services and products;

iv. to reward and award the professionals for their contribution;

v. to identify the library staff for further training and in-service training;

vi. to understand the program priorities;

vii. to understand the priority of information services;

viii. to understand the availability of alternatives;

ix. to assess professionals strengths and weaknesses;

x. to determine organization accountability;

xi. to provide accountability of resources;

xii. to accommodate and encourage creativity and originality shown by professionals;

xiii. to take career decisions;

xiv. to motivate employees to do their best;

xv. to maintain services consistent with the values of the library;

xvi. to improve services consistent with the values of the library;

xvii. to fairly evaluate competence of employees;

xviii. to provide effective feed back regarding performance to the employees;

xix. to provide professional with a clear understanding of job duties.

IMPORTANCE OF PERFORMANCE APPRAISAL IN LIBRARIES

Most of the libraries in the world have certain similarity in spite of the affiliation to institutions and purpose. The most common feature in the libraries is 'paucity' of funds and limited human resources. These reasons made the library scientists think towards the application of performance appraisal concept to overcome the above stated issues. A stage has reached that, the libraries have to offer variety of services to users' with the available staff and limited funds, which is definitely possible through the application of methods of performance appraisal among library staff. To offer various information services, the library personnel needs to be exposed to latest training in the fields of information technology, which is possible through performance appraisal. To maintain the quality and improve the quantity of the library services in the light of paucity of funds, the full utilization available library staff is one of the best solutions.

There is a performance appraisal in Higher Education environment. It is evident from the review of literature that the performance appraisal in libraries is not promising as most of the articles published are on status of the librarian but not on the application of performance appraisal in libraries. The contributors to this subject are mostly library educators, personnel in libraries and library administrators. Many of the researchers in this area have favoured the performance appraisal process as a viable organizational tool that helps to reach the goals and objectives of the library. some researchers expressed that the performance appraisal is an ingredient of management process. Although there are some articles on the process of conducting performance appraisal and the applications of methods of performance appraisal, their approach has been from a very superficial perspective. In academic libraries, the performance appraisal concept is not promising because of the lack of administrative support. Many changes that appeared in cataloguing, classification and information technology applications have forced libraries to offer training to library staff. Barbara Williams Jenkins[26] conducted a survey in 1990 and the survey reveals that most of the libraries are not providing training facilities to the library staff.

The performance appraisal concept is applied in American Libraries particularly in academic libraries in a more formalized way, employing annually or semi-annually[27]. The supervisors would fill the forms to assess the performance of each staff member. However no data is available regarding the application of performance appraisal in public and school libraries. In fact, the performance appraisal is more of an administrative and supervisory activity in American Library system. The American Library Association and ARL have issued collections of performance appraisal forms and guidelines.

Definitions of Performance Appraisal

Hayel defines performance appraisal as a "process of evaluating the performance and qualifications of the employees in terms of the requirements of the job for which they are employed, for the purposes of administration including placement, selection for promotions, providing financial rewards and other actions which require differential treatment among the members of a group as distinguished from actions effecting all members equally"[28].

Flippo puts it as a systematic, periodic, and an impartial rating on an employee's excellence in matters pertaining to his present job and to his potentialities for a better job.[29]

From the above definitions it is clear that performance appraisal is an important tool by which the organizations can review employee's performance; take corrective steps through training, interventions or placement decisions; reward good performance and attempt to take the employee performance at a higher level.

Need of Performance Appraisal in Libraries

1. to enhance institutional climate of libraries;
2. to facilitate the staff with in-service training periodically. It is necessary to improve the quality of service in the light of ever changing information services of libraries. In addition to this, the changes in information technology demands the librarian for in-service training;
3. to share the experiences between the librarian and the staff and also to understand the individual and institutional goals. The relationship between institutional and individual goals must be clearly articulated;
4. the success of performance appraisal mostly depends on attitude maintained by both the librarian and the library personnel being evaluated;
5. the performance appraisal would help to bring out hidden Human Resources.

A good performance appraisal programme helps to reach the goals and objectives of the library and allows the librarian for the future planning.

Objectives of Performance Appraisal in Libraries

Based on the objectives of performance appraisal stated by Management scientists, the following objectives are drawn suitable to libraries:

1. to enable the library to maintain inventory and to identify the training needs and aspirations;
2. to fix increments and develop a scientific method for promotion of library personnel;
3. to encourage the development of Library Professionals based on their performance;

4. to suggest solutions where the professional employee's performance is not up to the moral during the studied period;
5. to understand training and developmental needs of Library Professionals and to evaluate the effectiveness of such training and development programmes;
6. to plan career development, manpower planning based on potentiality of the library personnel;
7. to place library professional, to do the right kind of job in the right section of work.
8. to improve communication between the librarian and other professionals. So that a better understanding would develop between them which may help to reach the goals of the library. In this process the librarian would get an opportunity to understand the difficulties of other library staff and provide suitable solutions.
9. to provide adequate feedback on performance would be a key factor for comprehensive development of libraries.
10. to provide an opportunity for self-rectification of library personnel.
11. to serve as a basis for modifying or changing behaviour of library professional.

Functions of Performance Appraisal in Libraries

Keeping in view, the objectives of performance appraisal in libraries, the following functions are derived:

1. it should help the librarian to assess and understand the library professionals from time to time;
2. it should meet the training requirements of library personnel particularly in the context of Information Technology;

3. it should help the library professionals to know the bases for award of promotion and punishment.
4. it should minimize the distance between the librarian and other library professionals, which would help to reach the goals of the library;

Limitations of Performance Appraisal in University Libraries

The performance appraisal method has certain limitations, especially in University libraries, such as[30]

1. lack of evaluation skills;
2. technological changes;
3. scarce resources;
4. disregard for institutional goals and objectives;
5. Halo Effect;
6. Personal Bias and Central Tendency.

To accomplish performance appraisal, one of the difficulties is setting standards for performance. Many of the jobs and activities in libraries can't be quantified or measured easily. In addition to this, the performance standards in Indian Libraries are vogue. If the performance appraisal method is not applied properly, there is a danger that the professionals may loose confidence and faith in the library system.

Cook[31] (1995) mentioned age, ethnicity, physical appearance, attitudes, values and personal likes/dislikes, impression management, or some of the aspects which effects the quality of performance appraisal.

Tylor[32] (1998) also expressed the same opinion that performance appraisal is being more of on organizational curse than a tool. More or less, same opinion was expressed by Baker[33] (1988), Rendero[34] (1980) and Henderson[35] (1980) on performance appraisal.

In view of the above mentioned difficulties in the application of performance appraisal, and the little value it had in Indian libraries, in order to understand the services and activities in libraries, the only and best alternative is to apply the "Assessment Method".

ASSESSMENT METHODS[36]

To achieve the objectives of a library and to be in a position to use the system to the fullest extent, the organization has to choose an appropriate assessment method from the available alternatives. Depending on its requirements and objectives, the chosen method can be suitably modified. However, before deciding about an assessment method to be adopted in an organization/library, it is necessary to consider the following factors:

- what is to be assessed?
- who is to be assessed?
- the assessment experience of candidates
- how many candidates are likely to be assessed?
- cost of assessment tool.
- psychometric properties of the assessment instruments.

The following are the some common and professionally accepted assessment methods:

1. multiple choice;
2. work simulation;
3. key features/case study;
4. portfolio;
5. self-assessment;
6. supervisor evaluation;
7. structured Interviews.

Multiple Choice

This is one of the popular methods used in the assessment of people in various sectors and organizations. It is very useful to assess large number of employees in an organization. It is also proved to be cost-effective and efficient. In this method, a question is posed or a statement is made on which the employee is to respond. The candidate is given with a set of three, four or five options and is asked to choose one of the best answers to the given question or statement. Multiple-choice examinations are considered extremely well suited for assessing knowledge and its applications in the organizations and libraries.

Work Simulation

In this method the work is divided into five to fifteen encounters, questions, on each one may require five to ten minutes to complete. The employees are presented with standardized work place and are required to perform whatever interventions are necessary. Normally, at least one rater evaluates performance of an employee on pre-established criteria standards. In the absence of standards, particularly in Indian Academic Libraries, this method is not suitable to assess the library personnel.

Key Features/Case Study

This method is well suited for assessment of critical training skills and application of knowledge of employees. In some aspects, this method is similar to that of work simulation.

Portfolio

This method is popularly used in educational institutions and suitable to assess some aspects of occupational and professional practice. It is well suited to evaluate professional development of employees. This method is elaborate and time consuming, as it is developed by the employee, and includes key elements like history of work, history of education, evidence of continuing education and professional practice, evidence of competence designated specialty, etc. Since this method is very long and time consuming, it may not be suitable to assess large number of employees or professionals.

Self-Assessment

In this method, the employees answer the questions on their own on various aspects. Based on the response given by the employees, their competence and skills are assessed. The self-assessment method involves relatively low costs. In this method, a questionnaire is given to the candidates on various aspects, and the professionals, in turn, have to indicate their choice in three to five points rating scales.

Supervisor's Evaluation

There is a close similarity between self-assessment and supervisor evaluation method. In self-assessment method the employee himself rates his ability and skills whereas in supervisory evaluation method, the rating will be given by the supervisor. The supervisors evaluation is useful to assess the communication and performance based skills of employees. However, there is some scope for bias on the part of the evaluator.

Structured Interviews

The ability of researcher is the key factor in this method while gathering information from employees for assessment. In this method, a structured interview guide is used and there is no fixed frame to collect data or information as in the usual questionnaire method. So, the respondent and supervisor have the facility to express their opinions on different aspects freely. Since each respondent is to be assessed by the supervisor, it may take reasonably long time. Therefore, this method is suitable, if the number of respondents is few. The structured interview is better suited for evaluation of knowledge, ability and communication skills.

SELF-ASSESSMENT

Self-Assessment plays a vital role in the development of one's own career. Unless, an individual is interested in self-learning and self-development and make continuous efforts, he cannot develop himself in the profession. It requires a proper awareness about the latest changes in his own field, which is a necessary element in human force development. Such an effort should certainly include finding a way through which he may get proper growth, finding the possible directions of growth, choosing the ways through which he wants to grow and develop himself, experiencing the growth through the proper action plan, review and analyze the growth by continuous monitoring. Thus, for any employee, to develop his caliber/capabilities and perform a particular task associated with his role to the best of his ability, he must know, how well he can perform that particular function by identifying his capabilities as well as those qualities which are lacking in him to perform that function well. One can know about these actually by trying to perform that function, up to his level best and receiving feedback from superiors or others about his performance level and capability indicators. He may use this feedback and compare it with his own experience to identify his strength and weaknesses at a later stage. Then basing on that feedback, one can have a chance to make proper plans for developing the required capabilities with the assistance of his supervisors and others i.e., colleagues etc., if necessary. Thus, the individual can play a key role by determining his development and performance improvement and will be always helpful to any organization in achieving the goals and compete with similar organization. It is in this context, self-assessment plays a pivotal role in improving one's own performance and developing himself in a better way.

Definitions of Self-Assessment

Self-Assessment is the basic part of any assessment. An institution, evaluating its own activities, should formulate its objectives and tasks, and analyze its activities by applying different approaches, which will reveal its actual problems and foresees the ways of resolving them.[37]

Self-Assessment is used interchangeably with self-evaluation and self-study in the context of higher education quality. They all involve a process of self-reflection by the institution or sub-institutional unit being reviewed and the preparation of a document reflecting the self-reflection.[38]

"Self-Assessment is the process of critically reviewing the quality of one's own performance and provision"[39].

Self-Assessment is the process of "knowing your self". It involves taking an inventory of one's likes, dislikes, personal characteristics, values, wants and needs. It is the first part of the career planning process. Before you can decide what you want to be, you first have to discover what you are. People are constantly changing, growing and developing. Therefore, it is necessary for everyone to re-assess themselves periodically in relation to their career goals[40].

The *Oxford Advanced Learner's Dictionary* of current English defines Self-Assessment as "the process of judging your own progress, achievements etc."[41]

"Self-Assessment is the ability to decide on the degree to which a performance has achieved the target goal. This is based on published goals, measurable criteria and on submitted evidence"[42].

Self-Assessment is the process of gathering information about yourself in order to make about value, interest and personality inventories, skill assessments[43].

Value Inventories

The process of values clarification is a frequently used component of career exploration. It assists individuals in identifying priorities and it encompasses any activity that promotes self-examination. Values serve as a guide for behaviour and a basis for planning. Values are indicated in goals, attitudes, interests, feelings, activities, behaviour and even by problems. Relating values to work decisions and choices help a person to determine his or her reasons for wishing to work, the characteristics of occupations which are appeal them and their career goals. There are two types of values: intrinsic and extrinsic. The former is related to the work itself and what it contributes to society. The later includes external features, such as physical setting and earning potential.

Interests

Our interests are an important dimension of whom we are. By identifying what we really like and dislike, we are better able to determine the careers and environments that will satisfy in best our needs. Interest inventories can help us to measure and identify our likes and dislikes in a wide range of general activities and we can use this information to develop a personal interest profile. Our profile is then compared to the profiles of other individuals who successfully employed in specific occupational categories. A high degree of similarity between our interests and the interests of people in certain jobs might give us some ideas of possible careers to explore. Interest inventories do not, however, will tell us what we should or should not do or pursue. The instruments below offer tools to help us to define our interests.

Personality

The Merriam-Webster Dictionary[44] defines personality as "the complex of characteristics that distinguishes an individual or a nation or group; especially; the totality of an individual's behavioural and emotional characteristics".

Knowing our personality preferences can help us to make more informed career decisions. Individuals generally have a "default" way of living in the world; a preferred way of behaving and each of us is a combination of the four scales.

Skills

Knowing one's skills and abilities is an important factor in finding and fulfilling a job. When we are using the skills, we can enjoy the greater chance for job satisfaction.

"Self-Assessment is a process by which you learn more about your self-what you like and what you don't like, and how you tend to react to certain situations. Knowing these things can help you to determine which occupations and work situations could be better fit for you. You may recognize some of these tools if you ever worked with a career counselor or consultant"[45]

"A Self-Assessment should be the first step you take when choosing an occupation. Learning about yourself helps you to figure out what career to pursue"[46]

Purpose of Self-Assessment

The following can be considered as the purpose of Self-Assessment:

1. it provides the employee an opportunity to recapitulate:
    - the various activities he has undertaken in relation to different functions associated with his role;
    - his achievements and failures with regard to these;

- the capabilities he demonstrated and capabilities he felt as lacking in carrying out these activities and the various managerial and behavioral dimensions he demonstrated over the year.

2. to identify his own development needs and plan for his development in the organization by identifying the support he requires from his reporting officer and others in the organization.
3. to communicate to his reporting officer about his contributions, accomplishments, and reflections to enable him to view his performance in the right perspective and assess more objectively. This is a necessary preparation for improvement of plans.
4. it helps us to prepare for our review conversation with our supervisor.

Steps in Self-Assessment[47]

1. Employee reviews current job plan and development plan. The focus is on comparing planned goals with accomplished goals.
2. Employee receives and reviews any applicable multi-source feedback from other employees, customers or other feedback providers.
3. For each focus area, the employee describes:
   - What strategies were accomplished compared to planned;
   - The performance measures results versus planned;
   - What supervisor responsibilities were accomplished compared to planned;
   - Improvement opportunities focus area;
   - Any additional comments including any perceived

barriers or extenuating circumstances to accomplishing the focus areas, strategies, performance measures, and supervisor responsibilities. Also include any relevant feedback from others.

4. Based on the performance assessment, the employee makes a recommendation on his/her overall performance rating deserved.

Self-Assessment Methods[48]

Self-Assessment can take many forms, including:

- Writing conferences;
- Discussion(whole-class or small groups)
- Weekly self-evaluations;
- Self-assessment checklists and inventories;
- Employee-supervisor interviews.

Drucker's Self-Assessment Process[49]

This Self-Assessment process converts knowledge into effective action. This means engaging the board, the staff and your customers in a challenging process of organizational self-discovery. And as anyone who has been involved in a process of self-assessment or planning knows the quality of the process becomes very bit as important as the discoveries themselves. The Self-Assessment process is designed in three phases:

Phase-I: Preparing for Self-Assessment;

Phase-II: Conducting Self-Assessment Process;

Phase-III: Completing the Plan.

Drucker mentioned the fore most important questions in Self-Assessment guide as follows:

1. What are you doing?

2. Why are you doing it?
3. What you must do to improve an organization performance. Along with these, the author mentioned the following five essential questions:
   i. what is our mission?
   ii. who is our customer?
   iii. what does the customer value?
   iv. what are our results?
   v. what is our plan?

NOTES

1. Barrionuevo: http://www.uniovi.es/vicerrecturados.../colidad/ESOE/ proceedings.
2. *Oxford Advanced Learner's Dictionary of Current English.* New York, Oxford University Press, 1989, p.924.
3. Willace, Denny, P. and Boyce, Berr, R: Computer Technology and Interdisciplinary efforts – A discussion and Model Programme. *Journal of Education for Library and Information Science*, 27, 1986, p.159.
4. Metzr, W.P: What is Profession? *Seminar Reports*, 3(1), 1975, pp. 2-3.
5. Bayles, M.D: *Professional Ethics*, 2nd Ed. Belmont CA, Wordsworth, 1989, pp. 8-9.
6. Ezekwugo, C.M: A Tear for Education. *The Guardian* (A Nigerian Daily Newspaper), 1993.
7. Dawha, Emmanuel, M.K and Thambaiah, R.S: Professionalism and Librarianship in Nigeria. *Annals of Library Science and Documentation*, 41(3), 1994, p.112.
8. Windal, I. W. and Curley, R.N: The *Accounting Professional Ethics: Responsibility and Liability*. London, PHI, 1980, p.180.
9. Mason, Richard, O: What is an Information Professional. *Journal of Education for Library and Information Science*, 31(2), 1990, p.122.

10. Barette, William: *Irrational Man – A Study in Existential Philosophy*. Green Wood, Hartford Conn., 1994, p.5.

11. Blumer, Herben: *Preface in Professionalization* by H.M. Vollner and D.L. Mill. London, PHI, 1966, p.xi.

12. Lahiri Ramansu: *Professionalism and Research in Library and Information Science*. Ess Publications, 1995, p.4.

13. Davies, K (Quoted from B.K. Pussi): The Noble–the–teacher alone. *University News*, Delhi, 35(3), 1997, p.2.

14. Persons, T (Quoted from Kart and Rosenzurig's Book Organization and Management): *The Profession and Social Structure*. Free Press, 1964, pp.324-39.

15. Varalakshmi, R.S.R: Professional Challenges: Need for Attitudinal Changes among Librarian. *University News*, 37(11), 1999, pp.12-14.

16. Gopinath, M.A: Librarianship in Library Management. *IASLIC Bulletin*, 35(4), 1990, pp.140-141.

17. Dowlin, C.D: Education for the Electronic Library. *Drexel Library Quarterly*, 17(4), 1989, pp.77-90.

18. http://www.mazon.com/exec/obidos/tg/detail

19. Mohsin, S.M: *Attitude Concept, Formation and* Change. New Delhi, Wiley Eastern, 1990, p.2.

20. *ibid*.

21. National Assessment and Accreditation Council: Institutional Accreditation: Manual for Self-Study for Universities. Bangalore, Aatrey, 1997.

22. Peter, W.A: *Classroom Assessment*. New York, McGraw-Hill, 1994, pp.4-5.

23. Wehmeier, Sally: *Oxford Advanced Learner's Dictionary of Current English*, 6th Ed. New York, Oxford University Press, 2000, p.1159.

24. www.questionmark.com.com/UK/glossary.html

25. www.en.wikipedia.org/wiki/assessment.

26. Jenkins, B.W: Performance Appraisal in Academic Libraries. *Association of College and Research Libraries*, Chicago, IL, 1990, pp.236-245.

27. Johnson, M: Performance Appraisal of Librarians - A Survey. *College and Research Libraries*, 33, 1972, pp. 358-367.

28. Hayel, C: *Encyclopedia of Management*. New York, Reinhold Publishing Corporation, 1993, p.654.

29. Flippo, Edwin, B: *Principles of Personnel Management*. New York, McGraw-Hill, 1984.

30. Renekar, M and Steel, V: Performance Appraisal: Purpose and Techniques. *In*: Creth and Duda, F (Eds.), *Personnel Administration in Libraries*, New York, Neal-schumen, 1987.

31. Cook, M: performance appraisal and true performance. *Journal of Management Psychology*, 10(7), 1995, p.37.

32. Taylor, S: *Employee Resourcing*. Institute of Personnel and Development, London, 1998, p.185.

33. Baker, J: *Causes and Failure in Performance Appraisal and Supervision*. Quorum, New York, 1988, p.7.

34. Rendro, T: Consensus: Performance Appraisal Practices. *Personnel*, 12(6), pp.4-12.

35. Hendersons, R.: *Performance Appraisal: Theory and Practice*. Reston, VA, Prentice-Hall, 1980, p.33.

36. http:// www.asinc.ca/en/methods/index.htm

37. http://www.quality research international.com/glossary.

38. http://www.quality research international.com/glossary.

39. http://www.quality research international.com/glossary.

40. www. Soiec. State.nc.us/soicc/planning/cl.html

41. Wehmeier, Sally: *Oxford Advanced Learner's Dictionary of Current English*, 6th Ed. New York, Oxford University Press, 2000, p.1159.

42. Woods.R.Donald/www.chemeng.mcmaster.ca/mps/mps3-obj.pdf.

43. Saarinen, T: Systematic Higher Education Assessment and Development Impacts: Transilating the effort to meet the Need. *Quality in Higher Education*, 1(3), 1995, pp.223-224.

44. http://www.m-w.com/palm.htm

45. http:// www.riley guide.com/assessment.html.

46. www.career planning.about.com/self-assessment.

47. http://www.nashville.gov/finance/performance%20 management/page 1.5

48. http://www.eduplace.com/rdg/res/assess/selfmth.html

49. Drucker, Peter F: http://www. Leader to leader.org/ leaderbooks/sat/. process.html.

3

Review of Literature

For any research study, review of available literature is one of the important aspects. Review of Literature is a set of recent output on a particular area of a research and organized in a helpful sequence to strengthen the present research techniques. The main objective of review of literature is to understand the research activities that have taken place in a particular discipline and the area of research in particular. All the relevant literature available is reviewed here. The contribution of academicians, management scientists, research scholars, information scientists and library professionals on this topic in various dimensions has yielded in valuable set of research output. As this kind of research is new in the field of library and information science in India, an attempt is made to present review of all relevant literature published up to 2004.

The reviewed articles are grouped under three headings namely:

1. Performance Evaluation
2. Performance Appraisal
3. Self-Assessment

Under each topic, the reviewed articles are presented chronologically in ascending order.

PERFORMANCE EVALUATION

Hagerty[1] (1959) expressed that evaluation of employees is an art and not a science, and further that the pseudo accuracy of numerical ratings or of detailed adjective ratings is an opiate to the unsophisticated in personnel administration. The problem involved in measurement of effectiveness of an employee is explained. For example, the service of reference librarian is not measurable by the number of library users but by the quality of the service rendered due account being made of the volume of the demands put upon him. The issues involved in rating performance are mentioned at many times. The raters are unable to distinguish the difference between employee performance and employee potentiality. The raters are not aware of their short comings to make valid conclusions on performance evaluation of employees, such as (1) Halo effect (2) recent identity of performance are being overemphasized in the rating (3) senior employees are being over-rated and junior ones are under-rated 4) close subordinates are being given "the benefit of the doubt", and (5) his own trainees are not necessarily better than other employees.

Deprospo[2] (1971) traced out the development of performance evaluation in relation with the evaluation of man. The issue related to human force and scarce resources were discussed. The importance of using limited manpower to attain the goals is linked with performance evaluation, the special features of library staff and rendering information service to users, where the librarian's role is crucial to satisfy the user.

American Library Association's Co-ordination Committee on the revision of public library standards has made a statement on library personnel as "No library can render effective service without adequate and competent personnel. The library's unique function of serving as the unbiased nonpartisan bureau of information for the people calls for the personnel of highest competence and integrity.

The selection of qualified staff members for an institution and conditions under which they work are basic considerations in an institution dedicated to public service". The importance of appointing fulltime director to libraries where the staff is 150 and more was clearly stated.

All libraries should maintain a policy handbook and staff manual. The classification of personnel and their pay scales should be stated clearly. It is the responsibility of librarian to prepare a personnel policy defining job specification, salary scales, working days, coffee breaks, overtimes, illness, vacations, etc., The importance of two way communication was also realized as a reasonable ingredient in personnel evaluation. The concepts of rating were discussed at length. The trends in relation to performance evaluation were as follows:

- the traditional view has been enlarged to include how the individual functions as an integral part of the organizational system;
- organizations are becoming more concerned with the using of performance appraisal for planning and with a method for controlling poor performance ;
- the changing composition of the labour force has produced a decrease in the formal evaluations of supervisory personnel.
- theoretical research and development in the social and behavioural sciences have accelerated the growth of sophistication in Performance Appraisal.

The purpose of performance evaluation is, to improve performance; to achieve the relations between supervisor and sub-ordinates. Further, he stated the objectives of performance appraisal, and suggested a five step program to achieve these objectives by giving their advantages.

Evans[3] (1976) stated the importance of continuous performance evaluation for the success of all types of organizations or libraries. Performance evaluations are taken up for several reasons, out of which feedback of employees is one among them. The purpose of performance evaluation is to help both the employee and the organization in knowing about themselves. This activity should be taken in a positive manner rather than negative assumptions. The performance evaluation is not an on-going process and it is not easier always for the supervisor to discuss with their employees on their strengths and weaknesses. The author suggested the necessity of standards and consistency in applications. The author mentioned the Halo Effect while evaluating the performance of employees and suggested another method for appraisal of employees where in their services are compared with pre-determined standards. In this context, issues relating to the rating system were discussed. In the absence of clear standards on performance evaluation, it is impossible to know where the employee stands.

Cohen[4] (1989) states that believable information about staff members' job is necessary for performance evaluation. Performance evaluation is also necessary for promotion and disciplinary actions. Through this method, the supervisor has to provide a written record about an employee's performance. To understand the staff training requirements, supervisors can use this kind of performance evaluation of employees. It helps to have a better communication between the supervisor and staff members.

The Pitfalls involved in Performance Evaluation were stated as follows:

- Halo Effect: supervisor's ability in rating the job performance
- Central Tendency: Rating all employees as average
- Looser Rater: Rates everyone high
- Tight Rater: Rates everyone poor

- Recently error: Depends upon recent errors rather than total period
- Length of service bias: Tenured staff perform well
- Competitive rater: The supervisor determines staff members rating and how his own supervisor has evaluated him.

In performance planning, the necessity of job description and the responsibilities of staff members are stated. The employee may be delegated with responsibility. To develop a performance plan for both the supervisor and sub-ordinate staff, it should be jointly developed. The role and responsibilities of supervisor and employee are stated in order to make performance plan and goals. In performance evaluation, the importance of performance monitoring, performance evaluation is stressed up on.

Moore[5] (1992) opined that the performance of public libraries should be evaluated by community survey and user survey. In community survey, the author mentioned about the aims, data collection methods, and few sample questions which may be helpful to arrive at valid conclusions. The same methodology was followed in user survey too. In basic user survey, the following information was collected – reasons for the library visit for a particular piece of information, staff's co-operation, user's satisfaction about the available information and the services offered in library. Level two, measures the following:

- Check list;
- Attitudes survey;
- Depth interviews;
- Group discussions;
- Unobtrusive testing.

The aim of performance measurement is, to indicate the current progress of a library, to provide a means of assessing the efficiency with which resources are being used and to provide a basis for relating performance to the overall objectives and the services of library. The issues regarding performance of a public library were stated as: performance will depend on the nature of the community served by the library, the nature and scale of resources provided for that library services and finally the objectives within which the services are developed. The results of one country's public libraries need not be relevant to the public libraries of other country. The measurement should not be considered in isolation. For the measurement of library resources, IFLA has stated several standards.

Lancaster[6] (1993) stated the purpose of evaluation in relation to the library services offered and mention various methods for evaluation:

i. A Benchmark method to understand the performance, how to operate and measure the services in changing environment;

ii. Compare the performance and services of several libraries;

iii. Evaluation of information services is simplified to justify its existence;

iv. Evaluation is to identify the possible sources of failure or inefficiency in the services with a view to raise the level of performance.

The author stated the responsibility of manager according to 'Orr' as:

- To define the goals of organization;
- To obtain the resources needed to reach the goals;
- To identify the programs and services required to achieve the goals and to optimize the allocation of resources over these programs and services;
- To see that the resources allocated to a particular activity are used as wisely as possible.

Belcastro[7] (1998) opined that continuous improvement has become a key factor for the sustenance in all types of organizations. It is necessary for all types of libraries to deliver the highest quality of services. The prime motto is to prepare a performance evaluation method that measures the staff's work performance fairly, objectively and links their daily performance to the mission objectives. A frame provided for performance appraisal was as follows:

- Back ground – staff's overwhelming;
- The key is communicating expectations;
- The purpose of the appraisal;
- Focus is on the practical;
- Use of the appraisal system;
- The need for accountability for good library services is increasing.

A performance appraisal system based on the "expectations of quality service" not only provides the accountability to the library clients, customers, or patrons, but also it reinforces the value of services the library provides. Performance appraisal of the staff should be based on 'Behaviours' that can be 'Measured' not on 'Attitudes' that may be interpreted on 'Subjectively'.

Meera[8] (1998) studied the application of marketing concepts in Library and Information Centers, in order to make them as profit organizations. In this context, the importance of quality improvement programs, particularly performance measures are highlighted. Many changes are occurring in libraries to cope-up the information needs of the society. The evaluation of libraries was stated by giving the status and position of libraries in last 20 years. The user's requirement was shifted from book to information system. Keeping in mind all these aspects, to improve the quality of services, a kind of performance evaluation is said to be essential. To measure the functions of a library, two schools of thoughts are available, one believes that the benefits derived from a library cannot be measured and they are intangible. The other opinion is, if not all the library functions and services can be measured, then their performance can't be evaluated.

Town[9] (2000) stated the need for change of performance measurement system, if the library of an institution wants to perform effectively in the future. The relation between future performance and present performance approach should be highlighted, to achieve the goals of a library successfully and the development of libraries fairly which will depends on the staff and their development. This can be seen positively in TQM (Total Quality Management) environment, where total involvement of staff is required to achieve Excellence, Leadership, Teamwork, Staff involvement in improvement, staff competence and commitment, morale and culture, and staff development are all the critical areas for a successful library. To measure these areas, there is no agreement, but measurement of these services is necessary for performance assessment.

Creaser[10] (2001) studied the Introduction of Benchmarking Technique and its application in the libraries of U.K. She gave a series of steps to be followed to measure one's service. They are viz., selecting the aspects in benchmarking, finding suitable benchmarking points, identifying best practices, procedures which give rise to 'best practice', to measure the services and to assess the impact or exercise.

She also made an attempt to evaluate the services offered, sources of funding, etc., in U.K school libraries. Moreover, she made a note on the lack of standards and performance indicators for school library services, which are necessary for performance appraisal or evaluation.

Nelavagi[11] (2003) stated that performance evaluation is a process of quality assurance whereby an approved institution, personnel or a programme is critically appraised at regular intervals as to confirm whether the professionals meet the prescribed norms and standards or not. The changes coming into library profession and its impact on library services, lead to the need for performance evaluation to meet the goals. The evaluation of performance will predict the level and type of work, the individual' capability of performing in future and to adjust with the changing environment of modern Information Technology; and to the allocation and distribution of funds or rewards more fairly. The recognition of the contributions made by individuals, assistance to develop their full potential as quickly as possible, assistance to academic staff to reach the academic goals, assistance in the improvement of individual's performance, etc., were stated as the objectives of performance evaluation.

A criteria for the evaluation of library professionals was given and it includes:

- Teaching and research performance
- Scholarship and scholarly interests;
- Administrative success;
- Professionals and community interests;
- Educational attainment ;
- Reading;
- Individual personality;
- Outstanding achievements.

The performance evaluation is a continuous process and it helps to understand the strengths and weaknesses of library professionals as well as the infrastructural facilities of libraries.

Jackson Library Home[12] the University of North Carolina followed four levels for evaluating individual's performance:

1. Professional responsibilities/teaching effectiveness,

2. Research and creative activities,
3. Service activities and
4. Direct professional activities.

In professional responsibilities, the following issues should be considered – utilize the knowledge of professionals for developing the university curriculum and programs into library services and resources, library resources and research collections, use of bibliographic and information system, promoting library resources and services, assistance to development of research methodology for students and faculty, demonstrating written and oral communication skills, co-ordination of library services and resources, provision of electronic information, recruiting budgeting, etc., In research and creative activity, the scholarly writing and it's presentation, editing of books and journals, etc., were stated. The author identified many services and activities which were categorized under three types:

a) service to the library and university for the embracement of activities, which will sustain the University and enable it to carry out its academic goals;

b) service to the discipline, which will contribute to the function and effectiveness of the faculty member's profession, and discipline;

c) service to the external communities which will reach out to constituencies such as government agencies, industries and the arts where academic knowledge intersects with practical affairs and problem solving. The direct professional activities are much more well defined. The scope of activities, specific library developing initiatives, etc., is also mentioned.

As a conclusion, the importance of Performance Evaluation in libraries is stated and methods for evaluation are discussed. The problems involved in measurement of effectiveness of the professionals and their limitations are mentioned. The role of performance indicators, impact of Information Technology on libraries, purpose of evaluation, etc. were highlighted. For evaluation of performance in libraries a kind of standards are necessary. In the absence of established library standards, performance evaluation procedure cannot yield expected results.

PERFORMANCE APPRAISAL

Peele[13] (1970) made an attempt to rate the performance of employee in libraries and suggested two aspects:

1. the rating form and some guidelines for filling it in; and
2. the right of the librarian who is being rated to discuss or appeal a rating he believes to be biased.

The problems in rating method were discussed. The performance appraisal of professional staff, in the event of equal status with teaching staff is discussed thoroughly and suggested some measures to overcome the problems. The application of rating methods in academic libraries was also mentioned.

Johnson[14] (1972) stated that performance appraisal is one of the mechanisms to assess the individual's contribution and ability. The author conducted a study to compile information on performance appraisal of librarians in college and university libraries. The objectives of the study are as follows:

1) determine the approaches used in appraising librarians, together with the apparent success, or lack of success of these approaches;
2) compare the results with performance appraisal concepts expressed in recent literature;
3) draw conclusions, which could be helpful to those

responsible for the appraisal of professional personnel in libraries.

A kind of appraisal system was reported in 90 percent of the libraries surveyed, but no systematic method was followed there to assess the employee's ability. However, it included the casual observation of staff members by the director with no written records, and discussing with staff members about their performance based on the results obtained through the annually conducted performance appraisal.

The forms of assessment were mentioned in three categories.

1. rating sheet types;
2. forms identical to those used to evaluate the teaching faculty's performance;
3. forms designed to evaluate the special competencies of librarians.

Though the personnel appraisal was not taken, the promotion of staff was made or a salary was enhanced, based on a kind of appraisal. It was noted that, a kind of appraisal system was there but the method of appraisal varies among different libraries.

The opinions of various scientists on performance appraisal are stated as:

- supervisor should sharpen the contributing ability of subordinates;
- the scope of performance is grouping;
- the individual stands as an integrated part of the unit and the application of system approach to personal approach.

Due to cuts in budget, the libraries felt the necessity of appraisal system, the technique adopted by the librarians was similar to that of faculty. The author reported that 80 percent of the libraries are conducting the appraisal periodically and annually. The importance of continuous assessment is stated. In most of the libraries, the appraisal was linked with annual salary review, budget preparation, or determination of retention tenure, rank for the coming year. Out of the 130 libraries studied, 78 per cent have followed appraisal system by using forms; the rest of the libraries based on formal discussion or prepared return summary tenures. In all cases, the well-designed appraisal form may not yield a good result.

The 'Pros and Cons' of various personnel appraisal methods were stated - personal bias, central tendency, halo effect and logical error. The problems to understand the. phrases used in forms were mentioned in Management by Objectives of 'Peter F. Drucker'. The importance of MBO and advantages of self-evaluation methods were stated. The author advocates for five level rating scales for assessment. The professional status of librarians had its impact on Performance Appraisal in different libraries. If the appraisal is made by other than the immediate supervisor, the result was not disclosed to the employee immediately. The issues involved in rating scale were discussed.

Peel[15] (1972) discussed the issues involved in the evaluation of library personnel. In evaluation process, the importance of subjectivity is stressed on 'Halo Effect'. The difficulties involved in rating a person for promotions were stated and the limitations of objectivity method in evaluation are also discussed. The author concluded that, the objectivity method is not suitable to evaluate the performance of employees for promotion. The limitations of evaluation of employees by users of library were stated and concluded that they should not be considered. The author suggested "the result method" in which the junior and his supervisor should meet together to set performance goals and discusses the best means of meeting them, and over a period of time, they should meet again to evaluate the progress and the newly established goals which in turn is a performance review.

Berkner[16] (1979) stated the role of professional staff in academic libraries and up to what extent the services of the professional staff are more important than the major components of library such as - books, card catalogues, documents, etc., To provide access to information, the staff have to attend the works like, cataloguing, reference, inter library loan, administration, etc. To meet the goals of the library, the staff should be well trained and motivated. There is a need to maintain high standards of performance in libraries. The author stated the goals of the performance appraisal as follows:

- to improve performance in the present job;
- to provide basis for recommending for promotion, salary increase or dismissal;
- to give the employee a chance to know where he/she stands;.
- to develop an inventory of human resources for the use of management;
- to provide a method of counseling and encouraging the staff for future development.

The problems involved in the evaluation of subordinate staff by the supervisor were stated. MBO of Peter F. Drucker and his application for professional performance evaluation were highlighted:

In this method, the procedure for performance evaluation of staff was stated. The performance appraisal for staff development was stated, which includes discussions by the individual and the supervisor on job content, setting performance targets by the employee, review of these with the supervisor, establishment of evaluative check points, and appraisal of results.

The importance of interpersonal relationships among library staff were noted and these would be useful to measure the performance appraisal rather than by objective standards. In service-oriented fields like libraries, the goals of a library can be attained by many means but there is a danger in quantifying them.

The author stated a program proposal in nine steps.

1. Training of library supervisors,
2. Goal setting,
3. System interaction,
4. Refresher,
5. Individual Goal setting,
6. Critical incidents,
7. Review and analysis, and
8. Evaluation of the performance evaluation.

Evans[17] (1982) observed the quality and quantity of services offered by libraries in the light of paucity of funds. A common phenomenon in all libraries is to have more efficient and productive staff. So the performance of staff has become very important in this context. In American Academic Library System, a formal performance appraisal method is being followed annually or semi-annually and the supervisors would assess the performance of the subordinate staff. The productivity of all individuals is measurable up to some extent or evaluation of one person by another is as old as mankind it self. All libraries should have some formal plan for appraising it's each employee. The observations made on the basis of 'Business index and library literature' and the functions of performance appraisal in American organization were stated as; the process is essential for good management; the process is natural or normal; basis for granting or withdrawing employee economic benefits; important element of motivation; to understand strengths and weaknesses, etc. The goals of performance appraisal are stated as administration and behavioral goals. The issues involved in conducting performance appraisal were stated. The author concluded that performance appraisal is essential for good management and it is a means to control employee's job performance and thus it can effects the individual and organizational productivity.

Hodge[18] (1983) stated the issues and limitations of performance appraisal. In his view, the performance appraisal should include evaluator's judgments, job standards and criteria, organizational policy, legal requirements and evaluator's training. The functions of performance appraisal is to assist in personnel planning; to provide a basis for employment decisions, i.e., promotion, termination, merit pay, demotion, etc.; to guide job development; to provide performance feedback to employees; to elicit feedback from the employees; to serve as a basis for modifying or changing the behaviour; to determine the need for training and coaching. The application of rating technique in performance appraisal, the legal requirements related to performance appraisal system was stated. A criteria for developing or assessing a performance appraisal system is stated as; job analysis involves the duties and responsibilities; critical job factors; performance standards; precise and the use of unambiguous language; training for managers and supervisors, etc., The rating scale method was thoroughly discussed. Every employee should be provided with an opportunity to agree or disagree in writing regarding the approval statement and to comment if needed.

Seetaram[19] (1986) while discussing about the manpower planning in his book "Planning of Library and Information Systems", stated the impact of performance appraisal and listed the objectives according to 'Leck' as:

- to monitor performance;
- to plan for future performance;

- to identify potential;
- to assess profitability;
- to identify training needs;
- to counsel and motive;
- to assist with career and successive planning.

He opined that the same objectives need not be suitable to understand appraisal procedure in all organizations. A list of performance appraisal systems, which may be used in Special Library and Information Centers was given as below:

1. check list method,
2. ranking/grouping method,
3. open form system,
4. field review system,
5. critical Incident plan/system,
6. informal plan scheme,
7. self-appraisal.

Gopinath[20] (1990) stressed the need for co-operation between various components of libraries, which can be possible through the overall performance appraisal. The performance of any library depends mostly on library professionals and they act as a bridge between the users and utilization of library resources. The relation between productivity and performance was clearly stated. To bring out some possible changes in the behavior of professionals, the concept of performance diagnosis and approval system is necessary. This procedure certainly helps in understanding the critical aspects of job behaviour, employee behavior, etc. Guidelines for diagnosis and performance appraisal of library and information scientists' were stated. This process involves the rate of absenteeism, cost of spoiled work and the number of coded filing errors. He suggested a plan for performance appraisal which includes: the definition of work or a job to be performed; defining the units of job; the time taken for doing the jobs; the present performance levels of the library staff; improvement in the behaviour of library staff, consistency of the objects of library services: feed back for the performance of library staff.

Different varieties of performance measures are required to trace the work in different sections of the library. To understand the performance of library staff, broad performance criteria indicators are to be used. The details of jobs to be done in each section and the performance criteria were stated clearly. An attempt was made to relate five laws of library science with performance appraisal system. The performance of library should be towards the acquisition of information sources, meet the requirements of potential user, acquisition of documents and making them available at the earliest.

Gopinath[21] (1994) mentioned that, in order to satisfy the knowledge needs of users, their emotional needs, communication needs, economic needs and social needs are to be identified. It is necessary to consider that the library professionals should gain knowledge in the following skills:

1. Sociometric, scientometric, econometric, informetric, bibliometric and librametric techniques which one can use to gauge the variant relatives with interacting groups are librarians, information users and information resources,
2. Communication methods so as to discover constructional approach techniques to motivate, and to develop the information access processes,
3. Browsing techniques so that a searcher can have access to information without intermediation,
4. Sensing and measuring of values and address the

information relevant to problem solving or decision-making,

5. Perception of variance in value of information by individuals. It calls for indirect measures of performance of services. It entitles contextual or situational analysis and leads to help immediate and long-term needs of a seeker for information,
6. Knowledge of statistical quality control techniques and the capability to add quality to knowledge organization, retrieval, access, use and evaluation.

To meet the above goals, performance appraisal of the staff is necessary. To understand performance appraisal of the libraries, the relation between output performance and internal performance is to be examined.

Oldroyd[22] (1995) made an attempt to study the issues of staff training and development, and appraisal in an 'old' University library, 'The University of Nottingham Library', Nottingham, UK. The appraisal scheme covers only academic and academic related staff of the library. It was not related directly to reward structure, but provides an annual opportunity to the review and objective setting. The academic related staff in this library was reported as 20 percent. There was a need to apply the appraisal method for other staff also. The final appraisal method was not applied to staff, or interview annually by the team leaders on various aspects.

The importance of staff training and development, the commitment of senior management, positive perceptions among staff, etc., were highlighted to achieve the aims and objectives of the library.

The need for setting up training and staff development program was discussed. In these training programmes, new technologies like CD-ROM, OPAC, Networks, etc., should be included, particularly on-the-job training should be given to the library staff. Training should be imparted by the team leaders, managers and supervisors mostly, if necessary training may be given to this group known as "Training the trainers" through which they can educate the rest of the staff. At times, the staff may not come forward to have training program in which case they should be motivated in right perspective. It is not always easy to measure the benefit of training given to the employees. In libraries, the outcome of training at many times is not self evident, it happens so in service oriented institutions. The Fielden report recommended that staff should spend 5 per cent of their time in both performance and self-esteem. In training program, the following issues should be taken into account:

1. Money spent on each member of the staff.
2. Budget of staff training.
3. New computer system and amount to be spent on training.

Srivastav and Singh[23] (1996) opined that the promotions in higher education should be based on genuine and conscientious performance of teachers rather than on simple seniority. Further, they stated that the performance appraisal system is a process through which the behaviour and achievement of an individual teacher for a fixed period is to be measured and evaluated. The three main objectives of performance evaluation are listed as (1) the remedial objective (2) the developmental objective, and (3) the innovative objective. The limitations of Confidential Report, that permits a good amount of subjectivity, were listed as (i) superficial treatment, (ii) Ill-defined criteria and ambiguity, (iii) The raters' error (Leniency error, First impression, Halo and horn error, Stereo typing, Central Tendency Latest Behaviour and spillover error), (vi) Lack of feedback and performance standards. They also suggested some criteria for the evaluation of teaching, research and services.

Jorden[24] (1996) focuses light on staff appraisal in his book "Staff Management in Library and Information Work". According to 'Randell' three main objectives are:

1. Performance reviews
2. Potential reviews
3. Reward reviews

1. To improve the performance of the library and in particular the performance of individual members of staff. This incorporates the discovery of training needs, motivation of staff, counseling and shaping the behaviour of staff by praise and punishment.
2. To predict the level and type of work, the individual can do with their capability of performing in the near future.
3. To allocate and distribute rewards more fairly.

The author stated the following approaches of performance appraisal according to Judith Steward as:

- It must be appreciated that staff appraisal is a very personal and individual experience;
- The idea and benefits of appraisal need to be sold to staff;
- People prefer appraisal schemes with firm structure and framework;
- Training for interviewer and for those to be interviewed is of prime importance;
- The appraisal interview is an important occasion;
- The relationship between the appraiser and appraisee is critical.
- It is vital that discussions are rooted in reality and fact.

- The real benefit of staff appraisal lies in the regular and effective follow-up of agreed action plans.
- It is necessary to monitor, evaluate and develop appraisal schemes for their continuous success.

To improve the performance of library, it depends on performance of individual members of staff. The issues involved in potential reviews or reward reviews were stated. At the end a self-assessment form was given as model to assess the performance of staff in libraries.

Edwards and Williams[25] (1998) stated the scope of performance appraisal which is an activity between a supervisor and employee supervisors should discuss the employees problems with them while going to conduct performance appraisal. The boundaries of performance appraisal were stated and the evaluation process need not be about the job but the goals of the institution. Performance Appraisal in academic libraries is not a new concept in librarianship as reasonable amount of literature was published mostly on the status of librarians, but the studies on performance appraisal in libraries are not promising. The performance appraisal was based on a few distinct objectives of the libraries. The reason for the negligence of performance appraisal in academic libraries of USA was due to lack of administrative support. Till 1990, the performance appraisal concept was not applied in academic libraries in a systematic way.

The reasons for the need of having performance appraisal in academic libraries were stated as: enhance of environment in academic libraries, better communi-*cation, staff training, communication between employees and supervisors on a one-to-one basis, to train the staff on regular intervals, budget constraints and the staff, etc., The factors affecting the performance appraisal were stated as: lack of evaluation skills, technological changes, personal biases, scarce resources, disregard for institutional goals and objectives. The ability of supervisor is one of the important features in performance appraisal process.

Jabeen[26] (1999) mentioned the inherent relationship between the educational institutions and industries. The educational institutions are the source for the manpower that is required and utilized by many sectors. In this view, the role and importance of human resources are rightly realized. According to the author, performance appraisal is a very critical mechanism for the development of human resources with different focuses and purposes. The difference between evaluation of merit and performance appraisal was also stated clearly. The mechanism involved in performance appraisal is stated as:

- Appraisals are done by immediate superior and reviewed by the next in the hierarchy;
- Key performance areas are identified and departmental targets are set with mutual consent of both superior and the subordinate;
- Information to be used for appraisal is derived from all the possible sources including appraisal himself. They leave the appraise satisfied.
- Emphasis is on identifying the managerial skills and personality traits;
- Previous ratings are taken into consideration for current appraisals;
- Appraisals have a review discussion at the end;
- Uniform standard of appraisal is ensured through system of moderation by a committee;
- Appraisal system has separate components to identify potential differences and training needs and it is being done on demonstrated strengths and weaknesses in the current period.

The motivated and skilled staff of any organization would certainly achieve the objectives of the organization.

To make the personnel very perfect and excellent at the work place, the experiences of industries would be useful in education system. Therefore, the performance appraisal of staff is one of the important aspects, which should be used properly in order to achieve the goals of an institution.

Maharana and Panda[27] (2001) made an attempt to study the technological changes and their impact on academic libraries, particularly in the event of diminishing purchasing power in libraries. To improve the quality of information services, the services of library professionals are essentially to be assessed. As a result, the performance evaluation of professionals has become necessary. Performance Evaluation includes a clear definition of duties and responsibilities of the employees, establishment of performance standards and a reasonable understanding of expectations and goals. The objectives of performance evaluation were stated as: work towards the attainment of mission, goals and objectives of the library as well as the institution; inform the employees about their strengths, weaknesses and progress; improve individual and team performance and productivity; strengthen the work relationships and improve communications; develop employee skills; recognize accomplishments and good work; recommend employees for merit increases; and find out the training needs of employees. The criteria for Performance Evaluation includes job performance, professional development, contributions and types of performance rating skills were stated.

Martey[28] (2002) studied the Performance Appraisal of Blame Library, University of Ghana. The objectives of the study were stated as:

- Study the attitude of every employee to find out – opinion of the staff on appraisal system, criteria for measuring performance, interest of staff on promotion procedure, etc.,
- To analyzes contents of complete appraisal form (over 16 years period) with the aim of extracting the

following points – the commitment of staff, criteria for rating, raters and performance measures, objectives of performance, etc.,

- To find out whether the appraisal procedure used in the Blame Library provides an accurate way of knowing whether staff are really adequate for their job or not;
- To propose some guidelines for the design of a suitable procedure of the library.

The definition of performance appraisal given by various experts and components of the appraisal procedure were stated clearly. The components of appraisal procedure include an appraisal form having relevant performance criteria, appraisal interview and mutual trust and sincerity.

URL=http://www.libs.uga.edu/staff/appraisal.html[29] (2004), the importance of Performance Appraisal and its usefulness for the supervisors to evaluate the performance of their staff were given. The performance appraisal is one of the important tools to identify and to improve the existing conditions and skills of the employees. Some of the areas in purpose of performance appraisal are communication between employees and supervisors, employees work performance policies and practices, promotions, etc. The necessity of evaluation of supervisors by their employees was also one of the important factors to achieve the goals of performance appraisal.

As a conclusion, It is evident from this review that, the superiors should conduct Performance Appraisal or Performance Evaluation. However some of the authors suggested that, a Self-Assessment method is used to assess the library professionals, in view of the constraints like lack of established standards, guidelines, etc. Due to the paucity of funds, impact of information technology, the libraries have to make use of the available human resources and in such a case performance appraisal is necessary. Some authors have suggested different methods and procedures to conduct performance appraisal, which would bring together the resources of the library, and it's users, and those methods have also stated about the role to be played by the library staff. The problems and issues involved in performance appraisal are discussed.

Application of performance appraisal in Indian context is not possible because of the lack of set standards, which are comparable for deferent types of libraries that are functioning with different set of aims and objectives.

Self-Assessment

Peel[30] (1989) explained the methods of staff development and identified three scenarios (1) organizational hierarchy (2) develop ourselves (3) stimulate for development. Five essential ingredients are identified for the successful development viz., Mission, Environment, Relation, Infrastructure and Training (MERIT). The commitment of staff and its importance is highlighted. According to him, staff management would include both people and task dimensions. For the development of staff, the following are to be achieved – motivate them positively; improve their current job skills; preparing them for more responsible work. Staff development includes skill, time and effort. All techniques of management can't be applied at a point of time. Development includes target setting, delegation, secondment and job rotation, job enrichment and discipline. The essentials of development particularly will comprise of integrity, praise and encouragement, listening, involvement and working the job. For any organization, following are the major aspects of infrastructure - appraisalm counseling, career planning, remuneration, promotion and termination. The author mentioned the ways of training in addition to sending them to courses – on the job learning with coaching – reading and distance learning; special projects; workshops and seminars. The development of libraries is possible through appraisal process, job restructuring or improvement of work.

Siggins[31] (1992) predicted the problems to trouble the American Academic Libraries, particularly the declining income and rising costs, which force the management to use the scarce resources efficiently. This situation is same in Indian Academic Libraries. In spite of declining income in academic libraries, the services to be offered are increasing. At present, the storage and access to information in electronic form are the real issues in academic libraries. In the light of these constraints, various questions were raised such as - Change in the Library System, relation between staff and user, etc., to cope-up with changes, the improvement of the skills of the library staff is a way to meet the goals of the library without any further financial burden. Therefore, there is a need to assess the personnel from time to time. The relationship between job satisfaction and performance was discussed in different angles. It is stated that, job satisfaction has an impact on staff performance besides job related attitudes such as:

- Organizational Commitment;
- Job Involvement, etc;
- The importance of Training Programme and Professional Development;
- Empower the staff;
- Build an Effective Performance Management System;
- Fair Reward System;
- Identifying the Career paths; and
- Correct Organizational Weaknesses were discussed at length.

Nkereuwem[32] (1996) made an attempt to understand the gender issue and the performance of services in libraries. The issues of women performance and problems with supervisors were stated. Psychological issues between the supervisors and sub-ordinates, which may be common in performance evaluation, were stated. According to the author, success of men is attributed to their ability, whereas the success of women is attributed to their good luck. Gender difference would be more in the event of performance evaluated by supervisors with less or limited experience. Career advancement prospects of the sub-ordinate staff and supervisor's assessment method were also explained. The application of rating scale in performance evaluation is well explained. To arrive at conclusions, the author collected data from 747 librarians of Universities and Polytechnic colleges, etc., and out of the selected Universities nearly half were women librarians. Based on the analysis, necessary conclusions were drawn on various aspects.

Ogunrombi and Bentai[33] (1999) surveyed on staffing patterns in Nigerian University Library from 1981-1997 and concluded that, re-designing of jobs in the light of new technologies to meet the goals of libraries is certainly necessary. The re-designing will result in greater the differential of rules and the acceptance of how each of specific levels of skills, knowledge and abilities of staff can contribute to library services more effectively. In the light of budgetary limitations and increased cost of library materials, the importance of staff and their maximum effective use are discussed. The importance of job analysis and job re-structuring would help for a better staff pattern, in a way the importance of assessment of staff is realized in order to meet the goals of a library.

Barrionuevo (2002)[34] stressed upon the quality and efficiency of library services of universities and their evaluation. In this context, a pilot scheme for the assessment of "University Libraries in Andalusia 1999 – 2002" was taken up. The importance of assessment guide and self-assessment process for the assessment of library services was mentioned. The assessment guide developed by various agencies was mentioned. A model to evaluate academic libraries of Andalusia was given. The assessment of traditional and non-traditional activities of libraries and relation between the two types of activities was mentioned. The self-assessment method was discussed in three stages:

1. Self-assessment, undertaken by the Self-assessment committee, in accordance with the internal assessment guide;
2. External assessment, undertaken by a committee of external experts, in accordance with the guidelines set out in the external assessment guide;
3. TA final report was prepared by the Self-Assessment Committee, based on the findings of two previous reports.

Drucker[35] (2002) stated the importance of Self-Assessment tool and its purpose and the areas to be covered. The Drucker's Self-Assessment tool is discussed to assess the services of libraries. The nature of Drucker's Self-Assessment tool was also discussed. The requirements of library administrators before going for self-assessment were listed. The self-assessment process takes place in three phases; Phase-I: Preparing for self-assessment. Phase-II: conducting self-assessment process. Phase-III: Completing the plan. For comprehensive organizational self-assessment, two major options were given. Option A: two-group discussion, Option B: One group retreat. According to the author self-assessment tool can be adopted by any organization. The self-assessment process and its limitations should be thoroughly discussed before adapting by any organization.

Ustun[36] (2002) opined that human resources are the most important and costly element of information services. Further, the author stated that without qualified human resources and motivated personnel, there is no possibility of proper organization, in spite of the availability of qualitative information resources and Information Technology. The developments being taken place in Information Technology have highlighted the role of staff. A five-degree attitude scale was used to collect data. The relation between job satisfaction and measurement of individual assessment of the job was stressed upon. The author has thrown light on the relationship between productivity and job satisfaction, motivation from the standpoint of job satisfaction. He suggested a personal policy, which shows that the employees are to be valued, assessed, trusted and rewarded. Rewards should be given not to the person but to the job and it should be based on the standards of merit, which will be possible through assessment only.

Line[37] (2003) stressed the need for appraisal system in libraries and the problems that are likely to be occurred in the absence of any appraisal system. The procedure for assessing the staff by the supervisors is well stated that, self-evaluation is not the same as self-approval. So it does not meet this basic need. In self-approval method, the superior sets standards and judge the performance. The issues involved in development and establishing standards were thoroughly discussed as: who establishes the standards, are they generally accepted, would the staff agree with them, etc., and the limitation of self approval methods were also stated.

Self[38] (2003) made an attempt to study the University Libraries by considering score card metrics. He emphasized that the development of a library depends on many ingredients and one among them is self-assessment.

Walters[39] (2003) listed the advantages of user preference over traditional performance assessment as – response from both users and non-users. It was felt that the library's quality assessment would provide a valued measure of service quality; and the limitations of huge perceptions on performance assessment. The judgment of users on quality, potentiality of student is not always acceptable, as they are not experts. But the suggestions from them have proved at many times as useful to improve the quality of library services. The author listed some of the areas, which can be taken into account for the users' assessments as follows:

- Library staff should have the knowledge needed to answer patrons' questions;
- Library staff should understand the patrons' needs;
- Library staff were dependable when handling patrons' service problems;
- The library's website will enable the patrons to locate information on their own;
- The library's access tools will enable the patrons to find information on their own;
- Information is easily accessible for independent use by patrons;
- The library should maintain comprehensive print collections;
- The library should addresses patrons' inter disciplinary needs.

Curtes and Dean[40] (2004) have inspected 36 libraries, and focused on the activities of libraries from which they found some draw backs like: fall of visits, drop in loans, poor maintenance of staff, etc., In their report, a suggestion was made for the improvement of services as – to provide more number of books and information services; to improve accessibility through better opening hours; to share facilities with other services; and to address the perception that libraries simply did not match the ambience and accessibility of book shops. Further, it was stated that there was a danger of date generating targets. Also, a model for the assessment was mentioned in which the uniqueness of consistent Self-Assessment was highlighted. The necessity of annual performance assessment method to assess the staff was stated too. The performance of staff and their evaluation have greater impact and necessary to build better libraries.

Thebridge[41] (2004) stated the availability of evaluation models, measures and methods. Further, the author opined that the literature was not promising on the assessment of outcomes. The earlier studies made on evaluation of library services and activities were not satisfactory and proposed e-VALUED project (electronic valued) which was an evaluation tool kit to evaluate libraries (an evaluation model for Electronic Library developments). Primary aim of this project is to develop a tool kit for electronic library evaluation in Higher Education in UK. A survey was conducted to evaluate EIS (Electronic Information Services) of UK, accordingly a questionnaire was sent to 194 institutions both in print and web version. The EIS to measure performance in academic libraries was stated as:

- Library staff;
- Library operating expenditure;
- Library collection;
- Library loan transactions;
- Information services to groups;
- Library services in a typical week.

The limitations of electronic valued toolkit were stated as – gathering meaningful, purposeful, comparable data; acquiring methodological guidance and the requisite skills to plan and conduct assessments; managing assessment data; organizing assessment as a core activity; interpreting library trends data in the larger environmental context of user behaviour and constraints.

The author stated the process of assessment according to the Association of California Community Colleges as –

"ADICAC."

- **A**lign with relevant campus wide goals
- **D**efine these further by restating them as performance objectives
- **I**dentify performance indicators from the objectives
- **C**hart the performance indicators
- Collect, **A**nalyze and organize the data
- **C**ommunicate to the external audiences

The evaluated tool kit identified 8 areas to assess the Electronic Information System's (EIS) services as:

- Supports learning;
- Supports teaching;
- Supports research;
- Provision of range of resources;
- Effectiveness of EIS provision;
- Relation between internal and external factors;
- User needs;
- Staff career development.

Oltmanns[42] (2004) stressed the importance and benefits of assessment of performance and services of libraries. He assessed the organizational developments, performance, quality of services and a number of methods and tools used in libraries. Most of the methods are formal and empirical-based. He stressed the informal ways to assess the services of library to improve the quality. The author suggested the application of quantitative and qualitative methods to assess the performance in libraries. The outcome of assessment is to increase the staff's involvement in library activities and encourage them towards creativity. The purpose of assessment is to identify issues by development and understanding the mission and goals of the library. Any assessment is to develop a plan to tackle the issues and problems and also make the professionals more responsible through participation. The influence of information technology and its impact on libraries were rightly stated. The problems of economic and funding are discussed.

Pors and Others[43] (2004) conducted a survey on a "Sample of 411 employees to measure the quality of employment in libraries. The employment quality management tools are closely connected with accountability, effectiveness, value for money, empowerment, change, flexibility, incentives, motivation and evaluation". They made a comparison between the sample of UK and Denmark libraries to elicit data by applying the ranking method. They concluded that assessment of staff is a necessary item to meet the ever-changing goals of libraries.

www.ifla.org/iv/ifla66/papers/112-1[44] (2004), the Self-Assessment for library and information sector is stated and a model named "The library and information sector improvement model" (LISIM) is discussed. To improve the quality of library information services, the self-assessment method is one of the best among several other methods. Three-year strategic plans for public libraries to assess the services offered by them were stated. The self-assessment methods for public library services applied by the British Library Research and Innovation Centre was stated. Three approaches of self-assessment to assess library services are mentioned. Other self-assessment methods are cited.

http://www.eduplace.com/rdg/res/assess/selfmetch.html[45] (2004), Self-Assessment methods usually asked the students to review their work in order to have a clear idea on the topics learned. Each model may have a different methodology to assess the students' ability. To get right kind of results, The student should know the criteria of assessment. The feed back of the students would help to refine the instructional plan.

The self-assessment methods are discussed as mentioned below:

- Writing conferences;
- Discussions (whole – class or small groups)
- Reflection logs
- Weekly self-evaluations
- Self-assessment checklists and inventories
- Teacher-student interviews

As a conclusion, to meet the ever-changing goals, training for professionals, improvement of existing library services and introduction of new library services, understanding of gender issues, etc., the Self-Assessment of professionals would provide suitable solutions to achieve the goals of libraries. The self-assessment would help the professionals to understand themselves whether they fit for the job or not and understanding the ability and interests of professionals on various aspects is also possible through self-assessment. The advantages of self-assessment or the other methods of assessment are stated.

NOTES

1. Hagerty, Philip, E: Evaluation of Personnel. *In* Library Evaluation, Syracuse University, 1959, pp.21-29.
2. Deprospo, Ernest, R: Personnel Evaluation as an Impetus to Growth. *In* Library Trends, 20(1), 1971, pp.61-69.
3. Evans, Edward, G: Management Techniques for Librarians. Academic Press, New York, 1976, pp.202-207.
4. Cohen, Lucy R: Conducting Performance Evaluation. *In* Library Trends, 38(1), 1989, pp.41-49.
5. Moore, Nick: Measuring the Performance of Public Libraries: A draft manual Granthana. *In* Indian Journal of Library Studies, 3(2), 1992, pp.160-205.

6. Lancaster, F.W: If you want to evaluate your library, 2nd ed. Illinois, University of Illinas, Graduate School of Library and Information Science, Champangn, 1993, pp.35-40.

7. Belcastro, Patrica: Evaluating Library Staff – A Performance Appraisal System. *In* American Library Association, Chicago, 1998, pp.1-42.

8. Meera, B.M: Performance Measurement: A Criteria for Quality Improvement in Library and Information Services. *In* Library Science with a Stant to Documentation and Information Studies, 35(3), 1998, pp.149-156.

9. Town, Stephen, J: Performance or Measurement. *In* Performance Measurement and Metrics, 1(1), 2000, pp.43-54.

10. Creaser, Claire: Performance Measurement and Benchmarking for Schools Library Services. *In* Journal of Librarianship and Information Science, 33(3), 2001, pp.128-132.

11. Nelavigi, Savitha, M.: Performance Evaluation of Library Professionals: Need and Criteria. *In* SRELS Journals of Information Management, 40(1), 2003,pp.23-29.

12. http: Jackson Library: The University of North Carolina. Criteria for Merit evaluation and tenure of Librarians

13. Peel, David: Performance Ratings and Librarians rights. American Libraries, June 1970, pp.595-600.

14. Johnson, Marjorie: Performance Appraisal of Librarians – A Survey. *In* College and Research Libraries, 23(9), 1972, pp.358-367.

15. Peel, David: Evaluating Library Employees. *In* Library Journal, 97 (15), 1972, pp.2803-2807.

16. Berkner, Dimity, S: Library Staff Development through Performance Appraisal. *In* College and Research Libraries, 40(7), 1979, pp.335-344

17. Edward Evans and Bendict Rugaas: Another look at Performance Appraisal in Libraries. *In* Journal of Library Administration, 3(2), 1982, pp.61-69.

18. Hodge, Stanley, P: Performance Appraisals: Developing a Sound Legal and Managerial System. *In* College and Research Libraries, 44(4), 1983, pp.235-244.

19. Seetaram: Planning of Library and Information Systems. Ess Publications, 1989.

20. Gopinath, M.A: Performance Appraisal of the Library Professionals: A Normative approach. *In* Library Science with a Slant to Documentation and Information Studies, 27(3), 1990, pp.183-191.

21. Gopinath, M.A: Towards Performance Appraisal in Libraries. *In* Library Science with a Slant to Documentation and Information Studies, 31(4), 1994, pp.i-ii.

22. Oldroyd, Robert: Staff Development and Appraisal in an Old University Library. *In* Librarian Career Development, 3(2), 1995, pp.13-16.

23. Srivastav, A.K and Singh, T.B.: Performance Appraisal of the Faculty. *In* University News, 34(11), Nov. 1996, pp.3-6.

24. Peter Jordon: Staff Appraisal: Staff Management in Library and Information Work. New Delhi, Jaico, New Delhi, 1996, pp.141-162.

25. Edwards, Ronald G and Williams, Calvin J: Performance Appraisal in Academic Libraries: Minor Changes or Major Renovation. *In* Library Review, 47(1), 1998, pp.14-19.

26. Jabeen, Shagufta: Performance Appraisal System in Industries Implications to Education System. *In* University News, 37(30), 1999, pp.8-10.

27. Maharan, Balu and Panda, K.C: Performance Evaluation for Library and Information Professionals. *In* University News, 39(42), 2001, pp.5-8.

28. Martey, A.K: Appraising the Performance of Library Staff in a Ghanaian Academic Library. *In* Library Management, 23(8/9), 2002, pp.403-416.

29. URL=http://www.libs.uga.edu/staff/appraisal.html.

30. Peel, Malcolm: Developing Our Staff. *In* Aslib Proceedings, 41(10) 1989, pp.301-309.

31. Siggins, Jack A: Job Satisfaction and Performance in a Changing Environment. *In* Library Trends, 41(2), 1992, pp.299-315.

32. Nikereuwem, E.E: Job Performance Attributions and Career and Advancement Prospects for Women in the Academic

Libraries. *In* Librarian Career Development, 4(1), 1996, pp.18-24.

33. Orgunrombi, Samuel adewale and Bantai,R.C.: Appraising Staffing Patterns in a Nigerian University Library. *In* Library Career Development, 7(8), 1999, pp.77-84.

34. Barrionuevo:http://www.uniovi.es/vicerrecturados.../colidad/ESOE/proceedings.

35 Peter, D: http://www.leader to leader.org/leader books/sat/process.html.

36. Ustun, Ayse: Job Satisfaction in Information Centres: A Comparative Study in Instanbul. *In* Library Progress, 22(1), 2002, pp.1-23.

37. Line, Maurice B: Management Musings 14: We all Need Approval – even bosses. *In* Library Management, 24(8/9), 2003, pp.441-442.

38. Self, James.: From Values to Metrics: Implementation of the balanced score card at a University Library. *In* Performance Measurement and Metrics, 4(2), 2003, pp.57-63.

39. Walters, Williams, H: Expertise and Evidence in the Assessment of Library Services Quality. *In* Performance Management and Metrics, 4(3), 2003, pp.98-102.

40. Curtis, David and Dean Helen: Impact and Performance Measurement and Metrics. *In* Library Services, 4(2), 2003, pp.57-63.

41. The Bridge, Stella: The Evaluated Toolkit: Practical Evaluation Help for Academic Libraries. *In* Performance Measurement and metrics, 5(2), 2004, pp.72-80.

42. Oltmanns, Gail V: Organization and Staff Renewal Using Assessment. *In* Library Trends, Summer 2004 www.Ifla.org/iv/ifla66/papers/112-1

43. Pors, N. Ole, Pat Dixon, Heathu and Robson, Heather: The Employment of Quality Measures in Libraries: Cultural Differences, Institutional Imperatives and Managerial Profiles. *In* Performance Measurement and Metrics, 5(1), 2004, pp.20-27.

44. http://www.ifla.org/iv/ifla66/papers

45. http://www.eduplace.com/rdg/res/assess/selfmth.html

4

Study Design, Methodology and Profiles of Selected University Libraries in Andhra Pradesh

The present study is designed to elicit the views of Library Professionals on performance appraisal along with other relevant information. Basing on the available information, it is to be mentioned here that, in the libraries situated in Andhra Pradesh and for that matter in the country, the system or scheme of performance appraisal is not implemented and no where it is in vogue. In fact, the concept of 'performance appraisal' itself is relatively new to this area, although most of the personnel working in this field are aware of it and its consequences.

It is in this context, proposed to take-up this study in the lines of performance appraisal survey. The study is designed more or less as a self-assessment survey if not performance appraisal as it is not possible in the present context. Edwards and Williams[1] traced out certain issues in theoretical aspects of performance appraisal like supervisors unpreparedness, lack of interviewing skills, supervisors bias, morality in conduct of performance appraisal, etc. The application of performance appraisal in libraries of USA is not promising, where the library system is developed considerably. Therefore, the application of performance appraisal in Indian libraries is not practicable for several reasons to improve the quality of services and to the introduction of new services, and a kind of assessment of staff is necessary. Therefore, self-assessment method is opted to draw data from library professionals in this research work. Jordon[2] suggested in the first stage, staff would be given a chance to assess their own performance and survey was conducted in British academic library in 1992 on similar lines.

Barrionueo and Medana[3] also suggested a self-regulated method (self-assessment and external assessment method) to assess the staff from time to time in libraries. Accordingly, all the questions were framed in such a way, that giving scope for the respondent to assess himself the extent of his knowledge or ability or use with regard to different aspects of study ranging from simple general procedures to latest computer applications along with their views and opinions at appropriate contexts.

A study of this nature is surmised to yield some relevant and useful feedback is taken up among the academic libraries and accordingly, decided to conduct the survey among the University Libraries in the state of Andhra Pradesh. It is also planned to cover all the professionals working in these libraries for eliciting the needed information.

OBJECTIVES OF THE STUDY

The present study is taken-up with the following objectives:

1. To find out the views of the library personnel on appraisal system in general and the appraisal procedure used in their libraries if any, in particular.
2. To assess the professional activities and their areas of interest.

3. To understand the knowledge of the professionals on computer technology, printing and publishing technology and networking.
4. To understand the relations between professionals.
5. To understand strengths and weaknesses of professionals.
6. To understand training needs of library professionals.

METHODOLOGY

Once it is decided to conduct the survey on the University Libraries, the list of University Libraries in the state along with the number of professionals working in different cadres in each of the libraries is obtained. As per the information obtained, there are 17 Universities in the state and out of them 13 Universities are selected for the present study. The reason for not covering the remaining 4 is that they are only Deemed Universities. There is no similarity as far as the professionals and designations are concerned in the libraries between the Universities and Deemed Universities. The funding agency also differs between these Universities.

Questionnaires

After careful preparation of the study design, target group to be covered and objectives specified, the next step is to prepare the survey tools for obtaining required information. Keeping in mind the objectives of the study, an interview questionnaire is prepared after sequentially arranging the aspects to be covered. Provision is made in the questionnaire for recording the individual's response in a three-grade scale.

The finalized questionnaire was pre-tested in a near by University Library and after scrutinizing the responses and experiences, necessary modifications were made and the questionnaire is finally used for the survey.

Coverage

As already mentioned, 13 University Libraries from the State of Andhra Pradesh, India have been covered in the present study. In these libraries, altogether 215 professionals were contacted. Information on its year of establishment, number of persons contacted and number who have completely responded from these 13 Universities are shown in Table 4.1.

The main reason for the non-coverage of the remaining 43 individuals is, the non-availability of the respondents (15) and refusal (9) because of their personal reasons. The remaining 19 were covered, but excluded, as the information provided is not complete and only 172 were considered for analysis in the present study.

As the present coverage is 80 percent, it can be said that observations made from this study will have logical significance.

ANALYSIS OF DATA

The data thus obtained were analyzed using personal computers. Software used in the present analysis is SPSS 12.0 version. Observations made were presented under distinct sub-headings in proper tabulation format. Responses are presented as percentage distributions although the number in some categories is less. This was done to have an easy and clear understanding of the trends in the presentation. Hence, this limitation needs to be kept in mind when making generalizations using these observations.

The responses are analyzed and presented University wise and also by selected background characteristics like age, sex, professional qualifications and cadre in which they are working. These responses recorded for each question in three-grade scale were quantified by giving unit scores and a total score for each of the aspects is computed by adding

Table 4.1: Details Of University Libraries And Coverage

Sl. No.	Name of the University	Year of Establish -ment	No. of Professionals	
			Contacted	Fully Responded
Traditional				
1.	Osmania University (OU)	1918	13	10
2.	Andhra University (AU)	1926	50	41
3.	Sri Venkateswara University (SVU)	1954	26	20
4.	Nagarjuna University (NU)	1967	13	10
5.	Sri Krishnadevaraya University (SKDU)	1968	11	11
6.	University of Hyderabad (UOH)	1974	41	31
7.	Kakatiya University (KU)	1976	14	12
8.	Dr. B.R. Ambedkar Open University (BROU)	1982	7	5
9.	Sri Padmavathi Mahila Viswa Vidyalayam (PMU)	1983	6	6
10.	Potti Sriramulu Telugu University (PSTU)	1985	10	8
Professional				
1.	Acharya N.G. Ranga University (ANGRU)	1963	17	13
2.	Jawaharlal Nehru Technological University (JNTU)	1972	5	4
3.	N.T. Ramarao University of Health Sciences (NTRU)	1986	2	1

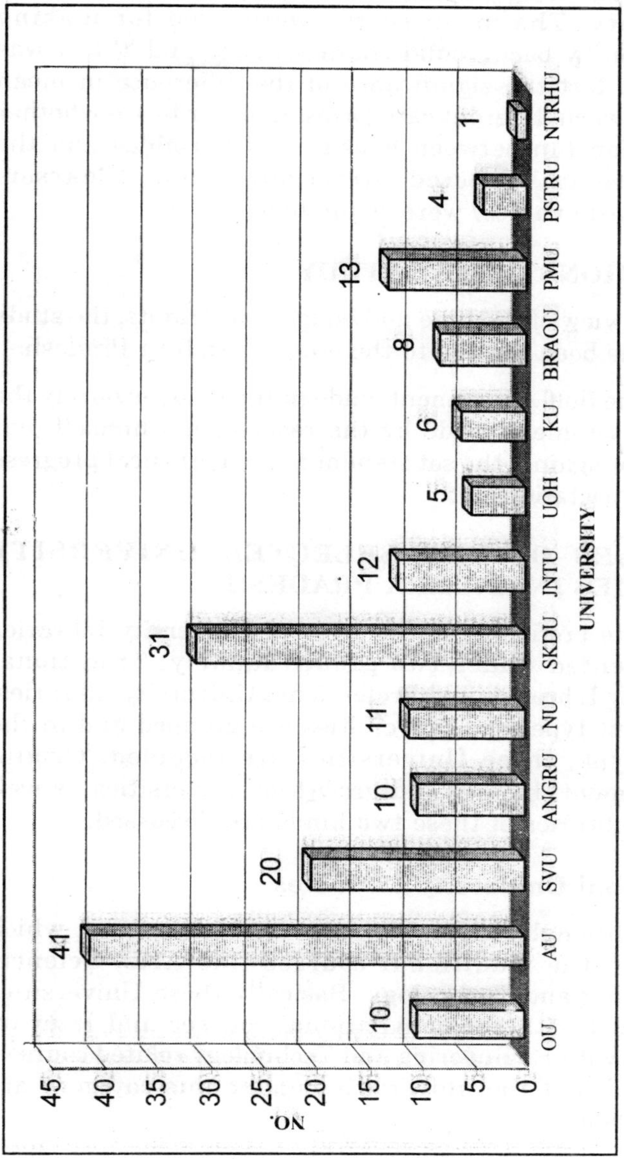

Fig. 4.1: Number of Library Professionals

up the scores of all responses under that particular aspect or category. The mean scores were used for making comparison by background characteristics and 't' test was applied to test the significance of the difference in mean scores between different categories. In order to see whether the relationship between background variables and the scores are in expected direction or not, 'Pearson' correlations(r values) were computed.

LIMITATIONS OF THE STUDY

1. In view of the time and budget constraints, the study has been limited to the state of Andhra Pradesh.
2. The Self-Assessment made in the study is purely the assessment made by the respondents himself, but not against the set standards are periodical progress expectations, etc.

PROFILES OF THE SELECTED UNIVERSITY LIBRARIES IN ANDHRA PRADESH

The profiles of the selected University Libraries are presented under two groups namely, Traditional University Libraries and Professional University Libraries. In the first type, ten Universities are grouped and in the second type, three Universities are included. Origin, establishment, history and growth of universities as well as their libraries of these two kinds are discussed.

Traditional University Libraries

Traditional Universities are the Universities, which deal with the traditional courses like Arts, Science, Engineering and Technology. Basically these Universities are started with the conventional courses and later on extended with Engineering and Technology related courses. The profiles of the universities under this category are detailed below:

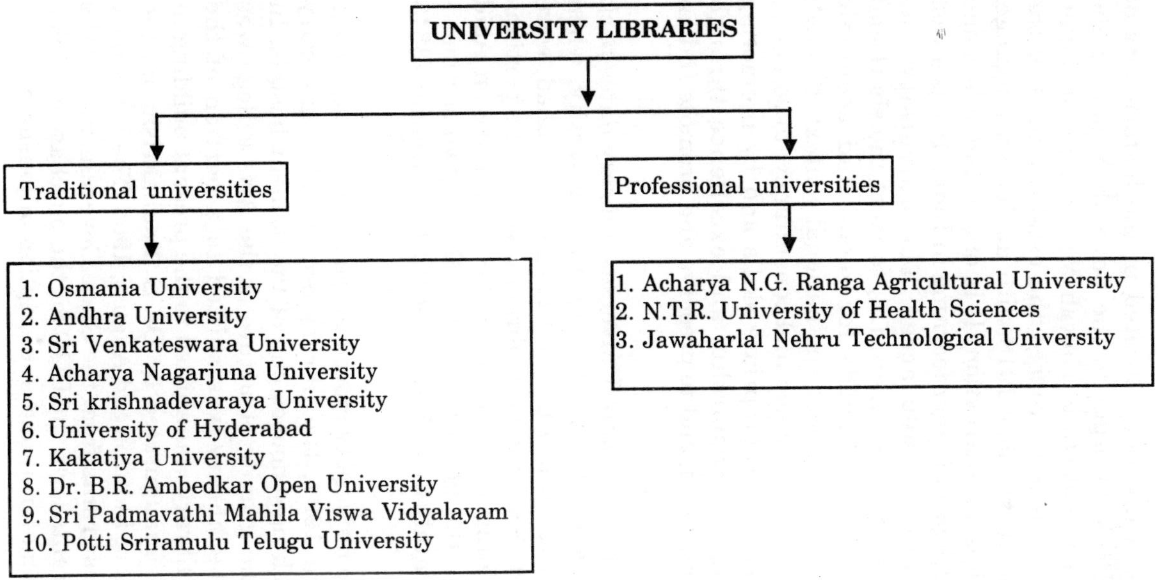
UNIVERSITY LIBRARIES
Traditional universities
Professional universities
1. Osmania University
2. Andhra University
3. Sri Venkateswara University
4. Acharya Nagarjuna University
5. Sri krishnadevaraya University
6. University of Hyderabad
7. Kakatiya University
8. Dr. B.R. Ambedkar Open University
9. Sri Padmavathi Mahila Viswa Vidyalayam
10. Potti Sriramulu Telugu University
1. Acharya N.G. Ranga Agricultural University
2. N.T.R. University of Health Sciences
3. Jawaharlal Nehru Technological University

Osmania University Library

"Osmania University" located in the historic city of Hyderabad, owes its orgin to the Seventh Nizam of the erstwhile Hyderabad state, Nawab Mir Osman Ali khan, who through a Firman ordered the establishment of the university on 7th October 1918 with an Indian language, Urdu as medium of instruction. It is one of the oldest and largest institutions of higher learning in India. It has a vast area of campus of 1600 acres. The university was established with the objectives, i.e., to meet the short and long term manpower needs for social and economic development in the regional and national context, through teaching, research, extension and consultancy; to empower youth by imparting appropriate skills and by promoting scientific temper, scholarship and excellence through teaching and research; and to preserve and promote Indian Culture and Heritage.

The origin of Osmania University Library dates back to 1918 along with the inception of the University, when the volumes of the Darul-Uloom College, Hyderabad, were acquired. In the beginning the library occupied the portions of rented building which Housed the University on Abid Road. In 1919, the library was divided into two sections - (1) the occidental (2124 Vols) and (2) the oriental (3313 Vols).

When the university moved to the present campus site at Adikmet in 1934, the library occupied a temporary building, which now houses one of the student hostels. In 1939, when the granite structure of the Arts college was completed, the library was shifted to a portion of the building. The library was shifted to the present building in 1963, and was inaugurated by Dr. S. Radhakrishnan, the then President of India on 3rd August, 1963. The University library receives grants from the State Government and the department grants form the UGC for the purchase of books, other reading material and subscription of journals.

The library has a collection of 4,90,356 Books(2003), 58,249 Bound Volumes (Journals), 6,473 Theses and Dissertations, 10,434 UN Documents, 6,428 Manuscripts, 272 Films and 11 CD ROM's. The library caters to the needs of P.G. students, research scholars, Teaching Faculty, Ministerial and Technical Staff who were enrolled as its members.

The Osmania University library functions throughout the year except on 7 National and public holidays. It works from 9.00 a.m. to 9.00 p.m. on all working days and from 10.00 a.m to 4.30 p.m on Sundays and other public holidays. During examination period, it functions till 11 o'clock.

The Library provides reference, S.D.I., documentation and bibliographical assistance to its users and Duplicating services such as Xerox facility is also available on a nominal payment.

The Vision of Osmania is a permanent exhibition of charts, photographs, official documents, campus plans, etc., depicting the history and development of the Osmania University. This is an attraction to the student community as well as visitors and other dignitaries who visit the Library.

The activities of the library are mostly computerized and the library is using "CDS/ISIS" and "SOUL" software for developing its database. This library has occupied place in the INFLIBNET project of the UGC. The library is planning to computerize all of its activities.

The University library has sanctioned posts of 22 professionals out of which thirteen are working at the time of conducting the survey. Among three these thirteen professionals, one is Librarians, one is Assistant Librarian and eleven are Library Assistants.

Andhra University Library

The Andhra University was constituted by an Act of the Madras Legislature, the Madras Act No.II of 1926. It came into existence as a result of a widely felt demand in the Telugu districts of the old Madras province for an institution which could help in the flowering of the rich heritage of the Andhras and their aspirations, both scientific and artistics, worthy of their great past. It was first established at the then Bezwada (Now Vijayawada) and shifted to Waltair (now Visakhapatnam) in September 1930 and in the year 1931-32, it began functioning in a building called the Hotel Cecill with an area of about 53 acres around it.

The Andhra University Library was started in 1927, with a nucleus collection of 4,500 books donated by Rao Bahadur Sri D. Lakshminarayana, a Philanthropist and Andhra Industrialist of Nagpur. The primary task of this library is to cater to the information needs of faculty, scholars and students of the resident university colleges. The name of the library has been changed to Dr. V.S. Krishna Library in 1968 as a token of respect to the former Vice-Chancellor Dr. V.S. Krishna who has shown keen interest in developing this library. Besides this main library, there are two more Branch Libraries i.e., Engineering college library and Law College Library in the campus to meet the specific information needs of the concerned colleges.

The Andhra University library is having a total collection of 4,20,000 documents at present. Out of which 2,50,000 are backsets of periodicals. The entire collection was kept in three categories as – Loan books, Reference books and special reference books, basing on the value and rarity of such collection. There are separate text book and quick reference sections for exclusive use and reference of users in the library. In addition, there are special collection of books donated by Dr. S. Radhakrishnan, Ex-President of India, Dr. K.V. Gopapalaswamy, Sri. A.V. Bhanoji Rao, etc. Each of the above collection is having its unique and rare reference value. There are 2,663 palm-leaf and paper manuscripts in the library. Most of them are donated by

Paravasthu family and others. They are very old and valuable. Most of them are in Sanskrit language covering various subjects. TOEFL cassettes along with books are available in the reference section for those appearing the TOEFL examination. The books and backsets of periodicals are arranged on the shelves by subject-wise with call numbers which are noted on the spine of the books as per the Dewey Decimal Classification system. The library catalogue is in card form and entries for each book are arranged in three sequences i.e., Author, Title and Subject in alphabetical order. One can easily identify the call numbers of a required book from any of the above three sequences in which cards are arranged in the catalogue.

The following services are offered in the library at present: Reference Service, Inter-Library Loan Service, Photocopying Service, Audio-Visual Service, E-Mail Service, Content Page Service, OPAC and UGC-INFONET Services.

The membership of the library is open to all the faculty, scholars and students of the University colleges. It is also open to certain cadres of university administrative staff. Besides, the library facilities are also available to the graduates and retired faculty of this university as deposited borrowers on the payment of prescribed fee. The library follows Open Access System.

The library consists of four floors and a cellar. It has an independent bindery. The library preserved its paper and palm leaf manuscripts in its cellar, they relate to the Vedas and the Upanishads of the yester centuries. All the other parts of the building are being used for Loan Section, Text Book Section, Reference Section, Technical Section, UGC-INFONET Section, Inter Library Loan Section and Special Reference Section. Automation of the University library has taken place and 50% of work has been completed. The library is using SOUL Software for its house keeping activities. Internet connectivity has been extended and open to staff and students on free of cost. The library was kept open on all the days except public holidays. It works from Monday through Saturday from 9.00 a.m. to 12.00 in the night.

There are 50 professional staff working in the University library at the time of survey, which includes one Deputy Librarian, three Assistant Librarians, thirty eight Library Assistants and eight Technical Assistants.

Sri Venkateswara University Library

Sri Venkateswara University was established in the temple town of Tirupathi, the holy abode of Lord Sri Venkateswara on 2nd September 1954, to meet the long felt desires and aspirations of the people of Rayalaseema region and Nellore district of Andhra Pradesh as an institution of post graduate learning and research. It is located in sprawling thousand acres with the picturesque sheshachala hill range of eastern ghats forming a back drop. Now the territorial jurisdiction of the university is confined to the districts of Chittoor, Cuddapa and Nellore. It is the 3rd biggest university in Andhra Pradesh.

The university library was started in the year 1955 with the small collection of 6700 books taken from the Sri Venkateswara College, Tirupathi, administered by Tirumala Tirupathi Devastanams. Initially the library was housed in one portion of the college main building. Later it was shifted to the present building which was inaugurated by late Dr. S. Radhakrishnan, the then president of India in July 1964. He described it as '*Tajmahal of South*'

The main library building was opened in the year 1964 with an area of 45,000 sq.ft. and a stacking capacity of 1,30,000 books and an extension wing was opened in 1982 with an area of 13,000 sq.ft. with a stacking capacity of 75,000 books. Thus, the present building has stacking capacity of 2,05,000 books. Additional space for stacking one lakh books is very much required.

The university library is centrally situated and easily accessible to all the departments in the campus and has steadily grown over the years and now, it has 3,23,489 documents (2003 -2004). The library subscribes to about 360 current journals of National and International importance. The library serves the information needs of the teaching faculty, research scholars and students of S.V.V College of Arts and Sciences and S.V.V. College of Engineering, Non-Teaching staff of the university and Deposit Borrowers numbering around 7000.

In order to provide better service to the users of the library, its huge and perennial growth of its collection has been arranged in such a manner that books and back volumes of journals on science and technology are housed in newly constructed extension building and books and back volumes of journals on social science, arts and humanities are housed in three floors of the stack area of the library building, so that readers may not find any difficulty in locating the documents of their choice. Besides book binding service, the library offers Reader's Advisory Service, Reference Service, Reprography Service and Inter- library loan facility. The library has competitive examinations cell providing books and journals relating to civil services, APPSC, GATE, TOEFL, GRE, GMAT, CAT and other competitive examinations. The library organized seminars and conferences also.

The library functions with 12 different sections to achieve functional efficiency. The sections are:

- Circulation Section
- Text book Section
- Periodical Section
- Book acquisition Section
- Children's Section
- Technical Section

- Competitive Examination Cell
- Reference Section
- Documentation Section
- Binding Section
- Loan Section
- Data Processing Section and
- Administrative Section

The library is kept open for readers between 8 a.m to 8 p.m. on all working days with the transactions at the circulation counter and on Sundays and holidays, the library function from 10 a.m to 5 p.m. for study and consultation purpose only. The library follows Open Access System. Books are classified using DDC and Catalogued using AACR.

The university library is a participating member in the INFLIBNET Programme of UGC. The UGC has provided Rs.6.5 lakhs (non-recurring grant) and Rs.1.72 lakhs (recurring grant) for computerization of the library under INFLIBNET Programme. The computer system was installed in the month of July 1996. About 15 professionals at various levels were trained in DOS, CDS/ISIS and ILMS in November 1996. The creation of database for thesis and dissertations consisting of 1914 records and database for serials (back volumes and current journals) consisting of 2169 records was completed. The creation of database for books (30,000 records created) is in progress.

The University has the professional staff of 26, out of which one Librarian, one Assistant Librarian, eighteen Library Assistants and six Technical Assistants are on rolls.

Acharya Nagarjuna University Library

Acharya Nagarjuna University is named after the great Buddhist Philosopher, Acharya Nagarjuna which was first started as PG center of the Andhra University at Guntur in 1967. It has grown into a full-fledged center of Higher Learning and was established as a University in 1976 to fulfill the needs of the people of the Krishna, Guntur and Prakasham Districts of Andhra Pradesh. The University and its affiliated colleges offer a vide variety of courses including Engineering, education, law, pharmacy, science, commerce and Arts. The University runs 24 academic departments offering 37 PG courses, 7 advanced research centres and also three extension centres at its main campus. It has two P.G centres at Nuzvid and Ongle. The University has completed 29 years of its existence on the date of survey.

The Andhra University Post Graduate Centre library, established in 1967 with its collection of 18,900 volumes, became the Acharya Nagarjuna University Library on 19th August 1976, which is named after late Dr.B.R.Ambedkar by the University recently as "AMBEDKAR MEMORIAL LIBRARY". The University Library remains the heart and soul of the university, though there has been a struggle to keep it current in the face of a staggering escalation in costs.

Presently the library is housed in its own magnificent building with three floors overlooking the main avenue of the university. The plinth area of the library is 2130 sqare meters. The book stack is located in the basement hall; current periodicals and back volumes collection in the first floor; text books, Dictionaries, Encyclopaedias and other quick reference material are located in the south wing; office in the North wing; and the circulation counter in the centre of ground floor. The library has over one lakh qualitatively rich and recent volumes and over 425 National and International Journals. It has also acquired some rare volumes of census, five year plans, District manuals, back volumes of periodicals in microfiche and microfilm.

The library is providing various services like:

1. Lending

2. Reference
3. Documentation
4. Reprography
5. Internet
6. Access to INFLIBNET databases
7. INFLIBNET services
8. Bibliographic services using CD-ROM Databases service.

Started its automation activity since 1988 with the recurring and non-recurring grants from UGC, data base of about 40,000 records are created using SOUL software and sent to INFLIBNET. Efforts are being made to access the Electronic Journals under UGC- INFONET Programme.

The Library has 18 sanctioned posts of professional staff at different levels, of which currently thirteen are working at the time of survey. Out of these professionals, one Librarian, one Assistant Librarian, eight Library Assistants and three Technical Assistants are working.

Sri Krishna Devaraya University Library

Sri Krishna Devaraya University had its beginning as the PG Centre of Sri Venkateswara University in the year 1968. It has gained its autonomy in the year 1976. Fulfilling the desires of the people of the region, the Post Graduate Centre was given the status of the University in the year 1981. Initially, Sri Krishna Devaraya University functioned as a unitary residential University. It was conferred the status of an affiliating university in the year 1987. Presently, it is catering to the higher educational needs of the revenue districts of Anantapur and Kurnool.

Sri Krishna Devaraya University has facilities for undertaking study and research through well-established library. The central library of the university is provided with a rich and varied collection of 1,14,000 books, 150 periodicals and 115 magazines. The clientele consists of teaching staff, Non-teaching staff, Research Scholars and students. The library functions from 8.30 a.m. to 8.30 p.m. on all working days and between 10.30 a.m. and 5.00 p.m. on all holidays.

The library has different sections to perform various functions of the library. It also has a separate section for helping the students to prepare for the competitive examinations at various levels. Besides lending of books and reference services, the library extends photocopying facility for the benefit of the users. INFLIBNET facility of UGC is offering a wide range of services, which is also available in the university library.

There are 11 professional staff working in the library. Out of which, one is Librarian, six are Library Assistants, and four are Technical Assistants.

The University of Hyderabad Library

The University of Hyderabad was established by an act of parliament on 2nd October 1974 as a Central University and is fully financed by the UGC. The University campus spread over a vast stretch of land measuring about 2,300 acres, 20 km from the city of Hyderabad. The university also a city campus popularly known as - "The Golden Threshold" - the residence of Late Sarojini Naidu, which was bequeathed to the University by her daughter, the late Padmaja Naidu. The main objective behind the establishment of the university is to disseminate and advancement of knowledge by providing instructional and research facilities in such branches of learning as it may deem fit and to take appropriate measures for promoting inter-disciplinary studies and research in the university.

The University Library started it's functioning from the "Golden Threshold", soon after the university was established. Full-fledged library services to the users started from the year 1976. Earlier, the library was in 3 different places catering to the needs of different schools. The library has been successfully catering to the needs of all schools of sciences, social sciences, humanities and management studies. A library unit has been functioning at the "Golden Threshold" to cater to the needs of S.N. School of performing arts, fine arts and communication and center for folk culture studies. The present library building named "Indira Gandhi Memorial Library" was inaugurated by Dr. S.D. Sharma, the then vice president of India in the year 1988.

The Library has a very rich collection of over 2.72 lakhs (2001) of volumes of comprising of monographs, reference works, Theses and Dissertations and back volumes of research periodicals. The library is subscribing to over 700 current periodicals and 50 popular magazines apart from good number of newspapers. Apart from the above, the library has over 2000 theses/dissertations accepted for the award of M.Phil/Ph.D degrees by the university. There is a moderate collection of over 2000 text books acquired under SC/ST book bank. In addition to the books and journals, the library has good collection of 16 mm education films in Science and Arts. In general, the Teaching and Non-Teaching Staff, Research Scholars and students of the university are the users of the library. In addition, the library has provision for the private section for R & D Institutions to become institutional members to use the library facilities for reference purpose.

The library is kept open throughout the year except on the following holidays - Republic Day, Independence Day, Gandhi Jayanthi, Holi, Vijaya Dasami and Deepavali. The library has been kept open from 8.00 a.m. to 10.00 p.m. on all working days and 10.00 a.m to 5.00 p.m. on holidays; and during examinations it works up to mid night.

The library works with the following sections:

(1) Acquisition Section,

(2) Technical Section,

(3) Periodical Section,

(4) Circulation Section,

(5) Computer Section,

(6) Stack Area,

(7) Binding Section,

(8) Reserve and SC/ST Book Bank,

(9) Golden Threshold Library, etc.

The library is offering the following services:

1. Reprographic Services,
2. Audio-Visual Services
3. Reader Services, i.e., the University Library is an institutional member of the NIRD Library, British Library, American Centre.
4. Institutional Membership, i.e. The Library has enrolled eight institutional members by collecting fee from these private laboratories and centres.
5. Book Binding Unit,
6. Library publications,
7. Training facilities and.
8. PGDLAN course on distance education mode.

The library started its automation activity in 1989 and it has the distinction of being the first university library in India to have fully automated house keeping activities using LIBSYS Software. The database is connected on to the campus-wide LAN (Local Area Network) for the benefit of network users of all the scholars/departments. The library has replaced its card catalogue with the OPAC. The library's proposal for creating a digital library was approved by the UGC.

The University library has sanctioned posts of 62 professionals, of these 41 are working at different levels and these professionals include one Librarian, one Deputy Librarian, seven Assistant Librarians, twelve Library Assistants and twenty Technical Assistants.

Kakatiya University Library

Facilities for Post Graduate Education for Telangana people were available only in Hyderabad until 1967. The UGC sanctioned eleven PG centres for the entire country during IV Plan Period, out of which Andhra Pradesh got three centers including the one at Warangal. With the sanction of PG Centre at Warangal under the control of Osmania University, it was established in 1967. The PG center was accorded autonomy in administrative and academic affairs by the Osmania University on 30th April, 1976. Finally, it was upgraded into Kakatiya University on the 19th August, 1976. The main objective behind the establishment of this university is to provide educational facilities to the people of Northern Telangana which was a backward region of Andhra Pradesh.

The present library of Kakatiya University made a modest beginning in the erstwhile PG Centre at Warangal in 1967 in a small room with a single clerk. The first book was accessioned in the annals of the library records in 18th November 1967. Antecedent to the formation of the university, the books were housed in the departments concerned with closed access system under the control of heads of departments.

A centralized library was established in 1982 by pooling the collection of erstwhile departmental libraries and introduced open access system in place of closed access system. The prime function of the university library is to provide study and research facilities to the students, research scholars and faculty members of the university. The credit goes to Late Prof. K. Venkata Ramaiah, the first Vice-Chancellor for his initiation, interest and materializing the plan in constructing a well planned and beautiful building for the university library in a central place of the campus. Comprising a plinth area of 20,000 sq.ft. With rich ventilation to house different sections, the university library building came into a physical reality in the year 1980. Prof. Jafar Nizam inaugurated the university library on 10th March, 1983 which is a land mark in the history of Kakatiya University.

The collection of the library is about 1.18 lakhs of (2001-2002) books, and 201(2001-2002) Journals of both Indian and foreign languages, 25,000 back volumes and 1800 Ph.D thesis and M.Phil dissertations. The library clientele includes teachers, research scholars and students. Further, it also serves the needs of thousands of students in distant learning mode and research scholars from Warangal, Khammam, Karimnagar and Adilabad districts, being the biggest library available in this area.

The Library works for 14 hours a day, kept open from 8.00 a.m. to 10.00 p.m on all working days. The library has the following sections to provide various types of services/ work to be performed. They are: 1. Administration Section 2. Acquisition Section 3. Technical Section 4. Reference and Text book Section 5. Periodicals Section .6. Stack section-Arts(S.S. Arts) 7. Technical Section 8. Stack Section – Science & Technology (SS – S & T) 9. Circulation Section 10. Competitive Examinations material cell 11. INFLIBNET-Database Management Internet Services, etc.

The University Library is providing the following services to its readers: 1. Reference Service 2. Document Delivery Service 3. Reprographic Service 4. Current Awareness Service 5. Career Guidance/Assistance Service 6. Library Orientation Service 7. Database search service and 8. OPAC

Ever since the establishment of the INFLIBNET , the university has been actively participating in its programmes. Selected by the INFLIBNET as one of the participant libraries in its nation wide network, the university library has received a grant of Rs.6.5 lakh for infrastructure facilities. A post of "Information Scientist" was also sanctioned for the purpose of automation of library activities. Both CDS/ISIS and SOUL packages of INFLIBNET have been successfully implemented by the library for the creation of data bases of books, theses and periodicals. The SOUL package developed by INFLIBNET is now being used to automate the in-house operations of the library. The university library claims a substantial share of 50,000 records of books and 1800 records of thesis in the INFLIBNET union catalogue and the bibliographical records are added to the National Union catalogue of books regularly. Bar-coding of these books is also completed.

Prof. T. Vasudev and Dr. K. Jaya Shankar, the then Vice-Chancellors of the University have equipped the library with technical/professional personnel for running the library on sound academic lines. The professional staff of the university library includes Deputy Librarian - one post, Assistant Librarians - Four posts, Library Assistants - five posts. With regard to academic contributions, the staff have presented a number of research papers at the national and regional conferences and also published books, articles and acted as resource persons, translators and course writers in the field of LIS. The staff of the library have actively participated in teaching assignments of Distant learning mode of Kakatiya University and Dr. B.R. Ambedkar Open University, Warangal centre and succeeded in imparting library education to students.

There are 14 professional staff working in the University library. These fourteen consists of one Librarian, two Assistant Librarians, eleven Library Assistants.

Dr. B.R. Ambedkar Open University Library

Dr. B.R. Ambedkar Open University, formerly known as Andhra Pradesh Open University, is the first Open

University in India. It was established by an act of A.P. State Legislature in 1982. Subsequently, the University was renamed as Dr. B.R. Ambedkar Open University in October 1992. Its primary objective is to provide opportunities for higher education to all sections of society and to cater to changing individual and social needs. The motto of the University is *'EDUCATION FOR ALL'*. The University offers 20 programmes in the Arts, Commerce, Science and Social Science faculties with an annual enrolment of about 1.25 lakhs (2003) of graduate students and 7000 P.G. students. The Headquarters of the university is located at Hyderabad.

The University Library was started in the year 1983. The central library is located at the main campus of the university at Jubilee Hills, Hyderabad. It has extensive premises in a plinth area of 9,510 sq. ft. in a building constructed in 1996. Study centers also have attached library cells to serve the needs of the widely scattered student population.

The library has a collection of about 1,23,000 Volumes at the central library and at the study Centers. The collection includes books, Non-book material like Audio - Video Cassettes, films, Charts, maps, modules, CD-ROM's, etc. The library is subscribing 209 current journals on various subjects. In addition to these collection, the library is subscribing for Newspapers, maintains Course material of Dr. B.R.A.O.U and special collection on Dr. B.R. Ambedkar. The membership of the university library is open to the university faculty, supporting staff, research scholars. However, students are allowed to use the library only for reference purpose on special request. Outsiders are also allowed for a short period to use the library for reference purpose with special permission of the librarian.

Library remains open on all the working days except second Saturday, Sunday and university notified holidays. The library timings are 10.30 a.m to 5.00 p.m. and services are available to the users from 11.00 a.m. to 4.30 p.m.

The available services in the library are Bibliographic Services, Inter-library loan Services, Reprographic Services. The course material is kept under reserve collection and they are available for reference only. All the in-house operations of the library are computerized. The library database is accessible to all the academic departments of the university through the LAN. The library LAN connects 11 systems in the library and 26 systems in the Academic branchs. The central library is also provided with an Internet connection. The cadre of the library professionals is on par with the teaching faculty of the University. The University library has 7 professionals on rolls at the time of conducting survey, out of these seven one Librarian, three Assistant Librarians and three Technical Assistants are working.

Sri Padmavati Mahila Viswavidyalayam Library

Sri Padmavati Mahila Viswavidyalayam was established in 1983 at Tirupathi. The campus of the University is spread out in an area of 138.43 acres. Sri Padmavati Mahila Viswavidyalayam is the only institution of Higher Learning in Andhra Pradesh devoted exclusively to Women's education. The objective of the university is to provide professional education to women in Andhra Pradesh and to make them self-reliant.

The University has a fully equipped central library housed in a spacious building. It has a large stack area of 46,000 volumes and 232 Journals. The University Library is kept open from 10.00 a.m. to 5.p.m on all working days.

The library has the following sections:

1. Book stack area
2. Circulation Section
3. Periodical Section
4. Technical Section

5. Reference Section
6. Binding Section, etc.

Library Automation and INFLIBNET Facility are available in the University, which facilitate networking with libraries in other institutions.

The University library has six professional staff, out of which one is Librarian, one is Assistant Librarian and four Librarian Assistants.

Potti Sreeramulu Telugu University Library

The establishment of Telugu University, on December 2, 1985 is a historic event, which marks the realization of a long cherished desire of the telugu speaking people nurtured over decades by the then Chief Minister of Andhra Pradesh Dr. Nandamuri Taraka Rama Rao by adopting a bill unanimously in the Andhra Pradesh State Legislative Assembly. Interestingly in 1997, the then Chief Minister Nara Chandra Babu Naidu has also adopted a bill in A.P. State Legislative Assembly to rename the University as P.S.T.U as a gesture of honour to Amarajeevi Potti Sreeramulu, an immortal great personality and patriot who fought for the formation of saparate Andhra State for Telugu people. It is also unique that the Telugu University is the second of its kind in the country to promote the language and culture of Telugu People.

Located in a prime central place and housed in Telugu Bhavanam Complex at Osmania University Campus, Hyderabad, the Telugu University Library established in the year 1985 has been serving its elite readers for one and half decades right from its conception. The university has two campus libraries one at Srisailam and the other at Rajahmundry and also a branch library at Lalithakalakshetram, Nampally, Hydrabad. Within a short span of time, it has emerged as one of the most resourceful libraries in the field of humanities.

Keeping the above objectives in view, the Central Library has equipped with rich resources, comprising of about one-lakh books, subscribing about 150 subject journals in Telugu and English. In addition, the library has acquired rare and unique collection of palm leaves, Mackenzie manuscripts, letters of C.P. Brown, microfilms / microfiche of Telugu dailies. The library has valuable collection of books received by donation, purchase of personal collection of elite and scholarly people.

The library is running with the following sections:

(1) Book Acquisition Section,

(2) Technical Section,

(3) Reference Section,

(4) Paper/Reading Section,

(5) Reprographic Services Section,

(6) Binding Section,

(7) Office Section etc. and the library is providing the following services

  (1) Reprographic Services,

  (2) Inter-Library Loan Services

  (3) Seminars and Publications,

  (4) Circulation of content pages to the respective teaching staff.

With the financial assistance provided by the INFLIBNET, Ahmedabad to the library, it is planned to create a qualitative database of entire holdings of P.S.T.U library and make it available for on-line access, under the scheme for National Networking of University Libraries in India.

Though inadequate in strength, the University Library including its branch and two campus libraries have well qualified staff, possessing the needed academic credentials and have contributed their efforts with committed zeal for the development and achievement of objectives of the library and information services.

There are sixteen sanctioned posts of professionals in the University library out of these 10 professionals are working at the time of survey. Among these, one Librarian, three Assistant Librarians, one Librarian Assistant, five Technical Assistants.

Professional University Libraries

Professional Universities are those, which deal with purely professional courses like Engineering and Technology, Health Sciences and Agriculture. The profile of libraries in these universities is given below:

Acharya N.G. Ranga Agricultural University Library

The proposal to set up an Agricultural University in Andhra Pradesh was taken up by Government of Andhra Pradesh in 1957 and a committee was appointed to consider the issue. Based on the recommendations of the committee, Andhra Pradesh Agricultural University Act was passed by the State Legislature in December 1963. The university has started it's functioning from 12th June, 1964. The name of the Andhra Pradesh Agricultural University has changed as Acharya N.G. Ranga Agricultural University with effect from 7th November 1996. Its Jurisdiction extends to the entire state of Andhra Pradesh and has a mandate for teaching, research and extension in Agriculture and Allied subjects. The university has 67 research stations. 06 Agricultural colleges, 03 veterinary colleges, 02 Home science colleges, one agricultural Engineering college, 01 Fisheries science college and 02 Agricultural Polytechnics.

From the inception of the university till 1980, the libraries continued to function as part of the respective constituent colleges under the control of respective principals. With the appointment of the university librarian in 1976, the library system was recognized with the following objectives.

(1) Be a clearing house of information on all the aspects of research and development in agriculture and allied subjects in the state.

(2) To acquire, organize and make available all types of documents including non-book materials on agriculture and allied subjects;

(3) To interact with the other information transfer agencies; and

(4) Be a partner in the integrated development of information services in the country as a whole and to act as a regional agricultural information Centre.

The university Central library is located at its main campus in Rajendranagar, Hyderabad. The University librarian leads this library.

The University library building was constructed with the carpet area of 4645 sq.mts with a potential to accommodate over 200 thousand books and has seating capacity of about 200 readers. The library functions from 8.00 a.m. to 8.00 p.m. on all working days. On Sundays and other holidays, it functions for 6 hours from 10 a.m. to 4 p.m.

The library is currently having the collection as follows: 51,910 Books, 16,019 back volumes, 6,055 thesis, 130 Reports and 500 periodicals are subscribed. The library user community is spread all over the state and includes scientists, undergraduates and postgraduates. Internet connectivity has been established through Videsh Sanchar Nigam Limited. A database is developed by using 'LIBSYS' software with a view to providing access to world agricultural literature, CAB Abstracts on CD-ROM's covering all the 45 abstracting Periodicals have been acquired.

The University library has 17 professional staff at different levels, out of these one Librarian, two Assistant

Librarians, two Senior Library Assistants, twelve Technical Assistants are working.

NTR University of Health Sciences Library

The NTR University of Health Sciences (known as University of Health Sciences) was established by the Andhra Pradesh Legislature Act No. 6 of 1986 at Vijayawada to provide training and Research on the Allopathic and Indian System of Medicine, Dentistry, Pharmacy and Nursing. The Main objectives in establishing this University are (1) To maintain a uniform curriculum in all the Institutions affiliated to it. (2) To conduct a common entrance examination to the courses in all the institutions affiliated there to, and (3) To improve the standards of Medical Education including research.

Since this University is continued for administrative activities and control of medical colleges affiliated, the University Library system is not similar to that of any universities in all respects. This library has considerably little collection and maintain by two professionals. In a way the library is not meant for any medical college. The number of users visit the library are also few. Therefore, there is no worth mentioned traditions and services available. However, for the benefit of longer medical community, MEDLINE and the library is moving towards automation. With the financial assistance obtained from Government of India, the University is networking all the Medical colleges and their libraries through APSWAN. This is already operational in many colleges and will be complete soon.

The University library has only two professional staff in the same cadre of Assistant Librarians to run its library.

Jawaharlal Nehru Technological University Library

Jawaharlal Nehru Technological University Library was established on 2nd October, 1972, by an act of state legislature. Rightly named after the ardent lover of Science

and Technology, Pandit Jawaharlal Nehru, the first Prime Minister of India, the University was established with the noble objectives of strengthening and improving the standards of Technological Education and making it relevant to the rural and industrial development of the country. Technological advancements and infrastructure facilitates determine the progress and prosperity of a nation. This is very much true in case of India, which has huge population growing at a rapid pace and vast natural resources largely remaining unexploited. Realizing that the promotion of technical education was the imperative need of the hour, "*Jawaharlal Nehru Technological University*", the first technological university of India - was established in Andhra Pradesh with head quarters at Hyderabad. The singular objective by the way of emphasis is on training and research in engineering and applied sciences. On its formation, the Government Engineering Colleges at Anantapur, Kakinada and Hyderabad, along with the Government College of Fine Arts and Architecture at Hyderabad, became its Constituent Colleges. These are back bone of the oldest Engineering Colleges of South India
The Library of erstwhile P.G. School was upgraded as the University Library from 1990. The University Library caters to the needs of Institute of Science and Technology, School of Information Technology, School of Management Studies, Academic Staff College, School of Continuing and Distance Education and JNTU College of Engineering, Kukatpally. The Library presently occupies a spacious three storyed building on the main campus of University at Kukatpally.

The University Library provides special services like CAS, SDI, Indexing and Abstracting along with the normal services like reference and referral, literature searching, bibliographic data and on-line services. The University Library has 48,000 books and subscribing to 128 technical journals in the subject fields of science, engineering, technology and management. The University Library has an Audio-Visual Library with two colour Television sets and

Video cassette Recorder with a small number of videotapes in subject fields viz., Engineering, Technology and Management.

The University has received grants-in-aid from AICTE, MHRD and UGC etc. The Library has 2 MBPS leased line Internet connectivity provided by UGC-INFONET. The Library was computerized using VTLS software with 4 SUN Servers, one network attached storage(NAS), 45 sunrays and 20 Pentium II &IV systems. The whole library is connected with LAN.

The University Library has created and maintains a computerized database in subject fields of Science, Engineering, Technology, and Management to meet the in-house needs. The library also plans to participate in the Local Area Network systems for sharing information resources with other libraries in twin cities.

The University Library is in the process of establishing a Digital Library to provide the web based expert lectures, e-Journals, e-textbooks and reference book services to all the engineering, pharmacy and architecture colleges under the control of JNT University. The library is kept open from 10.00 am to 8.00 pm in two shifts to enable the students and researchers to use the library resources.

The University library has five professional staff working at different levels, of which one is Librarian, two are Deputy Librarians and three are in the cadre of Assistant Librarians.

NOTES

1. Edwards, Ronald. G and Williams, Calrin. J: Performance Appraisal in Academic Libraries: Minor changes or major renovation. *In* Library Review, 47(1), 1998, pp.14-19.
2. Peter Jordon: Staff Appraisal: Staff Management in Library and Information Work. New Delhi, Jaico, 1996, pp.141-162.
3. Barrionueo:http://www.nniovi.es/vocerrectirados/colidad/ESOE/proceedings.

5

Observations of the Study

As already mentioned, the present analysis comprises of responses of 172 library professionals interviewed from 13 University Libraries from the state of Andhra Pradesh. The study is more or less designed in the form of a self appraisal of the respondents as all the questions were framed to elicit information on the extent of knowledge and use etc., instead of whether the individual is having the knowledge or he is using a particular method. Hence, scope is given for responding in varied levels such as to a great extent, to some extent and not at all. Thus the elicited information or responses of the individuals are recorded and presented in three-grade scale.

The three grade responses were quantified by giving unit scores and the mean scores computed for each of the aspect of study used to make comparisons by selected background characteristics like type of University, sex, age, professional qualifications and cadre of employment.

Another important aspect to be mentioned here is that, although the number of employees (N) from different Universities is small (less than 25), Percentages were considered for comparison. The responses presented in Percentage distribution only are discussed. This is done in order to make the comparisons easily understandable and also in view of the ease in presentation. This limitation needs to be kept in mind, while making any generalizations from these observations.

Observations made from the analysis are presented in two sections. The first section comprises background information and in the second, analysis of the different aspects studied are presented.

SECTION A: BACKGROUND INFORMATION

PROFILE OF THE RESPONDENTS

A brief profile of the respondents covered in the present study by selected characteristics is presented in Table 5.1.

About three-fourths (72%) of the respondents covered are males while the remaining 28 per cent are females. With the exception of PMU and NTRHU (where all the respondents covered are females), in all other 11 University Libraries, majority of the respondents are males.

Considering the age of the library professionals interviewed, it can be noticed that about 51 per cent are aged 46 years or below and the remaining 49 per cent are aged 47 years or above. This grouping is made considering mean age of the sample (46. years). It can be noticed that comparatively, the younger age group is more in ANGRAU, NU, UOH, BRAOU, PMU, PSRTU and NTRHU libraries while the reverse is true in the other six libraries.

It can also be seen that a majority (76%) of the respondents are having good professional qualifications i.e. MLISc., and above while the remaining 24 per cent have reported BLISc., or lower degrees such as DLSc, CLSc professional qualifications. In all the 13 University Libraries covered, the proportion of respondents reporting MLISc., and above qualification is more compared to those reporting BLISc., and below qualification.

Regarding cadre-wise distribution, about 21 per cent are in Cadre-I, which include Librarian, Deputy Librarian,

Table 5.1 : PROFILE OF THE RESPONDENTS
(Percentage Distribution of Respondents by selected Background Characters)

Background Character-istics	Name of the University													Total (N = 172)
	OU (N=10)	AU (N=41)	SVU (N=20)	ANGRAU (N=13)	NU (N=10)	SKDU (N=11)	JNTU (N=4)	UOH (N=31)	KU (N=12)	BRAOU (N=5)	PMU (N=6)	PSRTU (N=8)	NTRHU (N=1)	
Sex:														
Male	90	58.5	60	76.9	80	90.9	100	83.9	91.7	40	-	87.5	-	71.5
Female	10	41.5	40	23.1	20	9.1	-	16.1	8.3	60	100	12.5	100	28.5
Age:														
46 Years or below	40	19.5	50	76.9	80	36.4	25	58.1	50	100	83.3	100	100	51.2
47 Years or more	60	80.5	50	23.1	20	63.6	75	41.9	50	-	16.7	-	-	48.8
Professional qualification:														
BLISc or below	-	17.1	45	30.8	20	18.2	-	45.2	-	40	-	12.5	100	24.4
MLISc & above	100	82.9	55	69.2	80	81.8	100	54.8	100	60	100	87.5	-	75.6
Cadre :														
Cadre-I	10	12.2	10	23.1	10	9.1	100	25.8	25	60	33.3	37.5	100	21.5
Cadre-II	80	73.2	85	30.8	60	63.6	-	16.1	75	-	66.7	12.5	-	52.9
Cadre-III	10	14.6	5	46.2	30	27.3	-	58.1	-	40	-	50	-	25.6

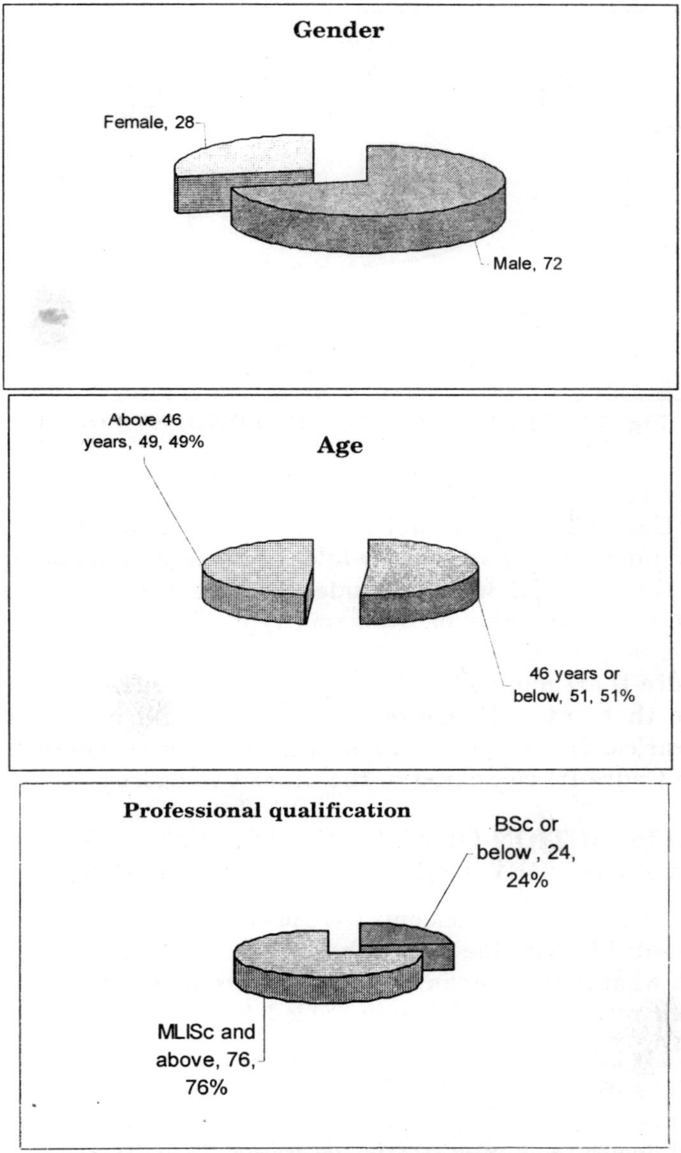

Fig. 5.1: PROFILE OF THE RESPONDENTS (contd.)

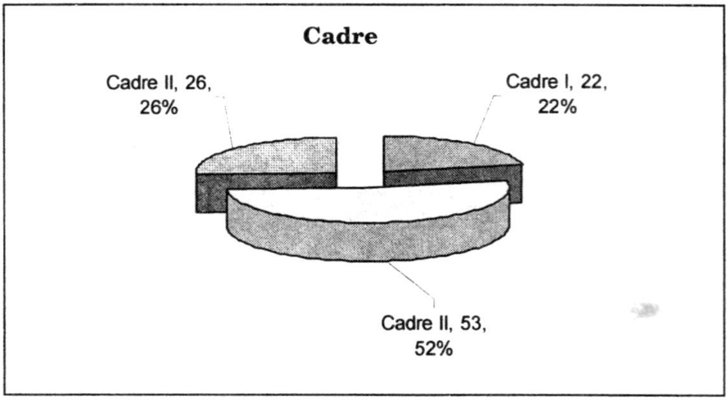

Fig. 5.1: PROFILE OF THE RESPONDENTS (contd.)

Assistant Librarian, Documentation Officer, 53 per cent are in Cadre-II which includes Library Assistants and Documentation Assistants while the remaining 26 per cent are in Cadre-III which includes Technical Assistants and other professionals of the same type. The general trend observed indicates that the proportion of respondents in Cadre-II are more followed by those in Cadre-III and Cadre-I in that order. However, in ANGRU, UOH and PSRTU libraries, the proportion of respondents covered is more from the Cadre-III compared to the other two cadres.

SATISFACTION OF THE RESPONDENTS WITH THE SECTION THEY ARE CURRENTLY WORKING

All the 172 respondents were asked to state whether they are satisfied with the section they are presently working and if not, what is their preferred section where they want to serve. Their responses are shown in Table 5.2.

It is observed that 148 out of the 172 respondents are quite satisfied with the section they are presently working and the remaining 24 have expressed their dissatisfaction and desire to change to other sections. This dissatisfaction is noticed to be more among males compared to females, slightly more among younger age group than the older age group, quite high among those with higher professional qualifications than those with lower professional qualifications and more among those in Cadre-II services compared to those in Cadre-I and Cadre-III services.

Regarding their preference of section in case of change, 8 out of the 24 reported preference for Technical section, 4 preferred Circulation section, 3 each preferred Computer and Periodical sections, 2 reported preference for Reference section while the remaining 4 expressed no preference for any particular section but want a change from the section they are presently working. These preferences indirectly indicate that the Computer and Technical areas are attracting the interests of the professionals and this direction is quite expected in the present era of automation and information technological development.

MEMBERSHIP IN PROFESSIONAL ASSOCIATIONS AND LIBRARY COMMITTEES

Information relating to the membership in professional associations and library committees as obtained from the 172 professionals selected in the study are shown in Table 5.3. It can be noticed that a majority of the respondents from all the University Libraries covered, with the exception of SKDU are having membership in professional associations. The proportion of respondents having membership in professional associations is more among males (61.8%) compared to females (49%). This proportion is slightly higher in younger age group (59%) than in the older age group (57%) and is more among those with higher professional qualifications (64%) than those with lower professional qualifications (41%).

The same proportion is more among those working in Cadre-I services (78%) compared to others working in Cadre-II (55%) and Cadre-III (48%) services.

Table 5.2 : Satisfaction of the Respondents with the Section They are Presently Working and Section Preferred To Change

(Distribution of Respondents by selected Background Characters)

Background Characters	Total No	No. not satisfied	Section preferred to work					
			Any Section	Circulation	Computer	Periodical	Reference	Technical
a) UNIVERSITY:								
OU	10	1	0	1	0	0	0	0
AU	41	4	1	0	0	1	1	1
SVU	20	2	1	0	0	0	0	1
ANGRAU	13	-	0	0	0	0	0	0
NU	10	3	0	1	0	1	0	1
SKDU	11	3	1	1	0	0	0	1
JNTU	4	-	0	0	0	0	0	0
UOH	31	7	1	1	3	0	0	2
KU	12	3	0	0	0	0	1	2
BRAOU	5	1	0	0	0	1	0	0
PMU	6	-	0	0	0	0	0	0
PSRTU	8	-	0	0	0	0	0	0
NTRHU	1	-	0	0	0	0	0	0

b) SEX:								
Male	123	18	4	1	2	2	2	7
Female	49	6	0	3	1	1	0	1
c) AGE :								
46 Years or below	88	11	1	2	3	2	0	3
47 Years or more	84	13	3	2	0	1	2	5
d) PROFESSIONAL QUALIFICATION:								
BLISc or below	42	2	0	0	0	0	0	2
MLISc and above	130	22	4	4	3	3	2	6
e) CADRE:								
Cadre-1	37	4	0	0	2	2	0	0
Cadre-2	91	14	3	3	0	1	2	5
Cadre-3	44	6	1	1	1	0	0	3

Table 5.3: Membership in Professional Associations and Library Committees
(Percentage Distribution of Respondents by selected Background Characters)

Background characters	N	Percentage having Membership in	
		Library committees	Professional associations
a) University:			
OU	10	60	20
AU	41	61	4.9
SVU	20	40	25
ANGRAU	13	53.8	30.8
NU	10	70	20
SKDU	11	18.2	-
JNTU	4	100	75
UOH	31	45.2	12.9
KU	12	91.7	33.3
BRAOU	5	60	20
PMU	6	83.3	33.3
PSRTU	8	87.5	37.5
NTRHU	1	100	-
b) Sex:			
Male	123	61.8	18.7
Female	49	49	18.4
c) Age :			
46 Years or below	88	59.1	21.6
47 Years or more	84	57.1	15.5
d) Professional qualification:			
BLISc or below	42	40.5	9.5
MLISc and above	130	63.8	21.5
e) Cadre:			
Cadre-1	37	78.4	45.9
Cadre-2	91	54.9	9.9
Cadre-3	44	47.7	13.6

Regarding the membership in library committees, it is noticed that the proportion reporting membership ranged from as high as 75 per cent in JNTU to none from SKDU library. An equal proportion of males and females (18%) have reported membership in library committees. This proportion is more among the younger age group (22%) compared to the older age group (16%) and is more reported by those with higher professional qualifications (22%) than those with lower professional qualification (10%). This proportion is high among those working in Cadre-I (46%) compared to those working in Cadre-III (14%) and Cadre-II (10%) services.

Most of the respondents reporting membership in professional associations speaks of their professional interest and interest in career development, while membership in library committees is dependent on specified stipulations of the organizations they are working and the choice of respondents is not involved. However, the observations indicate that these professionals can be involved more in library committees, so that their professional expertise can be better utilized for the development of the libraries.

AWARENESS OF PERFORMANCE APPRAISAL

Responses of the library professionals interviewed in the study to question like whether they are aware of performance appraisal? Whether such appraisal is implemented in their libraries? and whether they feel the need for performance appraisal? Are presented in Table 5.4.

It can be seen that most of the respondents (with the exception of those from SKDU library) from all the University libraries are aware of the concept of performance appraisal. This level of awareness ranged from a low of 18 per cent in SKDU library to a high of 88 per cent in PSRTU library, the lone respondent from NTRHU reporting the awareness of performance appraisal.

Table 5.4: Awareness of Performance Appraisal
(Percentage Distribution of Respondents by selected Background Characters)

Background Characters	N	Having Knowledge of Performance Appraisal	Reporting Implementation of Performance Appraisal in their Library	Feeling the Need for Perfromance Appraisal
a) UNIVERSITY:				
OU	10	50	-	50
AU	41	70.7	-	73.2
SVU	20	70	-	75
ANGRAU	13	61.5	-	61.5
NU	10	60	-	60
SKDU	11	18.2	-	18.2
JNTU	4	75	-	75
UOH	31	80.6	-	74.2
KU	12	75	-	83.3
BRAOU	5	80	-	80
PMU	6	83.3	-	83.3
PSRTU	8	87.5	-	75
NTRHU	1	100	-	100

b) SEX:				
MALE	123	66.7	-	64.2
FEMALE	49	73.5	-	79.6
c) AGE :				
46 Years or below	88	70.5	-	69.3
47 Years or more	84	66.7	-	67.9
d) PROFESSIONAL QUALIFICATION:				
BLISc or below	42	61.9	-	57.1
MLISc and above	130	70.8	-	72.3
e) CADRE:				
Cadre-1	37	83.8	-	81.1
Cadre-2	91	59.3	-	62.6
Cadre-3	44	75	-	70.5

This awareness is noticed more among females (74%) compared to males (67%). It is high among those in younger age group (71%) then in the older age group (67%) and is more among those with higher professional qualifications (71%) than among those with lower professional qualifications (62%). This level of awareness is observed to be more among those working in Cadre-I services (84%) compared to those working in Cadre-III (75%) and Cadre-II (59%) services. Interestingly, in none of the University libraries covered, such performance appraisal is reported to be implemented.

However, it is observed that a majority of the respondents from all the university libraries feel the need for performance appraisal. This feeling is expressed more by the females (80%) compared to the males (64%) and by more or less equal proportion from the younger (69%) and older (68%) age groups. However, more proportion of the respondents with higher professional qualifications (72%) expressed the need for performance appraisal compared to those with lower professional qualifications (57%). The proportion feeling the need for performance appraisal is found to be more among those working in Cadre-I services (81%) compared to their counterparts working in Cadre-III (71%) and Cadre-II (63%) services.

SECTION B: KNOWLEDGE, PRACTICE AND VIEWS OF RESPONDENTS ON PROFESSIONAL ACTIVITIES

All the 172 library professionals covered in the present study were interviewed for obtaining their levels of knowledge, extent of practice and views regarding the professional activities. The professional activities are categorized as below and the observations made from the study are presented in the same order.

Professional Activities

i) General Activities

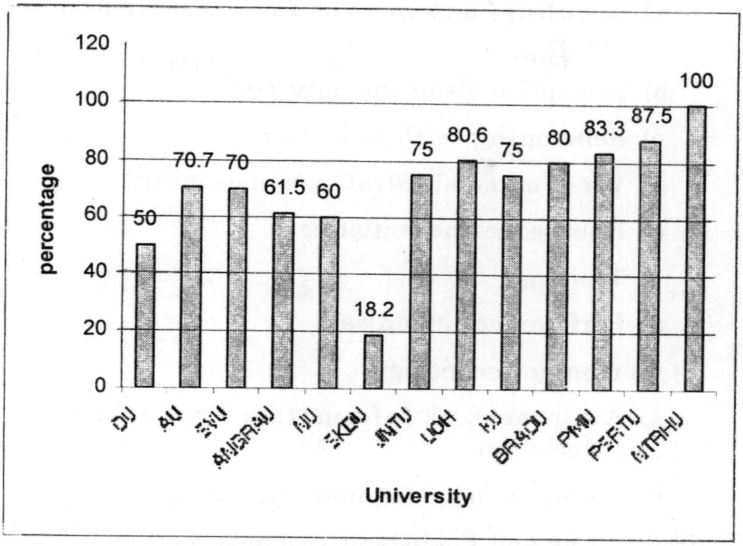

Fig. 5.2: Knowledgement of Performance

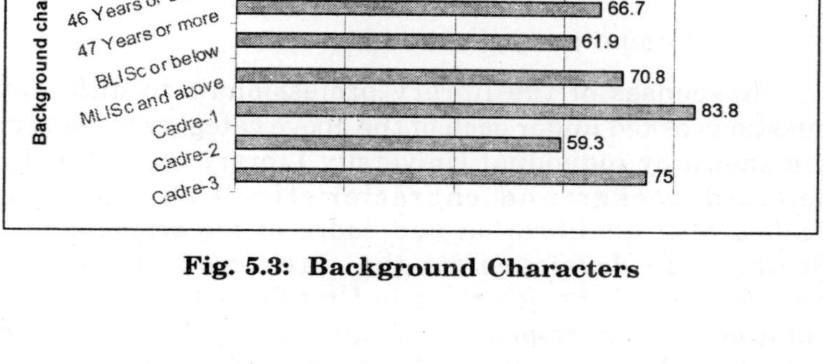

Fig. 5.3: Background Characters

a) Knowledge and views on Goals, objectives of the library.

b) Perception about the nature of job.

c) Relationship with co-workers.

d) Views on administration/management.

e) Knowledge and initiative.

f) Training.

g) Performance appraisal.

ii) Computer Technology

a) Awareness of Information Technology and automation.

b) Ability to use Computer Technology.

iii) Printing and Publishing Technology

a) Use of Computer Printing.

iv) Networking

a) Knowledge and use of networking.

v) Library Services

a) Awareness of general procedures.

b) Classification and cataloguing.

c) Computer applications.

Responses of the library professionals to different questions asked under each of the above category of aspects are shown by individual University Library as well as by selected background characteristics like sex, age, professional qualification and cadre of the respondents. Scores were developed for the three grade responses recorded for all the questions in Unit Scale by assigning a value of 3 for the response 'to a large extent', 2 for 'to some extent' and 1 for 'not at all'. Scores of all the related questions under one aspect are added-up and total scores for that aspect is computed. The total scores were used for comparison between the selected background parameters using means, standard deviation and 't' values. These were presented separately following the frequency tables for each aspect for all the categories of questions relating to the professional activities.

General Professional Activities

Questions on general professional activities are considered under seven sub categories and are presented separately for each sub-category.

Knowledge and views on objectives and goals of the library

Regarding the knowledge and views of the respondents about the objectives and goals of the library, five questions were asked and the responses are obtained in a three grade scale. These were presented by University Librarywise (Table 5.5) and by selected background characters (Table 5.6).

It can be noticed that about 98 per cent of the respondents are aware of the goals and objectives of the library. Out of these, nearly 69 per cent reported that they know the goals and objectives of the library to a large extent, while the remaining 29 per cent said that they know the goals and objectives to some extent. In total, respondents from all the university libraries have expressed this knowledge in more or less similar proportion. This knowledge is reported more by the males (99%) compared to the females (96%). All the respondents in the younger age group (46 years or below) and 96 per cent of those in the older age groups also expressed that they know about the goals and objectives of the library. This knowledge is reported by 95 per cent of those with lower professional qualifications and 99 per cent of those with higher

Table 5.5: Respondents' Views Regarding The Goals Of The Library
(Percentage Distribution of Respondents by University)

Extent of knowledge	Name of the University													Total (N = 172)
	OU (N=10)	AU (N=41)	SVU (N=20)	ANGRAU (N=13)	NU (N=10)	SKDU (N=11)	JNTU (N=4)	UOH (N=31)	KU (N=12)	BRAOU (N=5)	PMU (N=6)	PSRTU (N=8)	NTRHU (N=1)	
Extent of Knowledge about the goals and objectives of the library:														
To a large extent	50	53.7	95	69.2	70	72.7	100	54.8	75	60	100	100	100	66.6
To some extent	50	43.9	5	30.8	30	27.3	-	38.7	25	40	-	-	-	29.7
Not at all	-	2.4	-	-	-	-	-	6.5	-	-	-	-	-	1.7
Extent to which the goals and objectives are met:														
To a large extent	20	17.1	55	46.2	40	9.1	50	16.1	33.3	40	-	25	-	26.7
To some extent	70	78	40	30.8	60	90.9	50	74.2	58.3	60	100	75	100	66.9
Not at all	10	4.9	5	23.1	-	-	-	9.7	8.3	-	-	-	-	6.4
Extent to which the goals and objectives are fulfilled beyond the target:														
To a large extent	20	17.1	10	23.1	20	-	50	19.4	8.3	20	-	12.5	-	15.7
To some extent	80	58.5	90	53.8	60	90.9	25	64.5	58.3	80	83.3	50	100	66.9
Not at all	-	24.4	-	23.1	20	9.1	25	16.1	33.3	-	16.7	37.5	-	17.4

Extent to which the set individual goals are challenging enough making optimal utilisation of individual capabilities:														
To a large extent	30	29.3	60	7.7	20	36.4	50	29	33.3	60	66.7	87.5	100	37.2
To some extent	60	56.1	40	69.2	80	63.6	50	61.3	58.3	40	33.3	12.5	-	54.7
Not at all	10	14.6	-	23.1	-	-	-	9.7	8.3	-	-	-	-	8.1
Extent to which the set individual goals are realistic and attainable:														
To a large extent	20	14.6	60	23.1	10	27.3	50	41.9	58.3	40	50	25	100	33.1
To some extent	60	70.7	40	69.2	80	72.7	50	48.4	33.3	60	50	62.5	-	58.1
Not at all	20	14.6	-	7.7	10	-	-	9.7	8.3	-	-	12.5	-	8.7

Table 5.6: Respondents' Views Regarding the Goals of the Library
(Percentage Distribution of Respondents by selected Background Characters)

	Sex		Age		Perof. Qualification		Cadre			Total (N= 172)
	Male (N = 123)	Female (N=49)	46 Yrs or less (N=91)	47 Yrs or more (N=44)	Blisc or below (N=37)	MLISc & above (N=88)	Cadre 1 (N=84)	Cadre 2 (N=42)	Cadre 3 (N=130)	
Extent of Knowledge about the goals and objectives of the library:										
To a large extent	69.9	65.3	68.2	69	50	74.6	89.2	67	54.5	68.6
To some extent	29.3	30.6	31.8	27.4	45.2	24.6	10.8	31.9	40.9	29.7
Not at all	0.8	4.1	-	3.6	4.8	0.8	-	1.1	4.5	1.7
Extent to which the goals and objectives are met:										
To a large extent	26	28.6	29.5	23.8	26.2	26.9	35.1	26.4	20.5	26.7
To some extent	69.1	61.2	63.6	70.2	59.5	69.2	64.9	65.9	70.5	66.9
Not at all	4.9	10.2	6.8	6	14.3	3.8	-	7.7	9	6.4
Extent to which the goals and objectives are fulfilled beyond the target:										
To a large extent	17.1	12.2	18.2	13.1	14.3	16.2	29.7	12.1	11.4	15.7
To some extent	65	71.4	62.5	71.4	61.9	68.5	56.8	72.5	63.6	66.9
Not at all	17.9	16.3	19.3	15.5	23.8	15.4	13.5	15.4	25	17.4

Extent to which the set individual goals are challenging enough making optimal utilisation of individual capabilities:										
To a large extent	39	32.7	40.9	33.3	33.3	38.5	51.4	33.0	34.1	37.2
To some extent	53.7	57.1	53.4	56	54.8	54.6	45.9	54.9	61.4	54.7
Not at all	7.3	10.2	5.7	10.7	11.9	6.9	2.7	12.1	4.5	8.1
Extent to which the set individual goals are realistic and attainable:										
To a large extent	34.1	30.6	35.2	31	33.3	33.1	40.5	33	27.3	33.1
To some extent	58.5	57.1	58	58.3	54.8	59.2	54.1	58.2	61.4	58.1
Not at all	7.3	12.2	6.8	10.7	11.9	7.7	5.4	8.8	11.4	8.7

professional qualifications. All those working in Cadre-I services, 99 per cent from Cadre-II and 95 per cent from Cadre-III services have reported this knowledge.

To another question, to what extent the goals and objectives are met?, the response of nearly 94 per cent is positive. Nearly 67 per cent felt that the goals and objectives are met only to some extent while the remaining 27 per cent opined that they are met to a large extent. The Percentage of respondents reporting that the goals and objectives are met only to some extent is more in all the university libraries. This Percentage is observed to be more among the males (69%) compared to females (61%), more among those in older age group (70%) from those in younger age group (64%), more among the respondents with higher professional qualifications (69%) than those with lower professional qualifications (60%), more among those working in Cadre-III services (71%) compared to those working in Cadre-II (66%) and Cadre-I (65%) services.

In response to another question, about 83 per cent reported that the goals and objectives of the library are fulfilled beyond the stipulated targets. Out of these, nearly 67 per cent said that this fulfillment beyond targets is only to some extent while the remaining 16 per cent felt that it is to a large extent. In all the university libraries, the percentage responding with 'to some extent' is comparatively more. This percentage is more among the females (71%) compared to the males (65%) and is also more in the older age groups (71%) compared to the younger age groups (63%). The same response is found to be more among the library professionals with higher professional qualifications (69%) than those with lower professional qualifications (62%) and is also more among those working in Cadre-II services (73%) than among those working in Cadre-III (64%) and Cadre-I (57%) services.

To another question on individual goals, nearly 92 per cent of the respondents reported that the set individual goals are challenging enough making optimal utilization of the individual capabilities. Of these, about 37 per cent expressed that the individual goals are challenging to a great extent while 55 per cent felt that they are challenging only to some extent and the proportion feeling that the individual goals are challenging only to some is more in all the university libraries with the exception of SVU, BRAOU, PMU, PSRTU and NTRHU libraries, where the proportion responding with ;to a large extent' is more. This proportion responding with 'to some extent' is more among females (57%) than among males (54%) and more among those in older age groups (56%) than those in younger age groups (53%). This proportion is more or less equal (55%) in the respondents with high as well as low professional qualifications. However, this Percentage is more among those working in Cadre-III services (61%) compared to their counterparts in Cadre-II (55%) and Cadre-I (46%) services.

It is also noticed that about 91 per cent of the respondents also feel that the set individual goals are realistic and attainable. Of these, 58 per cent expressed that the goals are realistic and attainable only to some extent, while the remaining 33 per cent felt that it is to a large extent. In most of the university libraries, the proportion responding with 'to some extent' is more. This proportion is more among males (59%) than among females (57%) and more or less similar (58%) in the old and young age groups of respondents. This proportion is more among those with higher professional qualifications (59%) than among those with lower professional qualifications (55%) and is also more among those working in Cadre-III services (61%) compared to their counterparts working in Cadre-II (58%) or Cadre-I (54%) services.

As already mentioned, the responses recorded in the three-grade model are quantified by way of assigning unit scores. For each of the questions, the response 'to a large extent' is given 3 points, 'to some extent' is given 2 and 1 point is given to the response 'not at all'. The score points assigned to the five questions considered under this sub-category i.e. knowledge and views on goals and objectives are summed up and presented as scores for this aspect. The mean score along with standard deviation and computed 't' values by selected background characteristics are shown in Table 5.7.

Table 5.7: Mean Total Scores with Standard Deviation
(For Aspects Considered Regarding Goals & Objectives of the Library)

Background characters	N	Total score		't'	Sig.
		Mean	SD		
a) University Type					
Traditional	154	11.38	1.85	0.130	0.896
Professional	18	11.44	2.20		
b) Sex					
Male	123	11.48	1.85	0.994	0.322
Female	49	11.16	1.97		
c) Age					
46 Years or below	88	11.53	1.72	2.05	1.030
0.304					
47 Years or more	84	11.24			
D) Professional Qualification					
BLISc or below	42	10.90	2.17	1.934	0.055
MLISc and above	130	11.55	1.76		
e) Cadre					
Cadre-1	37	12.24	1.72	2.705[a]	0.008*
Cadre-2	91	11.26	1.91	0.969[b]	0.334
Cadre-3	44	10.93	1.77	3.362[c]	0.001*

* Significant values
a) t value for Cadre-1 × Cadre-2
b) t value for Cadre-2 × Cadre-3
c) t value for Cadre-3 × Cadre-1.

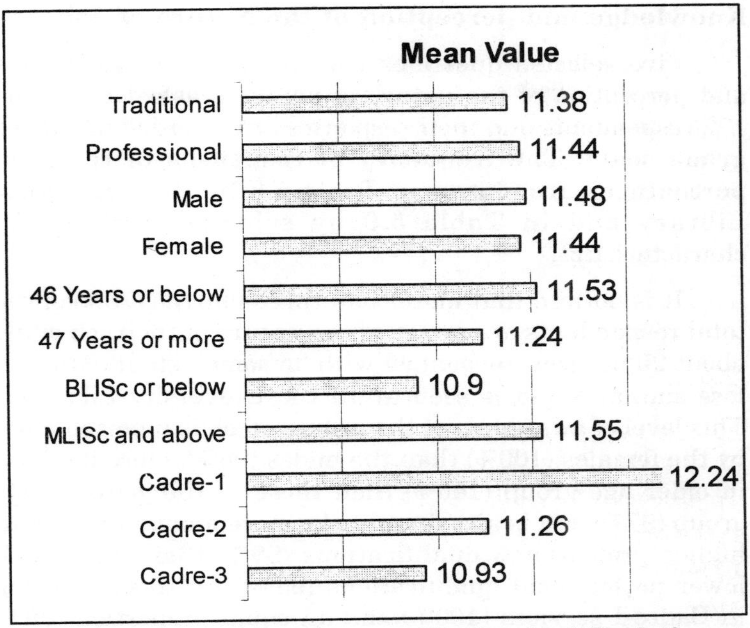

Fig. 5.4: Mean Total Scores with Standard Deviation

It is noticed that there exists very negligible difference in the mean scores computed for traditional and professional universities. The mean score are marginally higher for males than for females and for younger age group than the older age group. The difference in the mean score is a bit conspicuous when the professional qualifications are considered, those with higher qualifications recording better scores compared to those with lower qualifications. The differences in the mean scores are more pronounced when the cadre of these professionals is considered. The mean scores are higher for the Cadre-I compared to the Cadre-II and Cadre-III in that order. However, the computed 't' values revealed significant differences between the Cadre-I and Cadre-II as well as Cadre-I and Cadre-III. While the differences by university type, sex, age and professional qualifications are found to be statistically not significant.

Knowledge and perception of the Nature of Job

Five selected questions pertaining to the knowledge and perception of the nature of job were asked to all the 172 respondents and their responses are recorded in a three grade scale. The frequency of responses in terms of percentages are shown in Table 5.8 by the University Library and in Table 5.9 by selected background characteristics.

It is noticed that more than three-fourths (78%) of the total respondents are aware of the nature of their job while about 20 per cent responded with 'to some extent'. More or less similar trend is seen in all the University Libraries. This level of awareness of the nature of job is reported more by the females (100%) than the males (98%), more by those in older age group (100%) than those in the younger age group (97%) and is also found to be more among those with higher professional qualifications (99%) than those with lower professional qualifications (95%). All those working in Cadre-I services (100%) and an equal proportion (98%) from those working in Cadre-II and III services have reported that they are aware of the nature of their job.

In response to another question, about 98 per cent of the respondents reported that they are feeling doing an important job. Of these, 74 per cent expressed emphatically to the remaining 24 per cent. This type of feeling is expressed by all the respondents from all the University libraries, with the exception of a few from AU, SKDU and KU libraries. The proportion of respondents feeling that they are doing an important job is more among the males (99%) compared to females (96%), more among the younger age group (99%) than among the older age group (98%). This proportion is more or less similar (98%) among the respondents with high as well as low professional qualifications. This feeling is noticed more among those working in Cadre-III services (98%) compared to those working in Cadre-II (99%) and Cadre-I (97%) services.

To another question as to what extent the individuals know that their work relates to work in other sections of the library, a majority (98%) responded in affirmative – 53 per cent strongly and 45 per cent normally. With the exception of a few respondents from AU, NU and PSRTU libraries, respondents from all the university libraries know that their work relates to work in other sections of the library. This knowledge is seen to be more among males (98%) than the females (96%), equal among the younger (98%) and older age groups (98%). The proportion reporting this knowledge is more among those having lower professional qualifications (100%) compared to those having higher professional qualifications (97%). All the respondents working in Cadre-I services (100%) and 98 per cent each from Cadre-II and III services have also reported this knowledge.

Slightly more than half (52%) of the respondents reported that their given job assignment encourages initiative and originality to some extent while another 44 per cent felt that it encourages originality and initiative to a large extent and the remaining 4 per cent responded negatively. The proportion of respondents feeling that their given job assignment encourages initiative and originality is expressed slightly more by the males (97%) compared to the females (96%) and more by the younger age group (98%) than the older age group (95%). This proportion is also more among those with higher professional qualifications (98%) than those with lower professional qualifications (90%) and is also expressed more by those working in Cadre-II services (98%) compared to those working in Cadre-I and Cadre-III services (95 per cent each).

Nearly 94 per cent of the library professionals interviewed in the present study reported that their given job description is fair. Of which, 51 per cent responded with 'to some extent' while 43 per cent responded with 'to a great extent'. The same view is expressed by about 95 per cent of the males and 90 per cent of the females. The same

Table 5.8: Respondents' Views Regarding the Nature of the Job
(Percentage Distribution of Respondents by University)

Extent of knowledge	Name of the University													Total (N = 172)
	OU (N=10)	AU (N=41)	SVU (N=20)	ANGRAU (N=13)	NU (N=10)	SKDU (N=11)	JNTU (N=4)	UOH (N=31)	KU (N=12)	BRAOU (N=5)	PMU (N=6)	PSRTU (N=8)	NTRHU (N=1)	
Extent of Knowledge about the nature of work in the section:														
To a large extent	70	75.6	85	69.2	100	72.7	100	77.4	83.3	80	83.3	62.5	100	78.5
To some extent	30	24.4	15	15.4	-	27.3	-	19.4	16.7	20	16.7	37.5	-	19.8
Not at all	-	-	-	15.4	-	-	-	3.2	-	-	-	-	-	1.7
Extent to which the individual is feeling that he/she is doing an important job:														
To a large extent	80	70.7	80	61.5	70	72.7	75	71	91.7	80	66.7	87.5	100	74.4
To some extent	20	26.8	20	38.5	30	18.2	25	29	-	20	33.3	12.5	-	23.8
Not at all	-	2.4	-	-	-	9.1	-	-	8.3	-	-	-	-	1.7
Extent to which the individual knows that his/her work relates to work in other sections of the library:														
To a large extent	60	39	65	53.8	40	36.4	150	61.3	66.7	80	50	50	100	52.9
To some extent	40	56.1	35	46.2	50	63.6	50	38.7	33.3	20	50	37.5	-	44.8
Not at all	-	4.9	-	-	10	-	-	-	-	-	-	12.5	-	2.3

Extent to which the given job assignment encourage initiative and originality:														
To a large extent	40	39	50	38.5	30	27.3	50	51.6	41.7	60	83.3	37.5	100	44.2
To some extent	60	56.1	50	61.5	70	72.7	50	35.5	58.3	40	16.7	62.5	-	52.3
Not at all	-	4.9	-	-	-	-	-	12.9	-	-	-	-	-	3.5
Extent to which the given job discription is fair:														
To a large extent	60	31.7	65	53.8	20	18.2	25	45.2	41.7	80	50	37.5	-	42.4
To some extent	40	63.4	35	23.1	70	72.7	75	48.4	50	20	50	62.5	-	51.2
Not at all	-	4.9	-	23.1	10	9.1	-	6.5	8.3	-	-	-	100	6.4

Table 5.9: Respondents' Views Regarding the Nature of the Job
(Percentage Distribution of Respondents by selected Background Characters)

	Sex		Age		Perof. Qualification		Cadre			Total (N= 172)
	Male (N = 123)	Female (N=49)	46 Yrs or less (N=91)	47 Yrs or more (N=44)	Blisc or below (N=37)	MLISc & above (N=88)	Cadre 1 (N=84)	Cadre 2 (N=42)	Cadre 3 (N=130)	
Extent of Knowledge about the nature of work in the section:										
To a large extent	78	79.6	78.4	78.6	76.2	79.2	94.6	76.9	68.2	78.5
To some extent	19.5	20.4	18.2	21.4	19	20	5.4	20.9	29.5	19.8
Not at all	2.4	-	3.4	-	4.8	0.8	-	2.2	2.3	1.7
Extent to which the individual is feeling that he/she is doing an important job:										
To a large extent	77.2	67.3	75	73.8	76.2	73.8	83.3	71.4	72.7	74.4
To some extent	22	28.6	23.9	23.8	21.4	24.6	13.5	27.5	25	23.8
Not at all	0.8	4.1	1.1	2.4	2.4	1.5	2.7	1.1	2.3	1.7
Extent to which the individual knows that his/her work relates to work in other sections of the library:										
To a large extent	51.2	57.1	55.7	50	40.5	56.9	75.7	46.9	47.7	52.9
To some extent	47.2	38.8	42	47.6	59.5	40	24.3	50.8	50	44.8
Not at all	1.6	4.1	2.3	2.4	-	3.1	-	2.3	2.3	2.3
Extent to which the given job assignment encourage initiative and originality:										

To a large extent	45.5	40.8	46.6	41.7	45.2	43.8	54.1	40.7	43.2	44.2
To some extent	51.2	55.1	51.1	53.6	45.2	54.6	40.5	57.1	52.3	52.3
Not at all	3.3	4.1	2.3	4.8	9.5	1.5	5.4	2.2	4.5	3.5
Extent to which the given job discription is fair:										
To a large extent	44.7	36.7	46.6	38.1	43.5	41.5	48.6	40.7	40.9	42.4
To some extent	50.4	53.1	44.3	58.3	49.4	52.3	43.2	52.7	54.5	51.2
Not at all	4.9	10.2	9.1	3.6	7.1	6.2	8.1	6.6	4.5	6,4

proportion is found to be more among those in the older age group (96%) than those in the younger age group (91%) and is slightly more among those with higher professional qualifications (94%) than those with lower professional qualifications (93%). The same proportion is seen to be more among those working in Cadre-III services (95%) than those working in either Cadre-II (93%) or Cadre-I (92%) services.

Responses recorded in the three grade scale for all the above discussed five questions relating to the nature of job are quantified by giving unit scores to each of the responses. A score of 3 is given to response 'to a large extent' and in the same way a score of 1 is given to 'not at all'. Thus the maximum total score possible for all the five responses is 15 (3 × 5) and the minimum will be 5 (1 × 5). The mean total scores thus computed are shown in Table 5.10 by selected background characteristics.

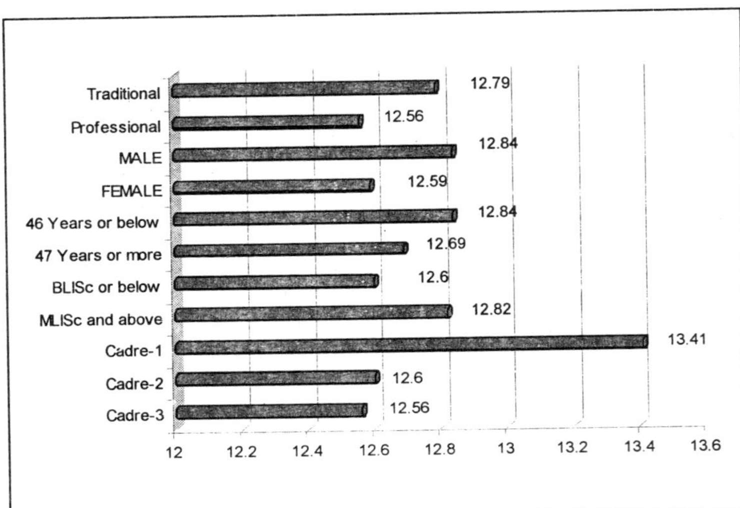

Fig. 5.5: Mean Total Scores with Standard Deviation

Table 5.10: Mean Total Scores with Standard Deviation
(For Aspects Considered Regarding
Views on Nature of the Job)

Background characters	N	Total score		't'	Sig.
		Mean	SD		
a) University Type					
Traditional	154	12.79	1.77	0.514	0.608
Professional	18	12.56	2.45		
b) Sex					
Male	123	12.84	1.81	0.787	0.433
Female	49	12.59	1.95		
c) Age					
46 Years or below	88	12.84	1.91	0.533	0.595
47 Years or more	84	12.69	1.78		
d) Professional Qualification					
BLISc or below	42	12.6	2.01	0.694	0.488
MLISc and above	130	12.82	1.79		
e) Cadre					
Cadre-1	37	13.41	1.57	2.298[a]	0.023*
Cadre-2	91	12.6	1.87	0.104[b]	0.917
Cadre-3	44	12.56	1.93	2.111[c]	0.038*

* Significant values
a) t value for Cadre-1 × Cadre-2
b) t value for Cadre-2 × Cadre-3
c) t value for Cadre-3 × Cadre-1.

It can be observed from the table that the mean scores recorded for this category of responses ranged between 12 and 13 and there is not much variation in the mean scores between the two types of universities or between the two sexes or between the two age groups or even the professional qualification groups. However, slight variation is observed among the three cadres of services with regard to three mean scores. Respondents of Cadre-I have recorded slightly better mean scores (13.41) compared to those of Cadre-II (12.60) and Cadre-III (12.56). The 't' value also indicates that there are significant differences between the Cadre-I and Cadre-II as well as between Cadre-I and Cadre-III with regard to the proportion of responses pertaining to the nature of job.

Relationship with Co-workers

Responses of the library professionals covered in the present study with regard to five selected questions relating to their relationship with their co-workers are presented in the three grade scale by university in Table 5.11 and by selected background characteristics in Table 5.12.

Regarding their relationship with superiors, a majority (85%) of the respondents reported that they are maintaining good relations with their superiors to a large extent, while 13 per cent said that they are maintaining good relations only to some extent. Only about 2 per cent reported that they are not at all maintaining good relationship with their superiors and this is reported from only 4 out of the 13 university libraries viz. AU, NU, SKDU and UOH. The proportion of respondents who are not maintaining good relationship with their superiors is more among the females (4%) than the males (2%), and more or less the same (2%) in younger as well as older age groups. It is more among those with lower professional qualifications (5%) than those with higher professional qualifications (2%). The same proportion is found more among those working in Cadre-III services (5%) than those in Cadre-II services (2%) and not reported by those in Cadre-I services.

In the same way, about 98 per cent of the respondents reported that they maintain good relationship with their subordinates. Of those, 74 per cent are maintaining good relationship with their subordinates to a large extent while the remaining 24 per cent are maintaining the same only to some extent. The proportion not maintaining good relationship with subordinates at all is only 2 per cent, all from AU, NU and PSRTU libraries. The proportion reporting that they are not at all maintaining good relationship with their subordinates is more among females (4%) compared to males (1%), more among the younger age group (2%) than the older age group (1%). This proportion is more among those with higher professional qualifications (2%) and none from those with lower professional qualifications. The same is found from 2 per cent each working in Cadre-III and Cadre-II services and none from those working in Cadre-I services.

About 96 per cent of respondents are maintaining good relationship with their peers, 59 per cent 'to a large extent' and 37 per cent only 'to some extent' and the remaining 4 per cent are 'not at all' maintaining good relationship with their peers. Those not maintaining good relationship with peers are from AU, SVU, UOH and PSRTU libraries. This proportion is more among females (4%) than among males (3%) and is slightly more in the older age group (3.6%) than the younger age group (3.4%). It is more among those with lower professional qualifications (4.8%) compared to those with higher professional qualifications (3.1%). This Percentage is more among those in Cadre-III services (9%) than those in Cadre-II services (2%) and nil among those in Cadre-I services.

Nearly 98 per cent of the respondents believe that good team-work and co-operation exists in their section. Of these, about 73 per cent felt that this sort of co-operation exists to a large extent while 25 per cent felt that it is only to some extent, while the remaining 2 per cent feel that good team work and co-operation does not exist in their section. This sort of negative response is reported from NU, SKDU and UOH libraries. This feeling is expressed more by the females (4%) than the males (2%) and the younger age group (5%). This proportion is more among those with low professional qualifications (5%) than those having high professional qualifications (2%) and more by those working in Cadre-III

Table 5.11 : Respondents' Views Regarding Their Relation With Co-workers (Percentage Distribution of Respondents by University)

Extent of knowledge	Name of the University													Total (N = 172)
	OU (N=10)	AU (N=41)	SVU (N=20)	ANGRAU (N=13)	NU (N=10)	SKDU (N=11)	JNTU (N=4)	UOH (N=31)	KU (N=12)	BRAOU (N=5)	PMU (N=6)	PSRTU (N=8)	NTRHU (N=1)	
Extent to which the individual is maintaining good relationship with Superiors														
To a large extent	100	78	95	92.3	70	72.7	100	77.4	91.7	80	100	100	100	84.9
To some extent	-	19.5	5	7.7	20	18.2	-	19.4	8.3	20	-	-	-	12.8
Not at all	-	2.4	-	-	10	9.1	-	3.2	-	-	-	-	-	2.3
Extent to which the individual is maintaining good relationship with Subordinates														
To a large extent	80	61	90	84.6	50	63.6	25	83.9	75	80	100	75	100	73.8
To some extent	20	36.6	10	15.4	40	36.4	75	16.1	25	20	-	12.5	-	24.4
Not at all	-	2.4	-	-	10	-	-	-	-	-	-	12.5	-	1.7
Extent to which the individual is maintaining good relationship with Peers														
To a large extent	60	51.2	65	69.2	60	54.5	50	58.1	41.7	80	83.3	75	100	59.3
To some extent	40	46.3	30	30.8	40	45.5	50	35.5	58.3	20	16.7	-	-	37.2
Not at all	-	2.4	5	-	-	-	-	6.5	-	-	-	25	-	3.5

Extent to which the individual believes that good team work and co-operation exists in his/her section														
To a large extent	20	17.1	55	53.8	20	27.3	75	16.1	50	40	16.7	37.5	-	73.3
To some extent	50	58.5	40	15.4	40	27.3	25	48.4	33.3	40	66.7	62.5	-	24.4
Not at all	30	24.4	5	30.8	40	45.5	-	35.5	16.7	20	16.7	-	100	2.3
Extent to which the individual discusses grievances freely with administration														
To a large extent	90	73.2	80	92.3	50	72.7	75	58.1	83.3	80	50	100	-	30.2
To some extent	10	26.8	20	7.7	40	18.2	25	38.7	16.7	20	50	-	-	44.8
Not at all	-	-	-	-	10	9.1	-	3.2	-	-	-	-	100	25

Table 5.12: Respondents' Views Regarding Their Relation With Co-workers
(Percentage Distribution of Respondents by selected Background Characters)

	Sex		Age		Perof. Qualification		Cadre			Total (N= 172)
	Male (N = 123)	Female (N=49)	46 Yrs or less (N=91)	47 Yrs or more (N=44)	Blisc or below (N=37)	MLISc & above (N=88)	Cadre 1 (N=84)	Cadre 2 (N=42)	Cadre 3 (N=130)	
Extent to which the individual is maintaining good relationship with Superiors										
To a large extent	88.6	75.5	88.6	81	83.3	85.4	86.5	84.6	84.1	84.9
To some extent	9.8	20.4	9.1	16.7	11.9	13.1	13.5	13.2	11.4	12.8
Not at all	1.6	4.1	2.3	2.4	4.8	1.5	-	2.2	4.5	2.3
Extent to which the individual is maintaining good relationship with Subordinates										
To a large extent	76.4	67.3	79.5	67.9	90.5	68.5	78.4	72.5	72.7	73.8
To some extent	22.8	28.6	18.2	31	9.5	29.2	21.6	25.3	25	24.4
Not at all	0.8	4.1	2.3	1.2	-	2.3	-	2.2	2.3	1.7
Extent to which the individual is maintaining good relationship with Peers										
To a large extent	60.2	57.1	65.9	52.4	66.7	56.9	73	54.9	56.8	59.3
To some extent	36.6	38.8	30.7	44	28.6	40	27	42.9	34.1	37.2
Not at all	3.3	4.1	3.4	3.6	4.8	3.1	-	2.2	9.1	3.5

Extent to which the individual believes that good team work and co-operation exists in his/her section										
To a large extent	73.2	73.5	77.3	69	66.7	75.4	75.7	75.8	65.9	73.3
To some extent	25.2	22.4	18.2	31	28.6	23.1	21.6	23.1	29.5	24.4
Not at all	1.6	4.1	4.5	-	4.8	1.5	2.7	1.1	4.5	2.3
Extent to which the individual discusses grievances freely with administration										
To a large extent	32.5	24.5	34.1	26.2	33.3	29.2	51.4	26.4	20.5	30.2
To some extent	44.7	44.9	44.3	45.2	38.1	46.9	37.8	40.7	59.1	44.8
Not at all	22.8	30.6	21.6	28.6	28.6	23.9	10.8	33	20.5	25

(5%) compared to those working in Cadre-I (3%) and Cadre-II (1%) services.

Only three-fourths (75%) of the respondents reported that they discuss grievances freely with the administration. Of these, 45 per cent do to some extent while 30 per cent do to a large extent. The remaining 25 per cent reported that they do not discuss their grievances at all with the administration. This proportion is significant in almost all the university libraries. this feeling is expressed more by the females (31%) compared to males (23%) and more by the older age group (29%) compared to the younger age group (22%). This proportion is more among those with lower professional qualifications (29%) than those with higher professional qualifications (24%) and is more among those working in Cadre-II services (33%) than those working in Cadre-III (21%) and Cadre-I (11%) services.

These three graded responses to the five questions relating to the individuals relation with their co-workers are quantified by assigning unit scores to the responses. Again, the maximum possible score is 15 and the minimum is 5. The mean scores for this category are shown in Table 5.13 by selected background characteristics.

Table 5.13: Mean Total Scores With Standard Deviation
(For Aspects Considered Regarding Views on Relations with Co-Workers)

Background characters	N	Total score		't'	Sig.
		Mean	SD		
a) University Type					
Traditional	154	12.81	1.72	1.368	0.173
Professional	18	13.39	1.69		
b) Sex					
Male	123	13.01	1.6	1.727	0.086
Female	49	12.51	1.95		

Background characters	N	Total score		't'	Sig.
		Mean	SD		
c) Age					
46 Years or below	88	13.11	1.68	1.95	0.053
47 Years or more	84	12.61	1.72		
d) Professional Qualification					
BLISc or below	42	12.98	1.67	0.476	0.635
MLISc and above	130	12.83	1.73		
e) Cadre					
Cadre-1	37	13.51	1.45	2.330[a]	0.021*
Cadre-2	91	12.74	1.81	0.452[b]	0.652
Cadre-3	44	12.59	1.63	2.668[c]	0.009*

* Signifiant values

a) t value for Cadre-1 × Cadre-2

b) t value for Cadre-2 × Cadre-3

c) t value for Cadre-3 × Cadre-1.

It is noticed that, with regard to the relationship with co-workers, respondents from professional universities recorded higher scores (13.39) than the traditional university libraries (12.81). Among the two sexes, the mean scores are higher for males (13.01) than the females (12.51) and higher for the younger age group (13.11) than the older age group (12.61). there is not much difference between the two professional qualification groups. The mean scores are found more for those working in Cadre-I (13.51) compared to those working in Cadre-II (12.74) and Cadre-III (12.59) services. However, the computed 't' values indicate no significant differences between the groups by type of university, sex, age group and professional qualification, but the differences between Cadre-I and Cadre-II as well as between Cadre-I and Cadre-III are found to be statistically significant.

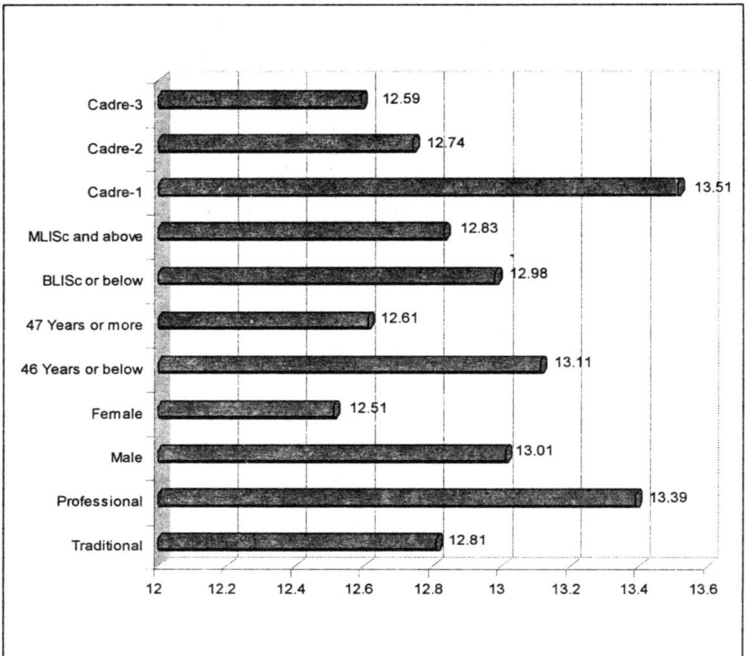

Fig. 5.6: Mean Total Scores With Standard Deviation

Views on Administration/Management

Four selected questions were asked with regard to their views on administration/management and the responses recorded in three graded scale are shown in Table 5.14 by university and in Table 5.15 by selected background characteristics.

About 85 per cent of the respondents believe that the library authority/management protect the individual's professional interest. Of these, 33 per cent expressed their belief to a great extent while 52 per cent expressed that it is only to some extent. The remaining 15 per cent say that the library authority/management is not at all protecting their professional interest. This feeling is reported by respondents from AU, ANGRAU, NU, SKDU, UOH, PMU and PSRTU libraries. The proportion of respondents believing that the authorities/management is protecting their professional interests is more among the females (90%) than the males (84%) and is more among the younger age group (90%) than the older age group (81%). This proportion is more among those with higher professional qualifications (88%) than those with lower professional qualifications (79%). This Percentage is much more among those working in Cadre-I (92%) than those working in Cadre-II (85%) and Cadre-III (82%) services.

In response to another question, about 98 per cent of the library professionals interviewed have reported that their superiors are having faith and confidence in their ability to do the assigned job. The remaining 2 per cent responded negatively in this regard and these are from AU, JNTU and UOH libraries. This sort of lack of confidence in superiors is reported only by the males (2%) and more from the older age group (2%) than the younger age group (1%). This proportion is same in the group with lower professional qualifications (2%) as well as those with higher professional qualifications (2%). The proportion with this kind of negative belief is much more among those in Cadre-I (5%) compared to those in Cadre-III (2%) services. Those in Cadre-II have not expressed this negative belief.

About 90 per cent of the total respondents reported that they believe that the administrators enforce rules equally for all the staff members. The remaining 10 per cent feel that the administrators are not at all enforcing rules equally to all the staff members. This feeling is recorded from AU, NU, SKDU, UOH, PMU and PSRTU libraries. This sort of negative feeling is reported more by the females (12%) than the males (9%), more by the older age group (11%) than the younger age group (9%) and more by those with lower professional qualifications (12%) than those with higher professional qualifications (9%). This proportion is less among those working in Cadre-I (8%) compared to those working in Cadre-II (10%) and Cadre-III (11%) services.

Table 5.14: Respondents' Views On The Mangement / Administration
(Percentage Distribution of Respondents by University)

Extent of knowledge	Name of the University													Total (N = 172)
	OU (N=10)	AU (N=41)	SVU (N=20)	ANGRAU (N=13)	NU (N=10)	SKDU (N=11)	JNTU (N=4)	UOH (N=31)	KU (N=12)	BRAOU (N=5)	PMU (N=6)	PSRTU (N=8)	NTRHU (N=1)	
Extent to which the library authority / management protects the individual's professional interest:														
To a large extent	40	17.1	55	46.2	30	18.2	75	29	58.3	40	33.3	25	-	33.7
To some extent	60	65.9	45	46.2	60	54.5	25	41.9	33.3	40	50	62.5	100	51.7
Not at all	-	17.1	-	7.7	10	27.3	-	29	8.3	20	16.7	12.5	-	14.5
Extent to which his / her immediate suprior has faith and confidence in his / her ability to do the assigned job:														
To a large extent	40	73.2	90	100	70	81.8	50	58.1	83.3	60	83.3	100	100	74.4
To some extent	60	24.4	10	-	30	18.2	25	38.7	16.7	40	16.7	-	-	23.8
Not at all	-	2.4	-	-	-	-	25	3.2	-	-	-	-	-	1.7
Extent to which the administrators enforce rules for all the staff members equally:														
To a large extent	50	26.8	70	69.2	10	36.4	100	25.8	50	60	33.3	25	-	40.1
To some extent	50	58.5	30	30.8	70	54.5	-	61.3	33.3	40	50	62.5	100	50
Not at all	-	14.6	-	-	20	9.1	-	12.9	16.7	-	16.7	12.5	-	9.9

Extent to which the individual discusses his / her doubts and problems related to job with superiors:														
To a large extent	40	19.5	70	61.5	30	36.4	75	35.5	41.7	40	50	37.5	-	39.5
To some extent	40	65.9	20	38.5	60	54.5	25	38.7	41.7	40	50	62.5	100	47.1
Not at all	20	14.6	10	-	10	9.1	-	25.8	16.7	20	-	-	-	13.4

Table 5.15: Respondents' Views on the Mangement/Administration
(Percentage Distribution of Respondents by selected Background Characters)

	Sex		Age		Perof. Qualification		Cadre			Total (N= 172)
	Male (N = 123)	Female (N=49)	46 Yrs or less (N=91)	47 Yrs or more (N=44)	Blisc or below (N=37)	MLISc & above (N=88)	Cadre 1 (N=84)	Cadre 2 (N=42)	Cadre 3 (N=130)	
Extent to which the library authority / management protects the individual's professional interest:										
To a large extent	31.7	38.8	39.8	27.4	35.7	33.1	40.5	31.9	31.8	33.7
To some extent	52	51	50	53.6	42.9	54.6	51.4	52.7	50	51.7
Not at all	16.3	10.2	10.2	19	21.4	12.3	8.1	15.4	18.2	14.5
Extent to which his / her immediate suprior has faith and confidence in his / her ability to do the assigned job:										
To a large extent	74.8	73.5	75	73.8	78.6	73.1	78.4	73.6	72.7	74.4
To some extent	22.8	26.5	23.9	23.8	19	25.4	16.2	26.4	25	23.8
Not at all	2.4	-	1.1	2.4	2.4	1.5	5.4	-	2.3	1.7
Extent to which the administrators enforce rules for all the staff members equally:										
To a large extent	40.7	38.8	47.7	32.1	31	43.1	56.8	37.4	31.8	40.1

To some extent	50.4	49	43.2	57.1	57.1	47.7	35.1	52.7	56.8	50
Not at all	8.9	12.2	9.1	10.8	11.9	9.2	8.1	9.9	11.4	9.9
Extent to which the individual discusses his / her doubts and problems related to job with superiors:										
To a large extent	38.2	42.9	40.9	38.1	40.5	39.2	51.4	38.5	31.8	39.5
To some extent	48	44.9	47.7	46.4	40.5	49.2	40.5	46.2	54.5	47.1
Not at all	13.8	12.2	11.4	15.5	19	11.5	8.1	15.4	13.6	13.4

To another question, about 47 per cent of the respondent said that they discuss their doubts and problems related to job with their superiors to some extent while 40 per cent do it to a great extent. The remaining 13 per cent say that they not at all discuss their doubts and job problems with their superiors. This negative response is recorded from OU, AU, SVU, NU, SKDU, UOH, KU and BRAOU libraries. This proportion is slightly more among males (14%) than among females (12%) and is more among the older age group (16%) than the younger age group (11%) and among those with lower professional qualifications (19%) than those with higher professional qualifications (12%). This negative response is reported more by those working in Cadre-II (15%) compared to Cadre-III (14%) and Cadre-I (8%) services.

The mean scores computed for these four responses under this category are shown in Table 5.16 by selected background characters.

It is noticed that the mean scores have shown some conspicuous difference between the professional (10.61) and traditional (9.35) type of universities and between the Cadre-I (9.97), Cadre-II (9.41) and Cadre-III (9.23) services. However, the variation is not much in the mean scores by sex, age group and also the professional qualification groups. The computed 't' values reveal statistically significant differences only between the two types of universities.

Knowledge and Initiative

Regarding the knowledge and initiative of the individuals, five selected questions were asked and the responses obtained were recorded in three grade scale. These were shown in Table 5.17 by the university and in Table 5.18 by selected background characteristics.

Nearly 94 per cent of the library professionals interviewed have reported that they are having the knowledge of latest trends in Library and Information Science.

Table 5.16: Mean Total Scores with Standard Deviation
(For Aspects Considered Regarding Views on Management / Administration)

Background characters	N	Total score		't'	Sig.
		Mean	SD		
a) University Type					
Traditional	154	9.35	1.81	2.486	0.005*
Professional	18	10.61	1.42		
b) Sex					
Male	123	9.44	1.8	0.497	0.62
Female	49	9.59	1.86		
c) Age					
46 Years or below	88	9.72	1.79	1.737	0.084
47 Years or more	84	9.24	1.82		
d) Professional Qualification					
BLISc or below	42	9.31	2.08	0.71	0.479
MLISc and above	130	9.54	1.73		
e) Cadre					
Cadre-1	37	9.97	1.86	1.586	0.115
Cadre-2	91	9.41	1.82	0.546	0.586
Cadre-3	44	9.23	1.72	1.869	0.065

* Signifiant values
a) t value for Cadre-1 × Cadre-2
b) t value for Cadre-2 × Cadre-3
c) t value for Cadre-3 × Cadre-1.

This knowledge was not reported by the remaining 6 per cent, who are from AU, SVU, ANGRAU, SKDU, UOH and BRAOU libraries. The proportion of respondents reporting knowledge of the latest trends in Library and Information Science is more or less the same (94%) among the males and females, but is slightly more in the younger age group (94%) than the older age group (93%). Difference between the groups with professional qualifications is striking as more of those with higher qualifications (96%) having knowledge compared to those with lower

Table 5.17: Respondents' Views on Their Knowledge And Initiative
(Percentage Distribution of Respondents by University)

Extent of knowledge	Name of the University													Total (N = 172)
	OU (N=10)	AU (N=41)	SVU (N=20)	ANGRAU (N=13)	NU (N=10)	SKDU (N=11)	JNTU (N=4)	UOH (N=31)	KU (N=12)	BRAOU (N=5)	PMU (N=6)	PSRTU (N=8)	NTRHU (N=1)	
Extent to which the individual is aware of latest trends in Library and Information Scienc:														
To a large extent	40	41.5	50	46.2	40	27.3	100	61.3	25	60	66.7	62.5	100	48.3
To some extent	60	48.8	40	46.2	60	63.6	-	35.5	66.7	20	33.3	37.5	-	45.3
Not at all	-	9.8	10	7.7	-	9.1	-	3.2	8.3	20	-	-	-	6.4
Extent to which adequate resources are made available for reaching the targets														
To a large extent	40	19.5	25	69.2	20	9.1	50	38.7	-	40	16.7	-	-	26.7
To some	50	73.2	75	30.8	80	90.9	50	54.8	91.7	60	83.3	62.5	100	67.4
Not at all	10	7.3	-	-	-	-	-	6.5	8.3	-	-	37.5	-	5.8
Extent to which the individual is aware of the administrative records														
To a large extent	80	56.1	75	92.3	80	63.6	75	83.9	75	100	100	87.5	100	75.6
To some extent	20	41.5	15	7.7	20	36.4	25	16.1	25	-	-	12.5	-	22.7
Not at all	-	2.4	10	-	-	-	-	-	-	-	-	-	-	1.7

Extent to which the individual makes suggestions to their superiors														
To a large extent	30	22	35	69.2	20	27.3	75	35.5	16.7	20	16.7	50	100	32.6
To some	40	65.9	40	30.8	60	36.4	25	29	66.7	60	83.3	37.5	-	47.7
Not at all	30	12.2	25	-	20	36.4	-	35.5	16.7	20	-	12.5	-	19.8
Extent to which the individual's suggestions are accepted and implemented														
To a large extent	30	14.6	25	38.5	10	9.1	50	19.4	16.7	-	16.7	50	-	20.9
To some extent	50	63.4	50	61.5	40	81.8	25	45.2	50	60	83.3	50	100	55.8
Not at all	20	22	25	-	50	9.1	25	35.5	33.3	40	-	-	-	23.3

Table 5.18: Respondents' Views On Their Knowledge And Initiative
(Percentage Distribution of Respondents by selected Background Characters)

	Sex		Age		Perof. Qualification		Cadre			Total (N= 172)
	Male (N = 123)	Female (N=49)	46 Yrs or less (N=91)	47 Yrs or more (N=44)	Blisc or below (N=37)	MLISc & above (N=88)	Cadre 1 (N=84)	Cadre 2 (N=42)	Cadre 3 (N=130)	
Extent to which the individual is aware of latest trends in Library and Information Science										
To a large extent	48.8	46.9	51.1	45.2	33.3	53.1	81.1	31.9	54.5	48.3
To some extent	44.7	46.9	43.2	47.6	52.4	43.1	16.2	60.4	38.6	45.3
Not at all	6.5	6.2	5.7	7.1	14.3	3.8	2.7	7.7	6.8	6.4
Extent to which adequate resources are made available for reaching the targets										
To a large extent	27.6	24.5	33	20.2	21.4	28.5	35.1	20.9	31.8	26.7
To some extent	68.3	65.3	61.4	73.8	73.8	65.4	62.2	73.6	59.1	67.4
Not at all	4.1	10.2	5.7	6	4.8	6.2	2.7	5.5	9.1	5.8
Extent to which the individual is aware of the administrative records										
To a large extent	71.5	85.7	73.9	77.4	76.2	75.4	86.5	75.8	65.9	75.6
To some extent	26.8	12.2	23.9	21.4	23.8	22.3	13.5	20.9	34.1	22.7
Not at all	1.6	2.1	2.3	1.2	-	2.3	-	3.3	-	1.7

Extent to which the individual makes suggestions to their superiors										
To a large extent	34.1	28.6	37.5	27.4	31	33.1	56.8	25.3	27.3	32.6
To some extent	43.9	57.1	43.2	52.4	35.7	51.5	40.5	53.8	40.9	47.7
Not at all	22	14.3	19.3	20.2	33.3	15.4	2.7	20.9	31.8	19.8
Extent to which the individual's suggestions are accepted and implemented										
To a large extent	21.1	20.4	20.5	21.4	19	21.5	27	17.6	22.7	20.9
To some extent	54.5	59.2	53.4	58.3	42.9	60	62.2	58.2	45.5	55.8
Not at all	24.4	20.4	26.1	20.2	38.1	18.5	10.8	24.2	31.8	23.3

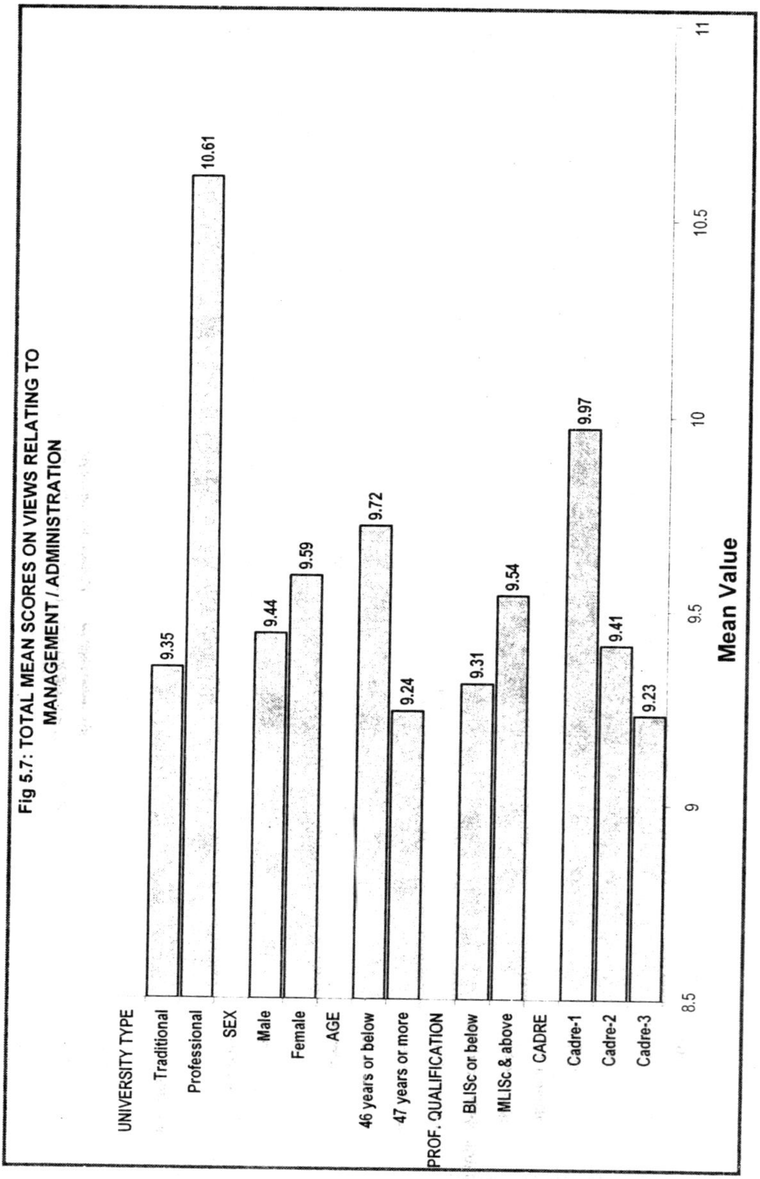

Fig 5.7: TOTAL MEAN SCORES ON VIEWS RELATING TO MANAGEMENT / ADMINISTRATION

qualifications (86%). This knowledge is also reported more by those working in Cadre-I services (97%) compared to those working in Cadre-III (93%) and Cadre-II (92%).

Only about 27 per cent of the respondents reported that adequate resources are made available for reaching the targets to a great extent while 67 per cent opined that the resources were made available only to some extent. The remaining 6 per cent who responded negatively are mainly from OU, AU, UOH, KU and PSRTU libraries. The proportion reporting the availability of adequate resources for meeting the targets is more among the males (96%) compared to the females (90%) and is more or less the same in the younger as well as older age groups (94%). Relatively more proportion of those having lower professional qualifications have reported the availability of resources (95%) than those with higher professional qualifications (94%). Availability of adequate resources is reported more by those working in Cadre-I services (97%) than those working in Cadre-II (94%) and Cadre-III (91%) services.

Knowledge about different types of administrative records like accession register, shelf list, Kardix etc. are reported by about 98 per cent of the respondents. Of whom, 75 per cent reported knowledge to a great extent and 23 per cent only to some extent. Only 2 per cent are lacking the knowledge and these are from AU and SVU libraries. Knowledge about the administrative records is reported more or less equally by the males and females while this knowledge is more among the older age group (99%) than the younger age group (98%). This knowledge is reported by all those having lower professional qualifications and those working in Cadre-I and Cadre-III services.

To another question on to what extent they make suggestions to their superiors, about 33 per cent stated that they make suggestions to their superiors to a great extent while 48 per cent expressed that they make suggestions only to some extent. Nearly 20 per cent said that they not at all make any suggestions to their superiors. All the respondents from ANGRAU, JNTU and PMU libraries reported that they make suggestions to their superiors. The proportion of respondents who make suggestions to their superiors is more among females (86%) compared to males (78%) and is slightly more among the younger age group (81%) compared to the older age group (80%). This proportion is found to be more among those with higher professional qualifications (85%) than those with lower professional qualifications (67%) and is much higher among those in Cadre-I services (97%) compared to those in Cadre-II (79%) and Cadre-III (68%) services.

Nearly 77 per cent of the respondents have reported that their suggestions are accepted and implemented. This expression is received from all the respondents from ANGRAU, PMU and PSRTU libraries. Those reporting that their suggestions are accepted and implemented is more among females (80%) compared to males (76%), more among those in older age groups (80%) than those in younger age group (74%), more among those having higher professional qualifications (81%) than those having lower professional qualifications (62%) and is much more among those working in Cadre-I services (89%) compared to those working in Cadre-II (76%) and Cadre-III (68%) services.

Responses recorded for these five questions related to the knowledge and initiative of the respondents are again quantified by way of assigning unit scores and all these were added up to obtain total score for this category on knowledge and initiative of the respondents. Here also, the maximum possible score is 15 and the minimum is 5. The mean scores are shown in Table 5.19 by selected background characteristics.

The mean score with regard to the knowledge and initiative of the respondents is found to be better for the professional university libraries and for those working in Cadre-I services compared to their counterparts. Variation in the mean scores is not much between the groups by sex or age group or professional qualification. The computed 't' value also indicates that there exists some statistically significant differences among the traditional and professional university libraries and also between Cadre-I and Cadre-II as well as Cadre-I and Cadre-III services with regard to the responses relating to knowledge and initiative of the respondents.

Table 5.19: Mean Total Scores with Standard Deviation
(For Aspects Considered Regarding Views on their Knowledge and Initiative)

Background characters	N	Total score		't'	Sig.
		Mean	SD		
a) University Type:					
Traditional	154	11.28	1.95	3.83	0.000*
Professional	18	13.11	1.6		
b) Sex:					
Male	123	11.45	1.97	0.247	0.805
Female	49	11.53	2.08		
c) Age :					
46 Years or below	88	11.57	2.01	0.653	0.515
47 Years or more	84	11.37	1.99		
d) Professional Qualification:					
BLISc or below	42	10.9	2.3	2.137	0.034*
MLISc and above	130	11.65	1.89		
e) Cadre:					
Cadre-1	37	12.68	1.53	4.471[a]	0.000*
Cadre-2	91	11.1	1.91	0.351[b]	0.726
Cadre-3	44	11.23	2.16	3.426[c]	0.001*

* Significant values
a) t value for Cadre-1 × Cadre-2
b) t value for Cadre-2 × Cadre-3
c) t value for Cadre-3 × Cadre-1

Views on in-service training and performance

All the 172 respondents were asked questions relating to their views on the in-service training, to what extent they have received in-service training and also to what extent they were deputed for training outside and to what extent they agree with rewards for standard performance and punishment for substandard performance. Their responses to these four selected questions are recorded in three grade scale and are shown in Table 5.20 by university and in Table 521 by selected background characteristics.

Nearly 95 per cent of the library professionals interviewed in this study felt that in-service training is necessary for the professionals. This includes 79 per cent who said that in-service training is necessary to a large extent and 16 per cent responding with 'to some extent'. The remaining 5 per cent opined that in-service training is not at all necessary for professionals. These negative responses are observed from OU, AU, SVU, ANGRAU, UOH and KU libraries. The proportion who feel that in-service training is necessary is more among males (95%) than females (94%), more among the older age group (96%) compared to the younger age group (93%), more among those with higher professional qualifications (96%) than those with lower professional qualifications (90%) and much more among those working in Cadre-III (98%) than those working in Cadre-I (97%) and Cadre-II (92%) services.

Only about 70 per cent of the total respondents reported receiving in-service training while the remaining 30 per cent did not. The proportion of respondents who did not receive any in-service training so for ranged from a low of 15 per cent in ANGARU to a high of 60 per cent in NU libraries. Those who did not report any in-service training is more among females (35%) than the males (28%), more among the younger age group (31%) than the older age group (29%), more among those with lower professional qualifications (41%) than those with higher professional

Fig 5.8: TOTAL MEAN SCORES ON VIEWS RELATING TO KNOWLEDGE & INITIATIVE

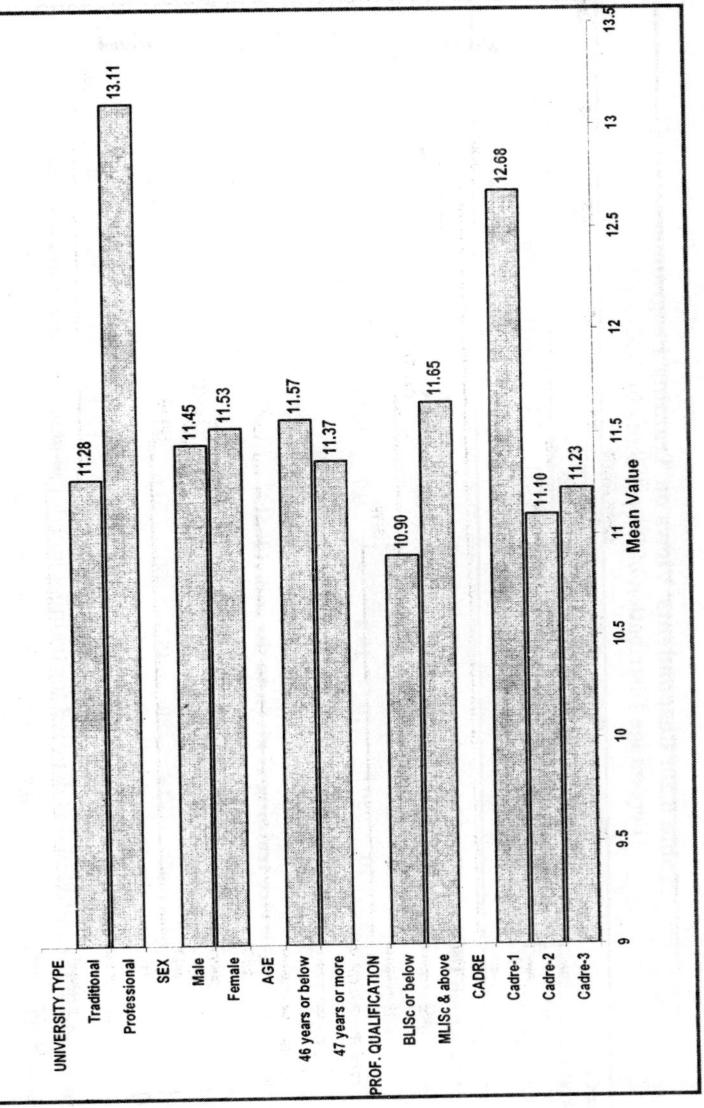

Table 5.20: Respondents' Views on Training Programmes
(Percentage Distribution of Respondents by University)

Extent of knowledge	Name of the University													Total (N = 172)
	OU (N=10)	AU (N=41)	SVU (N=20)	ANGRAU (N=13)	NU (N=10)	SKDU (N=11)	JNTU (N=4)	UOH (N=31)	KU (N=12)	BRAOU (N=5)	PMU (N=6)	PSRTU (N=8)	NTRHU (N=1)	
Extent to which the individual feels that inservice training is necessary for professionals:														
To a large extent	90	78	80	53.8	90	81.8	100	83.9	75	100	50	75	100	79.1
To some extent	-	19.5	10	30.8	10	18.2	-	9.7	16.7	-	50	25	-	15.7
Not at all	10	2.4	10	15.4	-	-	-	6.5	8.3	-	-	-	-	5.2
Extent to which inservice training is given to the individual:														
To a large extent	30	22	25	30.8	10	9.1	50	22.6	-	-	16.7	12.5	-	19.8
To some extent	50	53.7	45	53.8	30	45.5	50	51.6	41.7	60	66.7	62.5	100	50.6
Not at all	20	24.4	30	15.4	60	45.5	-	25.8	58.3	40	16.7	25	-	29.7
Extent to which the individual is deputed for training and development programmes elsewhere:														
To a large extent	20	14.6	10	30.8	10	9.1	100	12.8	-	20	50	12.5	-	16.9
To some extent	30	34.1	20	61.5	30	54.5	-	32.3	50	40	33.3	75	-	37.2

Not at all	50	51.2	70	7.7	60	36.4	-	54.8	50	40	16.7	12.5	100	45.9
Extent to which the individual agrees with rewards for standard performance and punishment for substandard performance:														
To a large extent	10	12.2	40	30.8	30	27.3	50	48.4	8.3	40	66.7	12.5	-	28.5
To some extent	20	56.1	25	30.8	30	27.3	50	32.3	50	40	16.7	62.5	-	38.4
Not at all	70	31.7	35	38.4	40	45.5	-	19.4	41.7	20	16.7	25	100	33.1

Table 5.21: Respondents' Views on Training Programmes (Percentage Distribution of Respondents by selected Background Characters)

	Sex		Age		Perof. Qualification		Cadre			Total (N= 172)
	Male (N = 123)	Female (N=49)	46 Yrs or less (N=91)	47 Yrs or more (N=44)	Blisc or below (N=37)	. LISc & above (N=88)	Cadre 1 (N=84)	Cadre 2 (N=42)	Cadre 3 (N=130)	
Extent to which the individual feels that inservice training is necessary for professionals:										
To a large extent	82.9	69.4	79.5	78.6	76.2	80	86.5	76.9	77.3	79.1
To some extent	12.2	24.5	13.6	17.9	14.3	16.2	10.8	15.4	20.5	15.7
Not at all	4.9	6.1	6.8	3.6	9.5	3.8	2.7	7.7	2.3	5.2
Extent to which inservice training is given to the individual:										
To a large extent	22	14.3	21.6	17.9	19	20	16.2	20.9	20.5	19.8
To some extent	50.4	51	47.7	53.6	40.5	53.8	67.6	44	50	50.6
Not at all	27.6	34.7	30.7	28.6	40.5	26.2	16.2	35.2	29.5	29.7
Extent to which the individual is deputed for training and development programmes elsewhere:										
To a large extent	18.7	12.2	20.5	13.1	16.7	16.9	27	14.3	13.6	16.9
To some extent	39.8	30.6	31.8	42.9	19	43.1	51.4	35.2	29.5	37.2
Not at all	41.5	57.1	47.7	44	64.3	40	21.6	50.5	56.8	45.9

Extent to which the individual agrees with rewards for standard performance and punishment for substandard performance:

To a large extent	27.6	30.6	28.4	28.6	28.6	28.5	37.8	24.2	29.5	28.5
To some extent	41.5	30.6	45.5	31	31	40.8	48.6	34.1	38.6	38.4
Not at all	30.9	38.8	26.1	40.5	40.5	30.8	13.5	41.8	31.8	33.1

qualifications (26%) and more among those working in Cadre-II (35%) services than those working in Cadre-III (30%) and Cadre-I (16%) services.

On the other hand, about 54 per cent of the respondents have reported that they were deputed for training and development programmes elsewhere i.e. outside the work place. The remaining 46 per cent did not report any such deputation. Those who were not deputed for training and development programmes ranged from a low of 8 per cent in ANGRAU library to as high as 70 per cent in SVU library. All the four respondents from JNTU reported such deputation. The proportion of respondents who were not deputed to training and development programmes outside the workplace are more among females (57%) compared to males (42%), more among younger age group (48%) compared to the older age group (44%), more among those with lower professional qualifications (64%) than those with higher professional qualifications (40%) and more among those working in Cadre-III services (57%) compared to those working in Cadre-II (51%) and Cadre-I (22%) services.

In response to another question on to what extent they agree with reward for standard performance and punishment for substandard performance, 29 per cent responded that they agree to a great extent and 38 per cent reported agreement only to some extent and the remaining 33 per cent said that they not at all agree with this sort of reward and punishment. The proportion of respondents reporting their agreement with such reward and punishment is more among males (69%) than females (61%), more among those in younger age groups (74%) compared to the older age groups (59%), more among those with higher professional qualifications (69%) than among those with lower professional qualifications (59%), and is much more among those working in Cadre-I services (86%) compared to those working in Cadre-III (68%) and Cadre-II (58%) services.

The mean scores computed by adding up the quantified responses with unit scores for all these four questions pertaining to the training programmes and performance is shown in Table 5.22 by selected background characteristics. The maximum possible score here is 12 and the minimum is 4.

Table 5.22: Mean Total Scores with Standard Deviation
(For Aspects Considered Regarding Views on Training Programmes)

Background characters	N	Total score		't'	Sig.
		Mean	SD		
a) University Type:					
Traditional	154	8.21	1.71	2.033	0.044*
Professional	18	9.11	2.35		
b) Sex:					
Male	123	8.46	1.76	1.873	0.063
Female	49	7.9	1.85		
c) Age :					
46 Years or below	88	8.39	1.97	0.625	0.533
47 Years or more	84	8.21	1.61		
d) Professional Qualification:					
BLISc or below	42	7.86	2.13	1.856	0.065
MLISc and above	130	8.45	1.67		
e) Cadre:					
Cadre-1	37	9.14	1.62	3.463[a]	0.001*
Cadre-2	91	8.01	1.68	0.589[b]	0.557
Cadre-3	44	8.2	2	2.276[c]	0.026*

*Significant values
a) t value for Cadre-1 × Cadre-2
b) t value for Cadre-2 × Cadre-3
c) t value for Cadre-3 × Cadre-1.

The mean scores for this category of responses are again found to be more for the professional university libraries (9.11) than the traditional university libraries (8.21), slightly more for males (8.46) than the females (7.90) and there is very minor difference between the younger (8.39)and older age groups (8.21). The mean score is more for those with higher professional qualifications (8.45) than those with lower professional qualifications (7.86). This mean score is more for those working in Cadre-I services (9.14) compared to those working in Cadre-III (8.20) and Cadre-II (8.01) services. However, the differences are found to be significant with regard to the type of university and cadre of the respondents only as indicated by the computed 't' values.

Views on performance appraisal

As already mentioned (Table 5.4), only 118 out of the 172 respondents have reported awareness about performance appraisal. All these 118 respondents were asked some selected questions regarding their views on implementation of performance appraisal. Again these responses are recorded in three grade scale and are presented in Table 5.23 by university and in Table 5.24 by selected background characters.

More than half of these respondents (53%) expressed that post-appraisal development activities are desired only to some extent, and 31 per cent felt that this sort of appraisal is desired to a large extent. The remaining 16 per cent felt that it is not at all desired. The proportion who feel that such post-appraisal is not desired ranged from 11 per cent in KU library to 67 per cent in JNTU library. The proportion of respondents with this kind of negative response is more among males (18%) than among females (11%), more among the older age groups (21%) than the younger age groups (11%), slightly more among those with higher professional qualifications (16%) than those with lower professional qualifications (15%) and much higher in those working in Cadre-I services (26%) compared to those working in Cadre-III (15%) and Cadre-II (11%) services.

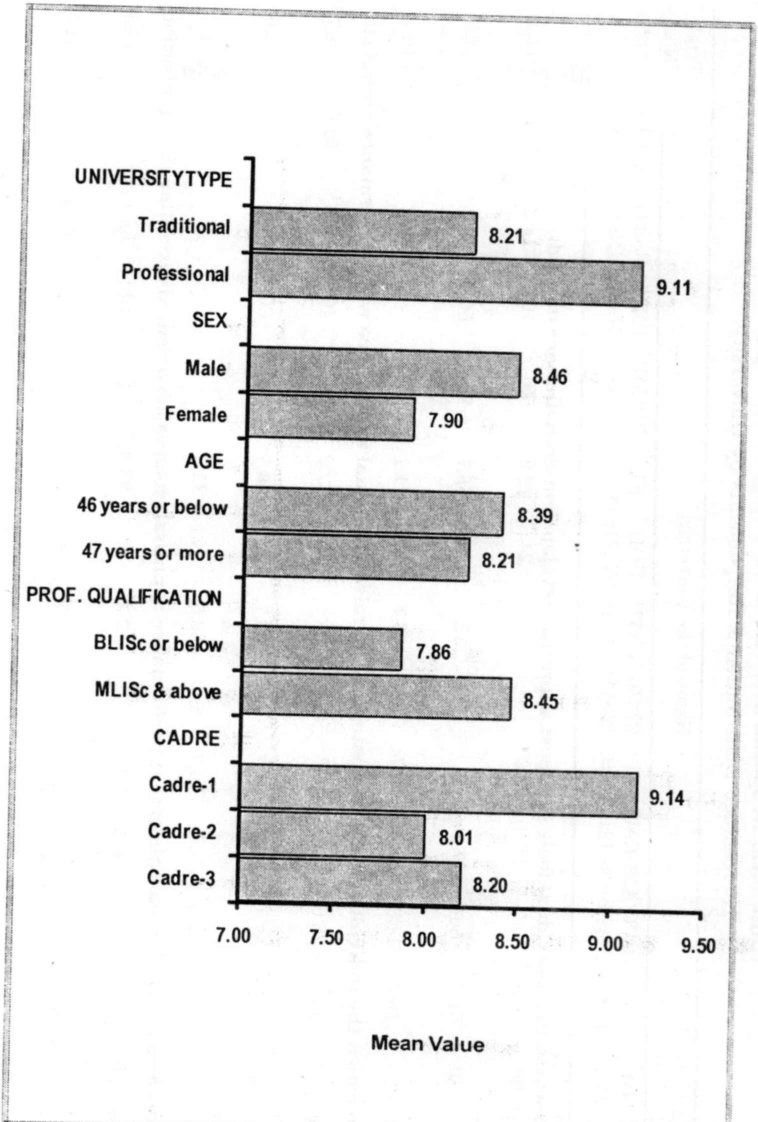

Fig. 5.8: Total Mean Scores onViews Relating to Training Programmes

Table 5.23: Respondents' Views On Performance Appraisal
(Percentage Distribution of Respondents by University)

Extent of knowledge	Name of the University													Total (N = 172)
	OU (N=10)	AU (N=41)	SVU (N=20)	ANGRAU (N=13)	NU (N=10)	SKDU (N=11)	JNTU (N=4)	UOH (N=31)	KU (N=12)	BRAOU (N=5)	PMU (N=6)	PSRTU (N=8)	NTRHU (N=1)	
Extent to which the individual feels that post appraisal development activities are desired:														
To a large extent	20	37.9	35.7	50	33.3	-	-	24	22.2	50	40	14.3	100	31.4
To some extent	60	51.7	50	37.5	50	50	33.3	56	66.7	25	60	71.4	-	52.5
Not at all	20	10.3	14.3	12.5	16.7	50	66.7	20	11.1	25	-	14.3	-	16.1
Extent to which the individual feels that potential appraisal has equal importance with performance appraisal:														
To a large extent	20	44.8	28.6	50	16.7	-	-	36	22.2	50	40	28.6	100	34.7
To some extent	80	48.3	57.1	50	66.7	50	66.7	52	66.7	50	60	71.4	-	55.9
Not at all	-	6.9	14.3	-	16.7	50	33.3	12	11.1	-	-	-	-	9.3
Extent to which the individual thinks that performance appraisal ensures job oriented discipline in organisation:														
To a large extent	20	37.9	50	62.5	83.3	50	33.3	52	33.3	25	80	57.1	100	48.3
To some extent	80	51.7	35.7	37.5	16.7	-	67.7	40	66.7	75	20	42.9	-	44.9

Not at all	-	10.3	14.3	-	-	50	-	8	-	-	-	-	-	6.8
Extent to which the individual agrees with the idea that qualitative factors should also be considered for performance appraisal:														
To a large extent	60	69	92.9	87.5	83.3	50	100	80	55.6	75	100	85.7	100	78
To some extent	40	31	7.1	12.5	16.7	50	-	20	44.4	25	-	14.3	-	22

Note: Respondents reporting no knowledge of Performance Appraisal were excluded.

Table 5.24 : Respondents' Views on Performance Appraisal
(Percentage Distribution of Respondents by selected Background Characters)

	Sex		Age		Perof. Qualification		Cadre			Total (N= 172)
	Male (N = 123)	Female (N=49)	46 Yrs or less (N=91)	47 Yrs or more (N=44)	Blisc or below (N=37)	MLISc & above (N=88)	Cadre 1 (N=84)	Cadre 2 (N=42)	Cadre 3 (N=130)	
Extent to which the individual feels that post appraisal development activities are desired										
To a large extent	26.8	41.7	27.4	35.7	42.3	28.3	38.7	37	15.2	31.4
To some extent	54.9	47.2	61.3	42.9	42.3	55.4	35.5	51.9	69.7	52.5
Not at all	18.3	11.1	11.3	21.4	15.4	16.3	25.8	11.1	15.2	16.1
Extent to which the individual feels that potential appraisal has equal importance with performance appraisal										
To a large extent	30.5	44.4	37.1	32.1	42.3	32.6	45.2	35.2	24.2	34.7
To some extent	59.8	47.2	58.1	53.6	42.3	59.8	48.4	57.4	60.6	55.9
Not at all	9.8	8.3	4.8	14.3	15.4	7.6	6.5	7.4	15.2	9.3
Extent to which the individual thinks that performance appraisal ensures job oriented discipline in organisation										
To a large extent	47.6	50	56.5	39.3	34.6	52.2	64.5	40.7	45.5	48.3

To some extent	47.6	38.9	41.9	48.2	46.2	44.6	32.3	50	48.5	44.9
Not at all	4.9	11.1	1.6	12.5	19.2	3.3	3.2	9.3	6.1	6.8
Extent to which the individual agrees with the idea that qualitative factors should also be considered for performance appraisal										
To a large extent	76.8	80.6	71	85.7	76.9	78.3	93.5	75.9	66.7	78
To some extent	23.2	19.4	29	14.3	23.1	21.7	6.5	24.1	33.3	22

Nearly 91 per cent of the professionals felt that potential appraisal has equal importance with performance appraisal. Of these, about 35 per cent agreed with this view to a large extent and 56 per cent to some extent. The remaining 9 per cent responded negatively. The proportion who felt that potential appraisal has equal importance with performance appraisal is more among the females (92%) than the males (90%), more among the younger group (95%) than the older group (86%), more among those with higher professional qualifications (92%) than those with lower professional qualifications (85%), more or less the same among those working in Cadre-I and Cadre-II services (93%) than those working in Cadre-III services (85%).

A majority of the respondents (93%) opined that the performance appraisal system ensures job oriented discipline in the organization. Of these, 48 per cent expressed their agreement to a large extent while the remaining 45 per cent only to some extent. Seven per cent of the total respondents answered negatively and these are mainly from AU, SVU, SKDU and UOH libraries. The proportion of respondents who feel that the performance appraisal system ensures job oriented discipline in the organization is more among the males (95%) than females (89%), more in the younger age group (98%) than the older age group (87%), more among those with higher professional qualifications (97%) than those with lower professional qualifications (81%) and more among those working in Cadre-I services (97%) than those working in Cadre-III (94%) and Cadre-II (91%) services.

All the 118 library professionals who are aware of the concept of performance appraisal have agreed with the idea that the qualitative factors should also be considered while making performance appraisal. A majority has agreed with this view to a large extent (78%) and the remaining to some extent (22%). The proportion of respondents reporting their agreement to a large extent is more among the females (81%) than males (77%), more by those in older age group

(86%) than those in the younger age group (71%), slightly more by those with higher professional qualifications (78%) than those with lower professional qualifications (77%), much more in those working in Cadre-I services (94%) compared to those working in Cadre-II (76%) and Cadre-III (67%) services.

Table 5.25: Mean Total Scores With Standard Deviation (For Aspects Considered Regarding Views on Performance Appraisal)

Background characters	N	Total score		't'	Sig.
		Mean	SD		
a) University Type:					
Traditional	106	9.56	1.49	0.947	0.346
Professional	12	10	1.91		
b) Sex:					
Male	82	9.49	1.47	1.218	0.226
Female	36	9.86	1.68		
c) Age :					
46 Years or below	62	9.74	1.43	1.044	0.299
47 Years or more	56	9.45	1.65		
d) Professional Qualification:					
BLISc or below	26	9.46	1.94	0.525	0.601
MLISc and above	92	9.64	1.41		
e) Cadre:					
Cadre-1	31	10.06	1.5	1.342a	0.183
Cadre-2	54	9.61	1.5	1.373b	0.173
Cadre-3	33	9.15	1.54	2.394c	0.020*

* Significant values
a) t value for Cadre-1 × Cadre-2
b) t value for Cadre-2 × Cadre-3
c) t value for Cadre-3 × Cadre-1.

Responses to the above four questions were quantified by way of assigning unit scores and the total scores were computed for this category of views on performance appraisal. Here, the maximum possible score is 12 and the minimum is 4. The mean scores are presented in Table 5.25 by selected background characteristics.

It is noticed that the total mean score ranged from 9.15 to 10.06 in different respondent groups. Variation or difference in mean total score is not much by type of university, sex, age group, or professional qualification group. Differences are a little conspicuous among the three cadre groups in the mean total scores. The computed 't' value also indicated that significant differences exist between the respondents working in Cadre-I and Cadre-III with regard to their agreement relating to the selected four statements pertaining to views on performance appraisal.

COMPUTER TECHNOLOGY

The recent developments in the field of Information Technology have brought in tremendous changes in the routine working of the libraries. The major intervention in this direction is the introduction of Computer Technology. This category mainly consensus information relating to the respondents' awareness about information technology, their views on library automation and their ability to use computer and communication technologies.

Awareness about Information Technology and views on Automation

Four selected questions on the extent to which the respondents are aware of Information Technology, extent to which they feel the necessity of library automation and also automation in housekeeping activities and extent to which they like to learn about library automation were asked and their responses recorded in three-grade scale are shown in Table 5.26 by university and in Table 5.27 by background characteristics of the respondents.

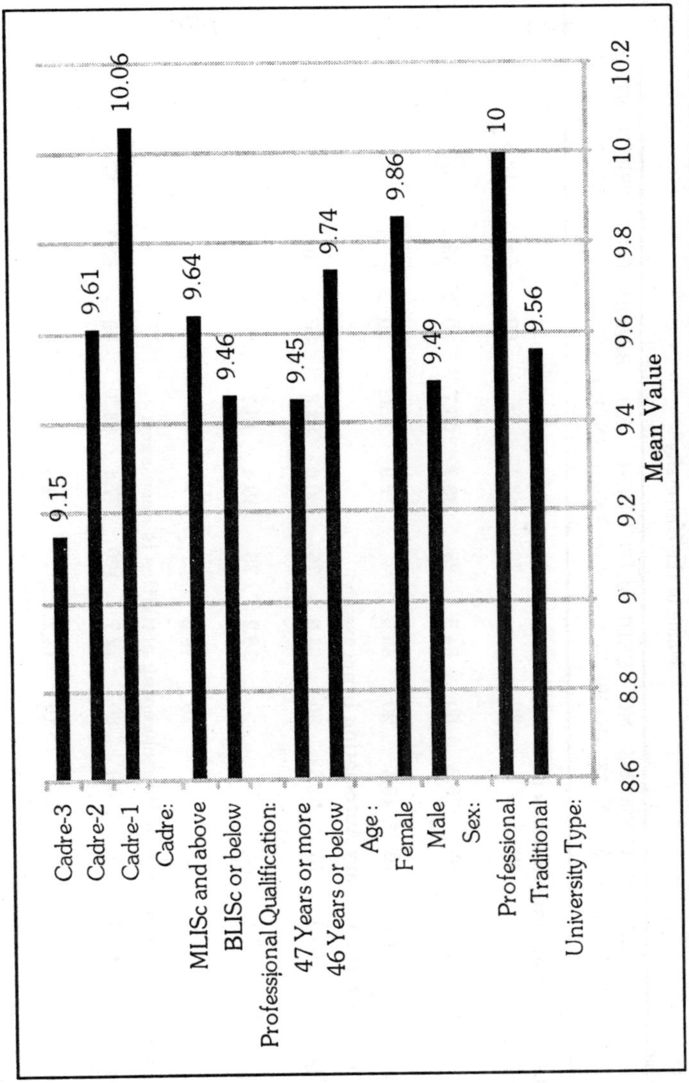

Fig. 9.10: Total Mean Scores on Views Relating to Performance Appraisal

Table-5.26 : Respondents' Awareness About Information Technology And Views On Automation
(Percentage Distribution of Respondents by University)

Extent of knowledge	Name of the University													Total (N = 172)
	OU (N=10)	AU (N=41)	SVU (N=20)	ANGRAU (N=13)	NU (N=10)	SKDU (N=11)	JNTU (N=4)	UOH (N=31)	KU (N=12)	BRAOU (N=5)	PMU (N=6)	PSRTU (N=8)	NTRHU (N=1)	
Extent to which the individual is aware of Information Technology:														
To a large extent	40	19.5	30	7.7	20	-	75	48.4	25	60	66.7	12.5	-	29.1
To some extent	30	53.7	60	76.9	60	54.5	25	38.7	66.7	20	33.3	62.5	100	51.7
Not at all	30	26.8	10	15.4	20	45.5	-	12.9	8.3	20	-	25	-	19.2
Extent to which the Library Automation is necessary:														
To a large extent	60	68.3	75	92.3	90	63.6	75	80.6	83.3	80	100	100	100	77.9
To some extent	30	29.3	25	7.7	-	18.2	25	19.4	16.7	20	-	-	-	19.2
Not at all	10	2.4	-	-	10	18.2	-	-	-	-	-	-	-	2.9
Extent to which Automation of Housekeeping activities is necessary:														
To a large extent	60	68.3	75	76.9	80	72.7	100	77.4	83.3	80	83.3	87.5	100	75.6
To some extent	40	29.3	15	23.1	10	18.2	-	22.6	16.7	20	16.7	12.5	-	21.5

Not at all	-	2.4	10	-	10	9.1	-	-	-	-	-	-	-	2.9
Extent to which the individual likes to learn about Library Automation:														
To a large extent	60	70.7	65	76.9	70	36.4	75	67.7	75	60	83.3	87.5	100	68.6
To some extent	30	24.4	25	15.4	20	45.5	25	29	25	20	16.7	12.5	-	25
Not at all	10	4.9	10	7.7	10	18.2	-	3.2	-	20	-	-	-	6.4

Table-5.27: Respondents' Awareness About Information Technology And Views On Automation
(Percentage Distribution of Respondents by selected Background Characters)

	Sex		Age		Perof. Qualification		Cadre			Total (N= 172)
	Male (N = 123)	Female (N=49)	46 Yrs or less (N=91)	47 Yrs or more (N=44)	Blisc or below (N=37)	MLISc & above (N=88)	Cadre 1 (N=84)	Cadre 2 (N=42)	Cadre 3 (N=130)	
Extent to which the individual is aware of Information Technology:										
To a large extent	29.3	28.6	30.7	27.4	16.7	33.1	54.1	22	22.7	29.1
To some extent	54.5	44.9	55.7	47.6	59.5	49.2	40.5	52.7	59.1	51.7
Not at all	16.3	26.5	13.6	25	23.8	17.7	5.4	25.3	18.2	19.2
Extent to which the Library Automation is necessary:										
To a large extent	79.7	73.5	80.7	75	73.8	79.2	86.5	72.5	81.8	77.9
To some extent	18.7	20.4	17	21.4	23.8	17.7	13.5	23.1	15.9	19.2
Not at all	1.6	6.1	2.3	3.6	2.4	3.1	-	4.4	2.3	2.9
Extent to which Automation of Housekeeping activities is necessary:										
To a large extent	78.9	67.3	76.1	75	66.7	78.5	81.1	73.6	75	75.6
To some extent	19.5	26.5	20.5	22.6	28.6	19.2	16.2	22	25	21.5
Not at all	1.6	6.1	3.4	2.4	4.8	2.3	2.7	4.4	-	2.9

Extent to which the individual likes to learn about Library Automation:										
To a large extent	70.7	63.3	69.3	67.9	61.9	70.8	81.1	64.8	65.9	68.6
To some extent	22.8	30.6	21.6	28.6	23.8	25.4	18.9	28.6	22.7	25
Not at all	6.5	6.1	9.1	3.6	14.3	3.8	-	6.6	11.4	6.4

In all, about 81 per cent of the respondents have reported that they are aware of Information Technology. Regarding the extent of awareness, 29 per cent said that they are aware of it to a great extent and 52 per cent said that they know to some extent. The remaining 19 per cent reported no knowledge about Information Technology. The proportion of respondents who do not have this knowledge ranged from 8 per cent in KU to 46 per cent in SKDU libraries. The proportion of respondents who are not aware of Information Technology is more among females (27%) compared to males (16%), more among those in older age group (25%) than those in younger age group (14%), more among those with lower professional qualifications (24%) than those with higher professional qualifications (18%) and more among those working in Cadre-II services (25%) than those working in Cadre-III (18%) and Cadre-I (5%) services.

A majority of the respondents (97%) agree that library automation is necessary. Of whom, 78 per cent agree to a great extent and 19 per cent agree to some extent. Only 3 per cent have opined that library automation is not at all necessary and these are from OU, AU, NU and SKDU libraries. The proportion of respondents who feel that library automation is not at all necessary is more among females (6%) than males (2%), more among those in older age group (4%) than those in younger age group (2%), slightly more among those having higher professional qualifications (3%) than those having lower professional qualifications (2%) and is slightly more among those working in Cadre-II (4%) services than those working in Cadre-III (2%) services. This response is not recorded from those working in Cadre-I services.

Regarding the necessity of automation in house-keeping activities, about 76 per cent felt that it is necessary to a great extent while 21 per cent said that it is necessary only to some extent. The remaining 3 per cent felt that automation is not at all necessary in housekeeping activities. The proportion of respondents who feel that automation is necessary in housekeeping activities is more among males (98%) than females (94%), slightly more in the older age group (98%) than those in the younger age group (97%), more among those having higher professional qualifications (98%) than those having lower professional qualifications (95%) and more among those working in Cadre-III (100%) services compared to those working in Cadre-I (97%) and Cadre-II (96%) services.

Nearly 94 per cent of the respondents expressed their desire to learn about library automation while the remaining 6 per cent reported that they not at all like to learn about library automation. The desire to learn about library automation is expressed by all the respondents from JNTU, KU, PMU and PSRTU libraries. The proportion of respondents willing to learn about library automation is slightly more among females (94%) than males (93%), more among those in the older age group (96%) than those in the younger age group (91%), more among those having higher professional qualifications (96%) than those having lower professional qualifications (86%), more among those working in Cadre-II (93%) services than those working in Cadre-III (89%) and all those working in Cadre-I services have reported their willingness to learn about library automation.

Responses to these four questions were quantified by assigning unit scores and the total scores were computed. The maximum possible score for this category of responses is 12 and the minimum is 4. The mean scores computed are presented in Table 5.28 by selected background characteristics.

The mean scores here have ranged from 9.74 to 10.95 in different groups of respondents. The differences in the mean score by type of university, by sex and by age are not significant, while the 't' value indicated statistically significant differences between those with higher professional qualifications and those with lower professional qualifications and also between those working in Cadre-I and Cadre-II as well as between those working in Cadre-I and Cadre-III services.

Table 5.28: Mean Total Scores With Standard Deviation (For Aspects Considered Regarding Awareness about I.T and views on Automation)

Background characters	N	Total score		't'	Sig.
		Mean	SD		
a) University Type:					
Traditional	154	10.16	1.67	0.983	0.327
Professional	18	10.56	1.29		
b) Sex:					
Male	123	10.33	1.41	1.632	0.105
Female	49	9.88	2.08		
c) Age:					
46 Years or below	88	10.28	1.6	0.71	0.479
47 Years or more	84	10.11	1.67		
d) Professional Qualification:					
BLISc or below	42	9.74	1.61	2.121	0.035*
MLISc and above	130	10.35	1.62		
e) Cadre:					
Cadre-1	37	10.95	1.33	3.230a	0.002*
Cadre-2	91	9.92	1.73	0.702b	0.484
Cadre-3	44	10.14	1.49	2.558c	0.012*

* Significant values
a) t value for Cadre-1 × Cadre-2
b) t value for Cadre-2 × Cadre-3
c) t value for Cadre-3 × Cadre-1.

Ability to use Computer and Communication Technologies

Under this category, questions relating to the knowledge and ability of the respondents to use computer and communication technologies are presented. Four selected questions were asked to all the respondents and their responses recorded in three-grade scale are presented in Table 5.29 by university and in Table 5.30 by selected background characteristics.

Availability of software packages/databases at their libraries is reported by a majority of the respondents (91%) and the proportion reporting this availability ranged from 64 per cent in SKDU to 100 per cent in OU, ANGRAU, NU, JNTU and PMU libraries. This indicates that in all the university libraries, the software packages/databases are available.

Regarding the knowledge of software/database management, nearly 30 per cent of the respondents reported having this knowledge to a great extent and 42 per cent reported having the knowledge to some extent. The remaining 28 per cent does not have the knowledge regarding software/database management. The proportion of respondents having no knowledge of software/database management ranged from 13 per cent in PSRTU to 50 per cent in OU and JNTU libraries. This proportion is the same (29%) among males and females, more among the younger age group (31%) than the older age group (26%), more among those with lower professional qualifications (31%) than those with higher professional qualifications (28%) more among those working in Cadre-II services (34%) than those in Cadre-III (27%) and Cadre-I (16%) services.

About 47 per cent of the respondents reported having the ability to design software packages for library housekeeping activities. Off these, 18 per cent are having this ability to a great extent while the remaining 29 per cent to some extent. The proportion having this ability to design software packages ranged from 20 per cent in BRAOU to 75 per cent in PSRTU libraries. This proportion of respondents having the ability to design software packages for the library are more among males (50%) than

Table-5.29: Use Of Computer Technology And Communication Technology
(Percentage Distribution of Respondents by University)

Extent of knowledge	Name of the University													Total (N = 172)
	OU (N=10)	AU (N=41)	SVU (N=20)	ANGRAU (N=13)	NU (N=10)	SKDU (N=11)	JNTU (N=4)	UOH (N=31)	KU (N=12)	BRAOU (N=5)	PMU (N=6)	PSRTU (N=8)	NTRHU (N=1)	
Percentage reporting availability of Software Packages / database at the library:														
	100	85.4	95	100	100	63.6	100	96.8	91.7	80	100	87.5	100	91.3
Extent to which the individual knows the Software / Database management of the Library:														
To a large extent	30	19.5	30	38.5	30	18.2	50	38.7	8.3	40	33.3	62.5	-	29.7
To some extent	20	46.3	35	38.5	40	36.4	-	45.2	66.7	40	66.7	25	100	41.9
Not at all	50	34.1	35	23.1	30	45.5	50	16.1	25	20	-	12.5	-	28.5
Extent to which the individual is having the ability to design software packages for library housekeeping activities:														
To a large extent	20	14.6	25	38.5	20	9.1	25	19.4	8.3	-	16.7	12.5	-	18
To some extent	20	24.4	10	23.1	20	27.3	-	41.9	41.7	20	50	62.5	100	29.1
Not at all	60	61	65	38.5	60	63.6	75	38.7	50	80	33.3	25	-	52.9
Extent to which the individual is able to use electronic sources of information:														

To a large extent	30	17.1	15	38.5	40	-	50	38.7	8.3	40	33.3	50	-	26.2
To some extent	10	48.8	45	53.8	30	45.5	50	41.9	66.7	40	50	37.5	100	44.8
Not at all	60	34.1	40	7.7	30	54.5	-	19.4	25	20	16.7	12.5	-	29.1
Extent to which the individual is able to use Communication Technology:														
To a large extent	30	17.1	20	38.5	40	-	75	41.9	8.3	40	66.7	37.5	100	29.1
To some extent	30	46.3	35	53.8	20	54.5	-	48.4	75	40	16.7	50	-	43.6
Not at all	40	36.6	45	7.7	40	45.5	25	9.7	16.7	20	16.7	12.5	-	27.3

Table 5.30: Use Of Computer Technology And Communication Technology
(Percentage Distribution of Respondents by selected Background Characters)

	Sex		Age		Perof. Qualification		Cadre			Total (N= 172)
	Male (N = 123)	Female (N=49)	46 Yrs or less (N=91)	47 Yrs or more (N=44)	Blisc or below (N=37)	MLISc & above (N=88)	Cadre 1 (N=84)	Cadre 2 (N=42)	Cadre 3 (N=130)	
Extent to which the individual knows the Software / Database management of the Library:										
To a large extent	31.4	18.4	36.4	22.6	26.2	30.8	43.2	24.2	29.5	29.7
To some extent	37.4	53.1	33	51.2	42.9	41.5	40.5	41.8	43.2	41.9
Not at all	28.5	28.6	30.7	26.2	31	27.7	16.2	34.1	27.3	28.5
Extent to which the individual is having the ability to design software packages for library housekeeping activities:										
To a large extent	19.5	14.3	19.3	16.7	23.8	16.2	10.8	19.8	20.5	18
To some extent	30.1	26.5	31.8	26.2	23.8	30.8	37.8	24.2	31.8	29.1
Not at all	50.4	59.2	48.9	57.1	52.4	53.1	51.4	56	47.7	52.9
Extent to which the individual is able to use electronic sources of information:										
To a large extent	28.5	20.4	36.4	15.5	23.8	26.9	37.8	18.7	31.8	26.2

To some extent	43.1	49	39.8	50	38.1	46.9	56.8	36.3	52.3	44.8
Not at all	28.5	30.6	23.9	34.5	38.1	26.2	5.4	45.1	15.9	29.1
Extent to which the individual is able to use Communication Technology:										
To a large extent	30.9	24.5	36.4	21.4	21.4	31.5	54.1	19.8	27.3	29.1
To some extent	46.3	36.7	39.8	47.6	47.6	42.3	37.8	39.6	56.8	43.6
Not at all	22.8	38.8	23.9	31	31	26.2	8.1	40.7	15.9	27.3

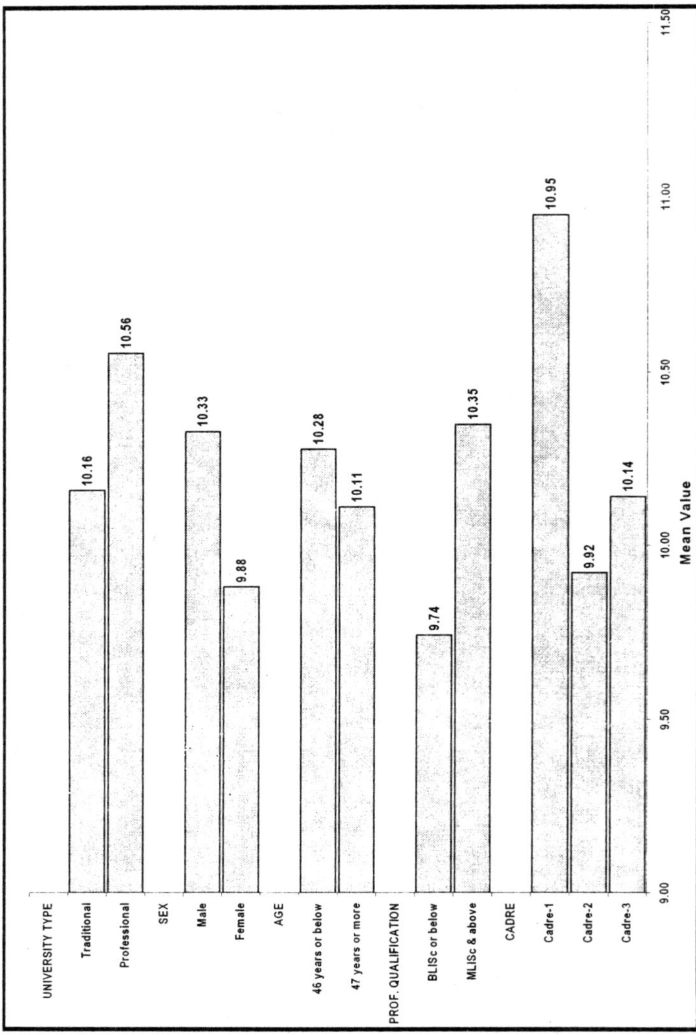

Fig. 5.11: Total Mean Scores on Awareness about I.T. & Views on Automation

the females (41%), more among the younger age group (51%) than the older age group (43%), slightly more among those with lower professional qualifications (48%), than those with higher professional qualifications (47%), more among those working in Cadre-III services (52%) than those working in Cadre-I (49%) and Cadre-II (44%) services.

The ability to use electronic sources of information to a large extent is reported by 26 per cent and to some extent by 45 per cent. In all, 71 per cent are having this ability and the remaining 29 per cent are not at all able to use the electronic sources of information. This proportion is nil in JNTU, only 8 per cent in ANGRAU and is 60 per cent in OU libraries. The proportion of respondents having the ability to use electronic sources of information is more among males (71%) than females (69%), more among the younger age group (76%) than the older age group (65%), more among those with higher professional qualifications (74%) than those with lower professional qualifications (62%), is much more among those working in Cadre-I services (95%) than those working in Cadre-III (84%) and Cadre-II (55%) services.

In all, nearly 73 per cent of the respondents have reported that they have the ability to use communication technology. Out of these, 29 per cent reported the ability to a great extent while 44 per cent had the ability to some extent only. The remaining 27 per cent are not able to use communication technology. This proportion ranged from 10 per cent in UOH to 46 per cent in SKDU libraries. The proportion of respondents having the ability to use communication technology is more among males (77%) than females (61%), more among the younger age group (76%) than the older age group (69%) more among those with higher professional qualifications (74%) than those with lower professional qualifications (69%), much more among those working in Cadre-I (92%) services compared to those working in Cadre-III (84%) and Cadre-II (59%) services.

Responses to these four questions are quantified by assigning unit scores and total score for this category of questions is computed. The maximum and minimum possible total scores are 12 and 4 for this category. The mean scores are presented in Table 5.31 by selected background characteristics.

Table 5.31: Mean Total Scores With Standard Deviation
(For Aspects Considered Regarding Use of Computer and Communication Technologies)

Background characters	N	Total score		't'	Sig.
		Mean	SD		
a) University Type:					
Traditional	154	7.53	2.46	1.97	0.050*
Professional	18	8.72	2.24		
b) SEX:					
MALE	123	7.83	2.48	1.511	0.133
FEMALE	49	7.2	2.38		
c) AGE :					
46 Years or below	88	8.01	2.53	1.984	0.049
47 Years or more	84	7.27	2.34		
d) PROFESSIONAL QUALIFICATION:					
BLISc or below	42	7.43	2.77	0.674	0.501
MLISc and above	130	7.72	2.36		
e) CADRE:					
Cadre-1	37	8.65	1.9	3.372[a]	0.001*
Cadre-2	91	7.07	2.58	2.088[b]	0.039*
Cadre-3	44	8.02	2.31	1.316[c]	0.192

* Significant values
a) t value for Cadre-1 × Cadre-2
b) t value for Cadre-2 × Cadre-3
c) t value for Cadre-3 × Cadre-1.

The mean scores ranged from 7.07 to 8.72 for different groups of respondents. There is a conspicuous differences in the mean score values between traditional and professional university libraries and these differences are found to be statistically significant. Although there is some variation in the mean scores between the groups by sex, age and professional qualification, these differences are not significant. However, the differences between Cadre-I and Cadre-II, Cadre-II and Cadre-III are found to be significant as can be seen from the computed 't' values.

PRINTING AND PUBLISHING TECHNOLOGY

Another important area of development, consequent to the changes due to development of information technology, is the printing and publishing technology. As the library automation is not complete in all the universities and is altogether a recent phenomenon, knowledge and ability to use computer printing technology is important in the regular activities of the library. Hence, only two selected questions were included in this category relating to the extent of use of computer printing technology.

Extent of use of Computer Printing Technology

Responses to questions on the extent of use of computer printing technology like printers, DTP, Electronic Publishing, Pagemaker, LCDs and VDUs and the extent to which they are using computer for making statements/ reports are presented in Table 5.32 by university and in Table 5.33 by selected background characters.

The ability to use computer technology like printers, LCDs and VDUs is reported by 64 per cent of the respondents. Of these, 23 per cent are using to a large extent and 41 per cent to some extent. The remaining 36 per cent are not at all using the computer printing technology. This proportion who does not use computer printing is seen to be ranging from 20 per cent in BRAOU to 55 per cent in SVU libraries. The proportion of respondents having the ability and using the computer printing technology is more

Table 5.32 : Extent Of Use Of Computer Printing Technology By The Respondents (Percentage Distribution of Respondents by University)

Extent of knowledge	Name of the University													Total (N = 172)
	OU (N=10)	AU (N=41)	SVU (N=20)	ANGRAU (N=13)	NU (N=10)	SKDU (N=11)	JNTU (N=4)	UOH (N=31)	KU (N=12)	BRAOU (N=5)	PMU (N=6)	PSRTU (N=8)	NTRHU (N=1)	
Extent to which the individual is using computer printing technology like Printers,LCDs,VDUs, DPT, PageMarker, e-Publishing:														
To a large extent	10	14.6	25	30.8	20	9.1	50	38.7	-	40	66.7	12.5	-	23.3
To some extent	40	43.9	20	46.2	30	54.5	50	35.5	58.3	40	33.3	62.5	-	40.7
Not at all	50	41.5	55	23.1	50	36.4	-	25.8	41.7	20	-	25	100	36
Extent to which the individual is using computer for making Statements / Reports:														
To a large extent	10	14.6	30	30.8	20	-	25	41.9	16.7	40	66.7	25	-	25
To some extent	40	46.3	25	61.5	40	72.7	75	35.5	66.7	40	33.3	62.5	100	46.5
Not at all	50	39	45	7.7	40	27.3	-	22.6	16.7	20	-	12.5	-	28.5

Table 5.33: EXTENT OF USE OF COMPUTER PRINTING TECHNOLOGY BY THE RESPONDENTS
(Percentage Distribution of Respondents by selected Background Characters)

	Sex		Age		Perof. Qualification		Cadre			Total (N= 172)
	Male (N = 123)	Female (N=49)	46 Yrs or less (N=91)	47 Yrs or more (N=44)	Blisc or below (N=37)	MLISc & above (N=88)	Cadre 1 (N=84)	Cadre 2 (N=42)	Cadre 3 (N=130)	
Extent to which the individual is using computer printing technology like Printers,LCDs,VDUs, DPT, PageMarker, e-Publishing:										
To a large extent	22.8	24.5	30.7	15.5	19	24.6	35.1	18.7	22.7	23.3
To some extent	43.9	32.7	35.2	46.4	33.3	43.1	51.4	33	47.7	40.7
Not at all	33.3	42.9	34.1	38.1	47.6	32.3	13.5	48.4	29.5	36
Extent to which the individual is using computer for making Statements / Reports:										
To a large extent	23.6	28.6	36.4	13.1	19	26.9	37.8	19.8	25	25
To some extent	49.6	38.8	40.9	52.4	45.2	46.9	54.1	39.6	54.5	46.5
Not at all	26.8	32.7	22.7	34.5	35.7	26.2	8.1	40.7	20.5	28.5

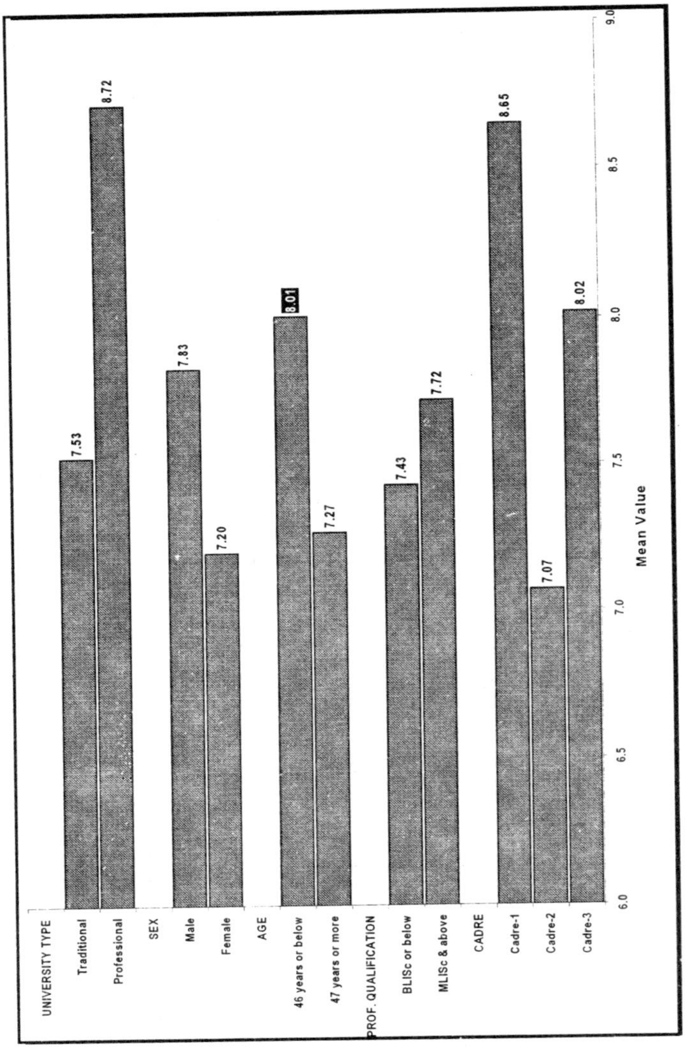

Fig. 5.12: Total Mean Scores on Views Regarding Use of Computer and Communication Technology

among males (67%) than females (57%), slightly more among those in the younger age group (66%) than those in the older age group (62%), more among those with higher professional qualifications (68%) than those with lower professional qualifications (52%), much more among those working in Cadre-I services (86%) than those working in Cadre-III (70%) and Cadre-II (52%) services.

Only 25 per cent of the library professionals interviewed in this study are using computer to a large extent for making statements/reports while another 47 per cent are using the same only to some extent, and the remaining 28 per cent are not at all using computer for making statements/reports. This proportion of respondents not using computer for making statements/reports ranged from 8 per cent in ANGRAU to 50 per cent in OU libraries. This proportion who are not using computer is more among females (33%) than males (27%), more in the older age group (35%) than the younger age group (23%), more among those with lower professional qualifications (36%) than among those with higher professional qualifications (26%) and much more among those working in Cadre-II services (41%) compared to those working in Cadre-III (21%) and Cadre-I (8%) services.

Here also, the responses obtained in three grade-scale were quantified by assigning unit scores for the two responses and total scores were computed. The maximum possible score for this category is 6 and the minimum is 2. The mean scores are shown in Table 5.34 by selected background characteristics.

The mean scores are seen to be ranging from 3.49 to 4.51 in different groups of respondents for this category. The mean scores are higher for professional universities (4.33) than the traditional universities (3.78), more or less similar for males (3.86) and females (3.78), more for the younger age group (4.10) than the older age group (3.56), slightly more for those with higher professional qualifications (3.93) than those with lower professional qualifications (3.55), but is higher (4.51) for those working in Cadre-I services compared to those working in Cadre-II (3.49) and Cadre-III (3.98) services. The computed 't' value indicates that statistically significant differences exist only between the Cadre-I and Cadre-II respondents with regard to the extent of use of computer printing technology.

Table 5.34: Mean Total Scores With Standard Deviation
(For Aspects Considered Regarding Extent of Use of Computer Printing Technology)

Background characters	N	Total score		't'	Sig.
		Mean	SD		
a) University Type:					
Traditional	154	3.78	1.45	1.558	0.121
Professional	18	4.33	1.19		
b) Sex:					
Male	123	3.86	1.39	0.355	0.723
Female	49	3.78	1.56		
c) Age :					
46 Years or below	88	4.1	1.51	2.52	0.013*
47 Years or more	84	3.56	1.3		
d) Professional Qualification:					
BLISc or below	42	3.55	1.47	1.511	0.133
MLISc and above	130	3.93	1.42		
e) Cadre:					
Cadre-1	37	4.51	1.17	3.756a	0.000*
Cadre-2	91	3.49	1.47	1.833b	0.069
Cadre-3	44	3.98	1.36	1.887c	0.063

* Significant values
a) t value for Cadre-1 × Cadre-2
b) t value for Cadre-2 × Cadre-3
c) t value for Cadre-3 × Cadre-1.

NET WORKING OF LIBRARIES

Networking of libraries is yet another important development consequent to the expansion of Information Technology. Networking in libraries is proved to be very useful and necessary because of its advantages such as scope for acquiring information in a relatively shorter period, access to information at different sources, scope for inter-library loan facilities, compilations and preparation of bibliographies etc. Hence, knowledge and skills in using this electronic media are very essential to the modern day library professionals.

Knowledge and ability to use network facility

Three selected questions relating to the knowledge and ability of the respondents in making use of the networking in the libraries were asked and the responses obtained in the three grade scale have been presented in Table 5.35 by university and in Table 5.36 by selected background characteristics.

A majority of the respondents (86%) have reported that their library is part of some network. This has been reported by more than 50 per cent of respondents from all the university libraries which indicates that all the university libraries are provided with some networking facility.

Interestingly, about 31 per cent of the respondents have reported that they are able to use the library network to a large extent and another 36 per cent only to some extent. The remaining 33 per cent said that they are not at all able to use the library network. This proportion of respondents who are not using the library network ranged from 13 per cent in UOH to 60 per cent in SVU libraries. The proportion not able to use the library network is more among the females (41%) than males (30%), more or less the same (33%) in the younger as well as older age group and also among the two groups with higher and lower professional qualifications, and much more among those

Table 5.35 : Respondents' Views On Library Networking
(Percentage Distribution of Respondents by University)

Extent of knowledge	Name of the University													Total (N = 172)
	OU (N=10)	AU (N=41)	SVU (N=20)	ANGRAU (N=13)	NU (N=10)	SKDU (N=11)	JNTU (N=4)	UOH (N=31)	KU (N=12)	BRAOU (N=5)	PMU (N=6)	PSRTU (N=8)	NTRHU (N=1)	
Percentage reporting that their library is part of some Network:														
	80	90.2	90	76.9	100	72.7	50	87.1	91.7	80	100	75	100	86
Extent to which the individual is able to use the library network:														
To a large extent	30	22	30	23.1	30	36.4	25	48.4	25	20	33.3	37.5	-	30.8
To some extent	20	41.5	10	53.8	20	9.1	50	38.7	50	40	50	62.5	100	36
Not at all	50	36.6	60	23.1	50	54.5	25	12.9	25	40	16.7	-	-	33.1
Extent to which the individual likes to know how to process the information and supply to user using the network:														
To a large extent	20	53.7	50	53.8	40	18.2	50	54.8	50	40	66.7	50	100	48.3
To some extent	30	31.7	40	38.5	50	45.5	25	38.7	33.3	40	33.3	37.5	-	36.6
Not at all	50	14.6	10	7.7	10	36.4	25	6.5	16.7	20	-	12.5	-	15.1

Extent to which the individual knows about 'Inflibnet – Infonet':

To a large extent	30	19.5	30	46.2	30	27.3	50	48.4	33.3	-	66.7	75	-	34.9
To some extent	30	58.5	35	38.5	30	36.4	25	35.5	33.3	80	33.3	25	100	41.3
Not at all	40	22	35	15.4	40	36.4	25	16.1	33.3	20	-	-	-	23.8

Table 5.36: Respondents' Views On Library Networking
(Percentage Distribution of Respondents by selected Background Characters)

	Sex		Age		Perof. Qualification		Cadre			Total (N= 172)
	Male (N = 123)	Female (N=49)	46 Yrs or less (N=91)	47 Yrs or more (N=44)	Blisc or below (N=37)	MLISc & above (N=88)	Cadre 1 (N=84)	Cadre 2 (N=42)	Cadre 3 (N=130)	
Extent to which the individual is able to use the library network:										
To a large extent	37.4	14.3	34.1	27.4	28.6	31.5	37.8	27.5	31.8	30.8
To some extent	32.5	44.9	33	39.3	38.1	35.4	43.2	29.7	43.2	36
Not at all	30.1	40.8	33	33.3	33.3	33.1	18.9	42.9	25	33.1
Extent to which the individual likes to know how to process the information and supply to user using the network:										
To a large extent	48.8	46.9	50	46.4	42.9	50	59.5	46.2	43.2	48.3
To some extent	36.6	36.7	33	40.5	42.9	34.6	29.7	36.3	43.2	36.6
Not at all	14.6	16.3	17	13.1	14.3	15.4	10.8	17.6	13.6	15.1
Extent to which the individual knows about 'Inflibnet – Infonet':										
To a large extent	39	24.5	42	27.4	26.2	37.7	59.5	25.3	34.1	34.9
To some extent	39	46.9	35.2	47.6	42.9	40.8	35.1	41.8	45.5	41.3
Not at all	22	28.6	22.7	25	31	21.5	5.4	33	20.5	23.8

working in Cadre-II (43%) compared to those working in Cadre-III (25%) and Cadre-I (19%) services.

Nearly 85 per cent of the respondents expressed their liking for knowing how to process the information and supply it to the user by using the network facility. About 48 per cent expressed this desire to a large extent while another 37 per cent to some extent. Only 15 per cent said that they are not at all interested in knowing the process using network. This proportion ranged from 7 per cent in UOH to 50 per cent in OU libraries. The proportion of respondents desiring to know the processing is slightly more among males (85%) than females (84%), more in the older age group (87%) than the younger age group (83%), slightly among those with lower professional qualifications (86%) than those with higher professional qualifications (85%) and more among those working in Cadre-I (89%) services compared to those working in Cadre-III (86%) and Cadre-II (82%) services.

Knowledge of 'Inflibnet – Infonet' to a large extent is reported by nearly 35 per cent and to some extent by about 41 per cent. In all, 76 per cent of the respondents are aware of 'Inflibnet – Infonet'. The remaining 24 per cent are not aware of the 'Inflibnet-Infonet'. Those who do not have this knowledge ranged from 15 per cent in ANGRAU to 40 per cent in OU and NU libraries. The proportion of respondents having knowledge of 'Inflibnet-Infonet' is more among the males (78%) than females (71%), more among younger age group (77%) than the older age group (75%), more among those with higher professional qualifications (78%) than those with lower professional qualifications (69%) and more among those working in Cadre-I services (95%) compared to those working in Cadre-III (79%) and Cadre-II (67%) services.

The mean scores computed by quantifying the responses with unit scores for this category of responses are shown in Table 5.37. The maximum and minimum possible scores for this category are 9 and 3.

Table 5.37: Mean Total Scores With Standard Deviation
(For Aspects Considered Regarding Views on Library Networking)

Background characters	N	Total score		't'	Sig.
		Mean	SD		
a) University Type:					
Traditional	154	6.38	1.91	0.72	0.473
Professional	18	6.72	1.67		
b) Sex:					
Male	123	6.59	1.89	1.848	0.066
Female	49	6	1.84		
c) Age :					
46 Years or below	88	6.53	1.99	0.82	0.413
47 Years or more	84	6.3	1.78		
d) Professional Qualification:					
BLISc or below	42	6.19	1.92	0.9	0.369
MLISc and above	130	6.49	1.88		
e) Cadre:					
Cadre-1	37	7.22	1.53	3.176a	0.002*
Cadre-2	91	6.05	2	1.263b	0.209
Cadre-3	44	6.5	1.75	1.945c	0.055

* Significant values

a) t value for Cadre-1 × Cadre-2

b) t value for Cadre-2 × Cadre-3

c) t value for Cadre-3 × Cadre-1.

The mean score for this category ranged between 6.00 and 7.22 for different categories of respondents and the difference between the mean scores of Cadre-I and Cadre-II respondents are revealed to be statistically significant. The differences between groups by type of university, sex, age, and professional qualifications are not much and are not significant. There are no significant differences between

Cadre-II and Cadre-III employees also with regard to the responses under this category.

KNOWLEDGE ABOUT LATEST TRENDS IN SERVICES

Because of the changing environment and invasion of electronic media, so many changes have come in the procedures relating to providing library services. Hence, knowledge about latest trends as well as knowledge in applying the new technical skills is an important aspect in to-day's library profession. In view of this, some selected questions relating to the knowledge of the respondents about some general procedures, knowledge in latest schemes of classification and cataloguing and also their extent of knowledge in computer applications were asked under this category.

Knowledge of Some General Procedures

Three questions on the respondents' knowledge regarding acquisition procedures, knowledge on preparation of accession register, knowledge regarding methods of charging and discharging, all pertaining to the general procedures were asked to all the respondents of the present study and their responses are shown in Table 5.38 by university and in Table 5.39 by selected background characteristics.

A majority of the respondents (99%) have reported the knowledge of acquisition procedures. Of whom, 68 present know the procedures to a great extent and 31 per cent to some extent. The remaining one per cent reported no knowledge about the acquisition procedures. These are mainly from AU and SVU libraries. All the female respondents and 98 per cent of the male respondents reported knowledge about the general acquisition procedures, while this proportion is the same (99%) in the two age groups. All the respondents having lower

Table 5.38: RESPONDENTS' KNOWLEDGE ON GENERAL PROCEDURES (Percentage Distribution of Respondents by University)

Extent of knowledge	Name of the University													Total (N = 172)
	OU (N=10)	AU (N=41)	SVU (N=20)	ANGRAU (N=13)	NU (N=10)	SKDU (N=11)	JNTU (N=4)	UOH (N=31)	KU (N=12)	BRAOU (N=5)	PMU (N=6)	PSRTU (N=8)	NTRHU (N=1)	
Extent to which the individual is having knowledge in Acquisition Procedures:														
To a large extent	80	46.3	90	76.9	40	45.5	75	74.2	75	100	66.7	87.5	100	67.4
To some extent	20	51.2	5	23.1	60	54.5	25	25.8	25	-	33.3	12.5	-	31.4
Not at all	-	2.4	5	-	-	-	-	-	-	-	-	-	-	1.2
Extent to which the individual is having knowledge on preparation of Accession Register:														
To a large extent	80	56.1	95	92.3	60	63.6	100	74.2	91.7	100	100	62.5	100	75.6
To some extent	10	39	5	7.7	40	27.3	-	22.6	8.3	-	-	25	-	20.9
Not at all	10	4.9	-	-	-	9.1	-	3.2	-	-	-	12.5	-	3.5
Extent to which the individual is having knowledge on the methods of Charging and Discharging:														
To a large extent	70	41.5	70	46.2	10	63.6	75	64.5	83.3	100	83.3	62.5	-	58.1
To some extent	30	51.2	25	53.8	90	36.4	25	35.5	16.7	-	16.7	25	100	39
Not at all	-	7.3	5	-	-	-	-	-	-	-	-	12.5	-	2.9

Table 5.39: Respondents' Knowledge On General Procedures
(Percentage Distribution of Respondents by selected Background Characters)

	Sex		Age		Perof. Qualification		Cadre			Total (N= 172)
	Male (N = 123)	Female (N=49)	46 Yrs or less (N=91)	47 Yrs or more (N=44)	Blisc or below (N=37)	MLISc & above (N=88)	Cadre 1 (N=84)	Cadre 2 (N=42)	Cadre 3 (N=130)	
Extent to which the individual is having knowledge in Acquisition Procedures:										
To a large extent	65.9	71.4	64.8	70.2	64.3	68.5	91.9	58.2	65.9	67.4
To some extent	32.5	28.6	34.1	28.6	35.7	30	8.1	39.6	34.1	31.4
Not at all	1.6	-	1.1	1.2	-	1.5	-	2.2	-	1.2
Extent to which the individual is having knowledge on preparation of Accession Register:										
To a large extent	74	79.6	73.9	77.4	66.7	78.5	97.3	73.6	61.4	75.6
To some extent	22	18.4	22.7	19	28.6	18.5	2.7	24.2	29.5	20.9
Not at all	4.1	2	3.4	3.6	4.8	3.1	-	2.2	9.1	3.5
Extent to which the individual is having knowledge on the methods of Charging and Discharging:										
To a large extent	56.9	61.2	54.5	61.9	52.4	60	81.1	54.9	45.5	58.1
To some extent	40.7	34.7	42	35.7	45.2	36.9	18.9	40.7	52.3	39
Not at all	2.4	4.1	3.4	2.4	2.4	3.1	-	4.4	2.3	2.9

professional qualifications have reported the knowledge of acquisition procedures. All the respondents working in Cadre-I and Cadre-III services and 98 per cent of those working in Cadre-II services also reported the knowledge of acquisition procedures.

Nearly 96 per cent of the respondents have reported that they are having the knowledge on preparation of accession register. Of these, 75 per cent know the procedure to a large extent and 21 per cent are having this knowledge to some extent. Those who have no knowledge on how to prepare the accession register is around 4 per cent and this proportion ranged from 3 to 13 per cent among OU, AU, SKDU, UOH and PSRTU libraries. Knowledge on preparation of accession register is reported more by the females (98%) than the males (96%), slightly more by the younger age group (97%) than the older age group (96%), more by those having higher professional qualifications (97%) than those having lower professional qualifications (95%). All those working in Cadre-I services, 98 per cent in Cadre-II and 91 per cent in Cadre-III services have also reported this knowledge.

Knowledge regarding methods of charging and discharging are reported by about 97 per cent of the respondents. Out of these, 58 per cent said that they know the methods to a great extent and 39 per cent know them only to some extent. The remaining 3 per cent are not aware of the methods of charging and discharging and all these are from AU, SVU and PSRTU libraries only. Knowledge of these methods is reported more by the males (98%) than the females (96%), more by the older age group (98%) than the younger age group (97%), more by those with higher professional qualifications (98%) than those with lower professional qualifications (97%) and all among those working in Cadre-I services, 98 per cent among those working in Cadre-III and 96 per cent among those working in Cadre-II services.

These responses were again quantified by assigning unit scores to the three graded responses recorded for these three questions under the category related to knowledge on general procedures. The maximum and minimum possible scores for this category are 9 and 3. The mean scores computed for this category by selected background characteristics are shown in Table 5.40.

Table 5.40: Mean Total Scores With Standard Deviation
(For Aspects Considered Regarding Knowledge on General Procedures)

Background characters	N	Total score		't'	Sig.
		Mean	SD		
a) University Type:					
Traditional	154	7.9	1.33	0.999	0.319
Professional	18	8.22	0.81		
b) Sex:					
Male	123	7.89	1.31	0.806	0.422
Female	49	8.06	1.23		
c) Age :					
46 Years or below	88	7.85	1.26	0.875	0.383
47 Years or more	84	8.02	1.31		
d) **Professional** Qualification:					
BLISc or below	42	7.76	1.28	1.01	0.314
MLISc and above	130	7.99	1.29		
Cadre-1	37	8.7	0.66	3.988[a]	0.000*
Cadre-2	91	7.78	1.34	0.678[b]	0.499
Cadre-3	44	7.61	1.33	4.520[c]	0.000*

* Significant values

a) t value for Cadre-1 × Cadre-2

b) t value for Cadre-2 × Cadre-3

c) t value for Cadre-3 × Cadre-1.

The mean score for this category of responses ranged from 7.61 to 8.70 in different categories of respondents. The mean score is more for the professional universities (8.22) than the traditional universities (7.90), more for females (8.06) than males (7.89), more for the older age group (8.02) than the younger age group (7.85), slightly more for those with higher professional qualifications (7.99) than those with lower professional qualifications (7.76) and is highest for those working in Cadre-I services (8.70) compared to those working in Cadre-II (7.78) and Cadre-III (7.61) services. However, the computed 't' value indicates that there exists significant differences in the proportion of respondents regarding these knowledge levels between Cadre-I and Cadre-II as well as between Cadre-I and Cadre-III services. Differences by type of university, sex, age and professional qualifications are not significant.

Knowledge on classification and cataloguing

Four questions were asked relating to the respondents knowledge regarding classification and cataloguing and their responses are recorded in three grade scale. These were shown in Table 5.41 by university and in Table 5.42 by selected background characteristics.

In all 93 per cent of the respondents reported that they know about the classification scheme followed in the library. Of these, nearly 63 per cent reported knowledge to a great extent and 30 per cent to some extent. The remaining 7 per cent do not know about the classification scheme followed in the library. These are from OU, AU, SVU, SKDU, UOH and PSRTU libraries. Knowledge of the classification scheme followed is reported more by the males (94%) than the females (90%), more by the younger age group (94%) than the older age group (92%), more by those with lower professional qualifications (95%) than those with higher professional qualifications (92%). All the respondents working in Cadre-I services, 91 per cent working in Cadre-II and Cadre-III Services are also aware of the classification scheme followed in the library.

About 81 per cent of the respondents know about the latest development in classification (DDC 21st Ed., DDC-CD etc). Out of these, 32 per cent reported knowledge to a great extent while 49 per cent reported it only to some extent. The remaining 19 per cent are not aware of the latest developments in classification. This proportion ranged from 10 per cent in OU and SVU to 40 per cent in NU libraries. Knowledge regarding the latest developments in classification is reported more among the females (88%) than males (78%), more or less the same (81%) among the younger and older age groups and also the two qualification groups. This knowledge is found to be more among those working in Cadre-I services (92%) than those working in Cadre-III (79%) and Cadre-II (77%) services.

Knowledge about the cataloguing code followed is reported by about 94 per cent of the respondents. This knowledge is reported to a great extent by 58 per cent and 36 per cent to some extent. Six per cent of the respondents are not aware of the cataloguing code followed. These are all from OU, AU, SVU, SKDU, UOH and PSRTU libraries. This knowledge is reported more by the females (96%) than the males (93%), more among higher professional qualifications (95%) than those with lower professional qualifications (93%) and it is complete (100%) among those working in Cadre-I services, 93 per cent among those working in Cadre-III and 92 per cent among those working in Cadre-II services.

Nearly 83 per cent of the respondents are aware of the latest developments in cataloguing (OPAC, MARC, CCF, Subject Headings etc.). This knowledge is reported to a great extent by 34 per cent and 49 per cent to some extent while 17 per cent of the respondents are not aware of the latest developments in cataloguing. This proportion ranged from 7 per cent in UOH to 40 per cent in NU libraries. This knowledge is reported more by the males (84%) than the females (82%), more among the older age group (84%) than the younger age group (82%), more among those with lower

Table 5.41: Respondents' Knowledge On Classification and Cataloguing
(Percentage Distribution of Respondents by University)

Extent of knowledge	Name of the University													Total
	OU (N=10)	AU (N=41)	SVU (N=20)	ANGRAU (N=13)	NU (N=10)	SKDU (N=11)	JNTU (N=4)	UOH (N=31)	KU (N=12)	BRAOU (N=5)	PMU (N=6)	PSRTU (N=8)	NTRHU (N=1)	(N = 172)
Extent of Knowledge about the Classification scheme followed:														
To a large extent	80	31.7	75	76.9	50	54.5	100	64.5	66.7	100	100	87.5	100	62.8
To some extent	10	53.7	20	23.1	50	36.4	-	29	33.3	-	-	-	-	30.2
Not at all	10	14.6	5	-	-	9.1	-	6.5	-	-	-	12.5	-	7
Extent of knowledge regarding the latest development in Class-ification (DDC 21st Ed., CD)														
To a large extent	30	12.2	35	53.8	30	27.3	50	41.9	8.3	40	66.7	50	100	32
To some extent	60	58.5	55	46.2	30	45.5	50	38.7	75	40	16.7	37.5	-	48.8
Not at all	10	29.3	10	-	40	27.3	-	19.4	16.7	20	16.7	12.5	-	19.2
Extent to which the individual knows about the Cataloguing code followed:														
To a large extent	70	26.8	75	61.5	40	54.5	75	67.7	75	100	83.3	62.5	-	57.6

To some extent	20	61	20	38.5	60	36.4	25	29	25	-	16.7	25	100	36.6
Not at all	10	12.2	5	-	-	9.1	-	3.2	-	-	-	12.5	-	5.8
Extent of knowledge regarding the latest developments in Cataloguing:														
To a large extent	20	17.1	35	46.2	30	36.4	50	41.9	25	40	83.3	62.5	-	34.3
To some extent	60	61	45	46.2	30	36.4	50	51.6	66.7	60	-	12.5	100	48.8
Not at all	20	22	20	7.7	40	27.3	-	6.5	8.3	-	16.7	25	-	16.9

Table 5.42: Respondents' Knowledge On Classification And Cataloguing
(Percentage Distribution of Respondents by selected Background Characters)

	Sex		Age		Perof. Qualification		Cadre			Total (N= 172)
	Male (N = 123)	Female (N=49)	46 Yrs or less (N=91)	47 Yrs or more (N=44)	Blisc or below (N=37)	MLISc & above (N=88)	Cadre 1 (N=84)	Cadre 2 (N=42)	Cadre 3 (N=130)	
Extent of Knowledge about the Classification scheme followed:										
To a large extent	61.8	65.3	68.2	57.1	52.4	66.2	91.9	53.8	56.8	62.8
To some extent	32.5	24.5	26.1	34.5	42.9	26.2	8.1	37.4	34.1	30.2
Not at all	5.7	10.2	5.7	8.3	4.8	7.7	-	8.8	9.1	7
Extent of knowledge regarding the latest development in Class-ification (DDC 21st Ed., CD)										
To a large extent	30.1	36.7	39.8	23.8	31	32.3	40.5	24.2	40.9	32
To some extent	48	51	40.9	57.1	50	48.5	51.4	52.7	38.6	48.8
Not at all	22	12.2	19.3	19	19	19.2	8.1	23.1	20.5	19.2
Extent to which the individual knows about the Cataloguing code followed:										
To a large extent	54.5	65.3	62.5	52.4	52.4	59.2	78.4	52.7	50	57.6
To some extent	39	30.6	33	40.5	40.5	35.4	21.6	39.6	43.2	36.6
Not at all	6.5	4.1	4.5	7.1	7.1	5.4	-	7.7	6.8	5.8

Extent of knowledge regarding the latest developments in Cataloguing:										
To a large extent	32.5	38.8	38.6	29.8	35.7	33.8	54.1	27.5	31.8	34.3
To some extent	51.2	42.9	43.2	54.8	50	48.5	40.5	49.5	54.5	48.8
Not at all	16.3	18.4	18.2	15.5	14.3	17.7	5.4	23.1	13.6	16.9

professional qualifications (86%) than those with higher professional qualifications (82%), much more among those working in Cadre-I (95%) than those working in Cadre-III (86%) and Cadre-II (77%) services.

The responses recorded in the three grade scale were quantified by assigning unit scores and total scores were computed adding-up all the scores for the four responses under this category. The maximum and minimum possible scores are 12 and 4. The mean scores are presented in Table 5.43. by selected background characteristics.

The mean score for this category ranged from 8.96 to 10.51 in different categories of respondents. The mean scores are more for the professional universities (10.39) compared to the traditional universities (9.26). Slightly higher scores are recorded among females (9.61) than males (9.28) and the mean scores are higher for the younger age group (9.61) than the older age group (9.13), more or less the same for those with higher and lower professional qualifications (9.4 and 9.3 respectively). The mean score is found to be highest for those working in Cadre-I services (10.51) compared to those working in Cadre-III (9.30) and Cadre-II (8.96) services. The computed 't' values indicate that significant differences exist between traditional and professional universities, between Cadre-I and Cadre-II employees and between Cadre-I and Cadre-III employees with regard to the knowledge on classification and cataloguing.

Knowledge on Computer Applications

Regarding the knowledge on computer applications, the respondents were asked four questions on the extent of knowledge of computer applications in acquisition section, circulation section, serial control and in office management. The responses to these four questions are recorded in three grade scale and are shown in Table 5.44 by University and in Table 5.45 by selected background characteristics.

Table 5.43: Mean Total Scores With Standard Deviation
(For Aspects Considered Regarding Knowledge on Classification and Cataloguing)

Background characters	N	Total score		't'	Sig.
		Mean	SD		
a) University Type:					
Traditional	154	9.26	2.08	2.24	0.026*
Professional	18	10.39	1.38		
b) Sex:					
Male	123	9.28	2.03	0.947	0.345
Female	49	9.61	2.09		
c) Age :					
46 Years or below	88	9.61	2.08	1.552	0.122
47 Years or more	84	9.13	2		
d) Professional Qualification:					
BLISc or below	42	9.26	2	0.421	0.674
MLISc and above	130	9.42	2.07		
e) Cadre:					
Cadre-1	37	10.51	1.41	4.213[a]	0.000*
Cadre-2	91	8.96	2.06	0.884[b]	0.378
Cadre-3	44	9.30.	2.15	2.952[c]	0.004*

* Significant values

a) t value for Cadre-1 × Cadre-2

b) t value for Cadre-2 × Cadre-3

c) t value for Cadre-3 × Cadre-1.

Nearly 36 per cent of the respondents know about the computer applications in acquisition section to a great extent and 42 per cent know about it to some extent. In all 78 per cent are having knowledge regarding computer applications in acquisition section. The remaining 22 per cent does not know about the computer applications in acquisition section. This proportion ranged from 3 per cent

Table 5.44: Respondents' Knowledge on Computer Applications
(Percentage Distribution of Respondents by University)

Extent of knowledge	Name of the University													Total (N = 172)
	OU (N=10)	AU (N=41)	SVU (N=20)	ANGRAU (N=13)	NU (N=10)	SKDU (N=11)	JNTU (N=4)	UOH (N=31)	KU (N=12)	BRAOU (N=5)	PMU (N=6)	PSRTU (N=8)	NTRHU (N=1)	
In Acquisition Section:														
To a large extent	40	19.5	20	53.8	20	18.2	25	51.6	33.3	40	83.3	62.5	100	35.5
To some extent	30	46.3	35	46.2	40	54.5	75	45.2	50	40	16.7	25	-	42.4
Not at all	30	34.1	45	-	40	27.3	-	3.2	16.7	20	-	12.5	-	22.1
In Circulation Section:														
To a large extent	20	14.6	25	53.8	10	18.2	25	61.3	16.7	40	33.3	62.5	-	31.4
To some extent	50	56.1	35	46.2	50	36.4	50	35.5	66.7	40	66.7	25	100	46.5
Not at all	30	29.3	40	-	40	45.5	25	3.2	16.7	20	-	12.5	-	22.1
In Serial Control:														
To a large	30	12.2	25	38.5	10	27.3	25	45.2	8.3	40	50	50	100	27.9

extent													
To some extent	40	56.1	25	53.8	50	9.1	50	45.2	75	40	50	37.5	-	45.3
Not at all	30	31.7	50	7.7	40	63.6	25	9.7	16.7	20	-	12.5	-	26.7
In Office Management:														
To a large extent	10	4.9	30	38.5	40	18.2	25	45.2	16.7	40	33.3	50	-	26.2
To some extent	60	46.3	40	23.1	30	27.3	75	48.4	58.3	40	66.7	37.5	100	44.8
Not at all	30	48.8	30	38.5	30	54.5	-	6.5	25	20	-	12.5	-	29.1

Table 5.45: Respondents' Knowledge On Computer ApPlications (Percentage Distribution of Respondents by selected Background Characters)

Extent of Knowledge of computer applications	Sex		Age		Perof. Qualification		Cadre			Total (N= 172)
	Male (N = 123)	Female (N=49)	46 Yrs or less (N=91)	47 Yrs or more (N=44)	Blisc or below (N=37)	MLISc & above (N=88)	Cadre 1 (N=84)	Cadre 2 (N=42)	Cadre 3 (N=130)	
In Acquisition Section:										
To a large extent	38.2	28.6	40.9	29.8	23.8	39.2	56.8	26.4	36.4	35.5
To some extent	39.8	49	39.8	45.2	50	40	37.8	42.9	45.5	42.4
Not at all	22	22.4	19.3	25	26.2	20.8	5.4	30.8	18.2	22.1
In Circulation Section:										
To a large extent	34.1	24.5	38.6	23.8	26.2	33.1	43.2	20.9	43.2	31.4
To some extent	44.7	51	42	51.2	45.2	46.9	48.6	48.4	40.9	46.5
Not at all	21.1	24.5	19.3	25	28.6	20	8.1	30.8	15.9	22.1
In Serial Control:										
To a large extent	29.3	24.5	35.2	20.2	23.8	29.2	40.5	19.8	34.1	27.9
To some extent	44.7	46.9	44.3	46.4	42.9	46.2	51.4	41.8	47.7	45.3
Not at all	26	28.6	20.5	33.3	33.3	24.6	8.1	38.5	18.2	26.7

In Office Management:										
To a large extent	30.9	14.3	35.2	16.7	23.8	26.9	37.8	17.6	34.1	26.2
To some extent	39.8	57.1	38.6	51.2	40.5	46.2	56.8	42.9	38.6	44.8
Not at all	29.3	28.6	26.1	32.1	35.7	26.9	5.4	39.6	27.3	29.1

in UOH to 40 per cent in NU libraries. Knowledge about computer applications in acquisition section is reported more or less in the same proportion by the males and females (78%), more by the younger age group (81%) than the older age group (75%), more by those with higher professional qualifications (79%) than those with lower professional qualifications (74%), much more by those working in Cadre-I services (95%) than those working in Cadre-III (82%) and Cadre-II (69%) services.

Knowledge regarding computer applications in circulation section is also reported by 78 per cent of the respondents. Of whom, 31 per cent had the knowledge to a great extent and 47 per cent know it only to some extent. The remaining 22 per cent are not having this knowledge and this proportion ranged from 3 per cent in UOH to 46 per cent in SKDU libraries. This knowledge is reported more among the males (79%) than the females (75%), more among the younger age group (81%) than the older age group (75%), more among those with higher professional qualifications (80%) than those with lower professional qualifications (71%) and much more among those working the Cadre-I services (92%) than those working in Cadre-III (84%) and Cadre-II (69%) services.

Only 73 per cent of the respondents have reported knowledge of computer applications in serial control. This knowledge is reported to be to a great extent by 28 per cent and to some extent by 45 per cent of the respondents. The remaining 27 per cent are not aware of the computer applications in serial control and this proportion ranged from 8 per cent in ANGRAU to 64 per cent in SKDU libraries. The proportion of respondents having knowledge of computer applications in serial control is more among males (74%) than females (71%), more among the younger age group (79%) than the older age group (67%), more among those with higher professional qualifications (75%) than those with lower professional qualifications (67%), much more among those working in Cadre-I services (92%) compared to those working in Cadre-III (82%) and Cadre-II (61%) services.

Knowledge about computer applications in office management is reported by 71 per cent of the respondents. Out of whom, 26 per cent had the knowledge to a great extent and 45 per cent had it only to some extent. The remaining 29 per cent of the respondents does not know about computer applications in office management. This proportion ranged from 7 per cent in UOH to 55 per cent in SKDU libraries. Knowledge about computer applications in office management is reported more or less the same proportion (71%) by the males and females, more among the lower age group (74%) than the older age group (68%), more among those with higher professional qualifications (73%) than those with lower professional qualifications (64%), much more among those working in Cadre-I services (95%) than those working in Cadre-III (73%) and Cadre-II (60%) services.

The three graded responses to these four questions on knowledge of computer applications are quantified by assigning unit scores and the total scores were computed for this category on knowledge of computer applications. The maximum and minimum possible scores for this category are 12 and 4. The mean scores by selected background characteristics are shown in Table 5.46.

The mean scores ranged from 7.45 to 9.51 among different categories of respondents. The mean scores are more among the professional universities (9.22) than the traditional universities (8.09), more among males (8.34) than the females (7.88), more among the younger age group (8.65) than the older age group (7.75), more among those with higher professional qualifications (8.36) than those with lower professional qualifications (7.74). The mean scores are highest (9.51) for those working in Cadre-I services than those working in Cadre-III (8.68) and Cadre-

II (7.45) services. The 't' values indicate that significant differences exist in the proportion of respondents between younger and older groups, between those working in Cadre-I and Cadre-II services as well as between those working in Cadre-II and Cadre-III services.

Table 5.46: Mean Total Scores With Standard Deviation (For Aspects Considered Regarding Knowledge on Computer Applications)

Background characters	N	Total score		't'	Sig.
		Mean	SD		
a) University Type:					
Traditional	154	8.09	2.65	1.752	0.082
Professional	18	9.22	2.02		
b) Sex:					
Male	123	8.34	2.69	1.054	0.294
Female	49	7.88	2.38		
c) Age :					
46 Years or below	88	8.65	2.65	2.285	0.024*
47 Years or more	84	7.75	2.5		
d) Professional Qualification:					
BLISc or below	42	7.74	2.43	1.35	
MLISc and above	130	8.36	2.65		0.179
e) CADRE:					
Cadre-1	37	9.51	2.24	4.309[a]	0.000*
Cadre-2	91	7.45	2.54	2.643[b]	0.009*
Cadre-3	44	8.68	2.54	1.547[c]	0.126

* Significant values

a) t value for Cadre-1 × Cadre-2

b) t value for Cadre-2 × Cadre-3

c) t value for Cadre-3 × Cadre-1.

TOTAL SCORE BY SELECTED BACKGROUND CHARACTERISTICS

The scores computed for all the 14 aspects of study are added to obtain total score for all the responses put together. The mean total scores by selected background characteristics are shown in Table 5.47.

Table 5.47 Mean Total Scores With Standard Deviation (All aspects studied)

Background characters	N	Total score		't'	Sig.
		Mean	SD		
a) University Type:					
Traditional	154	124.6	15.51	1.816	0.071*
Professional	18	131.67	16.57		
b) Sex:					
Male	123	126.14	15.3	1.051	0.295
Female	49	123.35	16.72		
c) Age :					
46 Years or below	88	127.28	16.24	1.666	0.098
47 Years or more	84	123.31	14.98		
d) Professional Qualification:					
BLISc or below	42	121.55	15.45	1.812	0.072
MLISc and above	130	126.57	15.67		
e) Cadre:					
Cadre-1	37	136.32	12.45	5.428[a]	0.000*
Cadre-2	91	121.18	15	1.275[b]	0.205
Cadre-3	44	124.73	15.54	3.6582[c]	0.000*

* Significant values

a) t value for Cadre-1 × Cadre-2

b) t value for Cadre-2 × Cadre-3

c) t value for Cadre-3 × Cadre-1.

The mean total score ranged from 121.18 to 136.32 in different categories of respondents. The mean total score is more for professional universities (131.67) than the traditional universities (124.60), slightly more among the males (126.14) than females (123.35), more among the younger age group (127.28) than the older age group (123.31), more among those with higher professional qualifications (126.57) than those with lower professional qualifications (121.55). The mean total scores are highest among those working in Cadre-I services (136.32) than those working in Cadre-III (124.73) and Cadre-II (121.18) services. The computed 't' values reveal that significant differences exist only between those working in Cadre-I and Cadre II as well as between those working in Cadre-I and Cadre III services.

Comprehensive presentation of the mean scores and mean total scores for all the 14 aspects of the study by background characteristics

The mean scores computed for all the 14 aspects considered in the study are presented in Table 5.48 along with the mean total scores by different background characters in order to have a comprehensive picture.

Considering the selected background characteristics like type of university, sex, age, professional qualification and Cadre, it is noticed that for almost all the aspects, the maximum and minimum mean scores are recorded in the case of cadre groups. In all the cases, the highest mean score are observed for those working in Cadre-I services. This group obviously is the more experienced, qualified and aged among the three as per the general understanding and there is not surprise in observing highest mean scores for this group. For most of these study aspects, the minimum or lowest mean scores are observed for the Cadre-III or Cadre-II groups and the reason for this may be there are the workers at lower strata comparatively, relatively young, comparatively less experienced and include both technical and non-technical employees. That is why, among these two, the mean scores for knowledge and use of technical aspects are higher for Cadre-III than those in Cadre-II.

Coming to the next important aspect i.e. the professional qualification – obviously, the mean scores are expected to be more for those with higher qualifications than those with lower qualifications as all the aspects of study are on the extent of knowledge and use of different practices and technologies. The same observation is made here and the mean scores for all the aspects are found to be more for those with higher professional qualifications than those with lower professional qualifications. However, the difference between the two groups varied basing on the type of response.

Age and sex are the two aspects, which show very little effect on the responses reflected in the form of the computed mean scores. These two variables have not revealed any clear association with any of the aspects considered as the mean scores showed variation in these two groups. However, the difference in the mean scores is not much under these two groups.

Type of university is observed to be another important variable, which is presenting a lot of variation in the computed mean score values for all the aspects of study. The mean scores are more for professional universities compared to the traditional universities for all the aspects of study. This observation is also in the expected direction as the work environment in terms of infrastructure facilities, other facilities and scope for exposure to latest developments are relatively better in professional universities compared to the traditional universities.

Hence, it appears that the mean scores based on self-assessment with regard to this extent of knowledge and use regarding different aspects considered in the present study are more influenced by the variables like type of university, professional qualification and cadre in which they are

Table 5.48 : Mean Scores and Mean Total Score for All the 14 Aspects of Study by Selected Background Charaters

Aspect of study	Type of University		Sex		Age group	
	Traditional	Professional	Male	Female	46 and below	47 and above
1	2	3	4	5	6	7
1. Goals and objectives of the library	11.38	11.44	11.48	11.16	11.53	11.24
2. Nature of job	12.79	12.56	12.84	12.59	12.84	12.69
3. Relationship with co-workers	12.81	13.39	13.01	12.51	13.11	12.61
4. Views on Management/Administration	9.35	10.61	9.44	9.59	9.72	9.24
5. Knowledge and initiative	11.28	13.11	11.45	11.53	11.57	11.37
6. Views on training programmes	8.21	9.11	8.46	7.9	8.39	8.21
7. Views on performance appraisal	9.56	10	9.49	9.86	9.74	9.45
8. Awareness about IT and automation	10.16	10.56	10.33	9.88	10.28	10.11
9. Use of computer & communication technology	7.53	8.72	7.83	7.2	8.01	7.27
10.Use of computer printing technology	3.78	4.33	3.86	3.78	4.1	3.56
11. Views on library networking	6.38	6.72	6.59	6	6.53	6.3
12. Knowledge on general procedures (service)	7.9	8.22	7.89	8.06	7.85	8.02
13. Knowledge on classification & cataloguing	9.26	10.39	9.28	9.61	9.61	9.13
14. Knowledge on computer applications	8.09	9.22	8.34	7.88	8.65	7.75
15. Total Score	124.6	131.67	126.14	123.35	127.28	123.31

Aspect of study	Professional qualifications		Designation		
	BLISc and below	MLISc and above	Cadre-I	Cadre-II	Cadre-III
1	8	9	10	11	12
1. Goals and objectives of the library	10.9	11.55	12.24	11.26	10.93
2. Nature of job	12.6	12.82	13.41	12.6	12.56
3. Relationship with co-workers	12.98	12.83	13.51	12.74	12.59
4. Views on Management/Administration	9.31	9.54	9.97	9.41	9.23
5. Knowledge and initiative	10.9	11.65	12.68	11.1	11.23
6. Views on training programmes	7.86	8.45	9.14	8.01	8.2
7. Views on performance appraisal	9.46	9.64	10.06	9.61	9.15
8. Awareness about IT and automation	9.74	10.35	10.95	9.92	10.14
9. Use of computer & communication technology	7.43	7.72	8.65	7.07	8.02
10.Use of computer printing technology	3.55	3.93	4.51	3.49	3.98
11. Views on library networking	6.19	6.49	7.22	6.05	6.5
12. Knowledge on general procedures (service)	7.76	7.99	8.7	7.78	7.61
13. Knowledge on classification & cataloguing	9.26	9.42	10.51	8.96	9.3
14. Knowledge on computer applications	7.74	8.36	9.51	7.45	8.68
15. Total Score	121.55	126.57	136.32	121.18	124.73

working and factors like age and sex have comparatively lesser influence.

Correlation between Background variables and the computed scores for different aspects of the study

In order to see whether the relation between the selected background variables and the scores computed for different aspects of the study are in expected direction or not. Pearson's correlation coefficients ('r' values) are computed and these were presented in Table 5.49.

Bivariate correlations were computed for the 15 scores and five background variables as shown in the table. For type of university, traditional universities were given a value of 1 and 2 is given for professional universities. For sex, males are given 1 and females 2. Age is taken as a continuous variable. For professional qualification groups, higher qualification group is given 1 and 2 is given for lower qualification group. For cadre, Cadre-1 is given 1, 2 for Cadre-2 and 3 for Cadre-3 the computed scores for the 15 aspects are taken as they are.

A careful observation of the values reveal that none of the 'r' values is nearer to even 0.5 which indicate very week relationship between the background variables and the aspects of study, although some of the values are statistically significant.

These values also indicate that Cadre, type of university, professional qualification and age are having some influence on the responses to the questions relating to the 15 aspects of study in the same order. Significant correlations were observed between cadre and 8 of the 15 study aspects. The negative sign is recorded because, the cadres are recorded as 1,2,3 from higher to lower. For example the first observation implies that knowledge on goals and objectives of the library decreases with increase in Cadre (i.e. from 1 to 3). In other words, those in Cadre-I will have better knowledge. In the same way type of university has shown significant relation with 3 of the 15 aspects, professional qualification with 2, age with 1 and sex with none of the study aspects.

In general, the observations do not show any deviation from the expected directions and can be said that the various aspects considered in the study are influenced mostly by the cadre in which they are working, type of university, professional qualification and age of the individual in that order.

Table 5.49: Pearson Correlation Coefficients (R Values)
(For scores on different aspects and selected background characteristics)

Scores on aspect of study	Type of University	Sex	Age	Professional qualification	Cadre
1 2	3	4	5	6	
01.Goals and objectives of the library	0.01	-0.076	-0.048	0.147	-0.234**
02. Nature of job	-0.039	-0.06	-0.026	0.053	-0.149
03. Relationship with co-workers	0.104	-0.131	-0.097	-0.036	-0.179*
04. Views on management/ administration	-0.213**	-0.038	-0.079	-0.054	0.138
05. Knowledge and initiative	0.282**	0.019	-0.016	0.162*	-0.236**
06. Views on Training Programme	0.154	-0.142	-0.008	0.141	-0.166*
07. Views on performance appraisal	0.015	0.123	-0.077	0.114	-0.154*
08. Awareness about IT and views on automaton	0.075	-0.124	-0.076	0.161*	-0.158*
09. Use of computer and communication technologies	0.149	-0.115	-0.13	0.052	-0.071
10. Extent of use of computer printing technology	0.119	-0.027	-0.142	0.115	-0.112
11. Views on library networking	0.055	-0.14	-0.06	0.069	-0.117
12. Knowledge on General procedures related to services	0.076	-0.062	0.073	0.077	-0.282**

13. Knowledge on classification and cataloguing	0.169*	-0.072	-0.085	0.032	-0.19
14. Knowledge on computer applications	0.133	-0.081	-0.217**	0.103	-0.09
15. Total Score	0.138	-0.08	-0.114	0.138	-0.235**

* Correlation is significant at the 0.05 level (2 tailed)
** Correlation is significant at the 0.01 level (2 tailed)

6

Summary, Conclusions and Suggestions

The Human resource component in industries and organizations is one of the important factors, which play a key role in achieving the objectives and goals of the organizations. The recent developments, particularly technology, is another factor, which influences both the human resources and the product. The people working in industries and organizations have to learn the latest developments in their area of interest from time to time in order to improve the quality of product. In such situations, the employees are to be assessed about their capabilities either by the superior or by himself. During this process, the capabilities and weaknesses of employees would be ventilated and the required changes could be suggested.

The objectives of university libraries made the professionals to improve their professional skills from time to time, in order to attend the information requirements of library users. So, learning the developments in information technology has become a continuous process for information storage, process and dissemination among library professionals.

The growth and development of universities and their libraries are significant during the post-independence period, due to the recommendations of various commissions and committees appointed for this purpose. Consequently, the University Grants Commission(UGC) was established in the year 1956, a body responsible for the development of universities and colleges in India.

In the present study, selected university libraries in Andhra Pradesh are grouped in to two, viz. traditional and professional. Out of the 13 university libraries selected, 10 fall in the category of traditional and the remaining 3 in professional category.

The UGC is providing annual grants to university libraries and supporting the libraries in many ways. The university libraries also get grants from university managements. All these efforts are made mainly to offer commendable information services to users in university libraries.

The importance of assessment of library services and programmes is realized in the recent past. The information requirements can be satisfied to the expectations of users with the application of the available information technology. Therefore, the library professionals should mould their attitude and come forward to equip themselves with the latest developments in information technology.

The Oxford Advanced Learner's Dictionary of Current English defines profession as "Occupation, one requiring advanced education and special training".

It is also defined as: "Concerned with the specialized knowledge and skills, and these attitudes, standards and values, which together contribute to competence in the conduct of our vocation".

Bayles suggests that there are three features to a profession-

(1) extensive training;

(2) a significant intellectual component;

(3) a trained ability that puts one in a position to provide an important service to society.

For every profession to have its impact on society, it must have an organized body, which has control over its field and clients.

There are many ways to assess the caliber of the professionals. According to Richard O. Mason, the main focus should be on two key areas, those are:

(1) Professionals possess specialized knowledge; and

(2) They use this knowledge in the service of others.

Most of the definitions on profession reveal reasonable importance to specialized knowledge and regular improvement of specialized skills. The professionals in library and information science should therefore, inculcate the habit of learning new knowledge and develop skills of IT from time to time.

One of the important elements of profession is 'code of ethics/professional behavior'. It must be guided by a code of professional ethics ordained by the professional group as a body and accepted by the professionals as their guiding principles so far as their professional performance and conduct are concerned.

In any profession the responsibilities are not static, so also in LIS profession. The prime responsibility of any profession is to respond positively to environmental change, which influences the behaviour of professionals. The LIS professionals should keep themselves concerned with the on-going developments and changes taking place in the profession.

Attitude is the most important factor in human life. It applies to every sphere of life, relating to one's personal or professional life. William James of Harvard University said, 'the greatest discovery of my generation is that human beings can alter their lives by altering their attitudes of mind". The foundation of success is being dependant on the personal attitude of the individual. There are three major factors, which determine the attitude - Environment, experience, and education.

Assessment means the process by which the grades are assigned to employees or library professionals in Library and Information Centers. Assessment is a mechanism for providing library professionals with data for improving their skills to achieve the goals and objectives of the library. In a way the assessment mechanism provides a feed back to both library staff and library administrators. In simple words, the process of collecting, synthesizing, and interpreting information to aid in decision making is called 'Assessment'.

Assessment is essential in order to develop standards in libraries to focus on goals and objectives of libraries, to monitor the quality of information services and products, to reward and award the professionals for their contribution, to identify the library staff for further training and in-service training, to understand the availability of alternatives, to assess professionals strengths and weaknesses, to provide professional with a clear understanding of job duties, to fairly evaluate competence of employees and to motivate employees to do their best.

Most of the libraries are facing problems like limited funds and limited human resources and at the same time the libraries have to offer a variety of services to the satisfaction of users. In order to meet this objective, the professionals need training on latest aspects in information technology. The standard of a library is rated, considering the quality of services offered. To improve the quality of services, the staff should be given training on latest developments in handling of information.

PERFORMANCE APPRAISAL AND LIBRARIES

Hayel defines Performance Appraisal as a "process of evaluating the performance and qualifications of the employees in terms of the requirements of the job for which they are employed, for the purposes of administration including placement, selection for promotions, providing financial rewards and other actions which require differential treatment among the members of a group as distinguished from actions effecting all members equally".

The reasons for implementing performance appraisal in libraries are - to enhance institutional climate of libraries, to facilitate the staff with in-service training periodically. It is necessary to improve the quality of service in the light of ever changing information services of libraries. In addition to this, the changes in information technology demands the librarian for in-service training and to share the experiences between the librarian and the staff and also understand the individual and institutional goals.

Functions of performance appraisal in libraries are - it should help the librarian to assess and understand the library professionals from time to time, it should meet the training requirements of library personnel particularly in the context of Information Technology, it should help the library professionals to know the bases for award of promotion and punishment and it should minimize the distance between the librarian and other library professionals which would help them to reach the goals of the library.

Performance appraisal method has certain limitations such as - lack of evaluation skills, technological changes, scarce resources, disregard for institutional goals and objectives, halo effect and personal bias & central Tendency

In view of the above mentioned limitations in application of performance appraisal and the little value it had in Indian Libraries in order to understand the services and activities in libraries, the only and best alternative is to apply the "Assessment Method".

ASSESSMENT METHODS AND LIBRARIES

The following are the some common and professionally accepted assessment methods: multiple choice, work simulation, key features/ case study, portfolio, self-Assessment, supervisor evolution and structured Interviews.

Self-Assessment is a method used continuously in the area of choice. In this method the employees have to assess themselves with their peers in order to stand in the main stream and help the organization to meet the set goals and objectives.

Self-Assessment is the basic part of any assessment. An institution evaluating its own activities should formulate its objectives and tasks, analyze its activities by applying different approaches which will reveal its actual problems and foresees the ways of resolving them.

Self-Assessment is used interchangeably with self-evaluation and self-study in the context of higher education quality. They all involve a process of self-reflection by the institution or sub-institutional unit being reviewed and the preparation of a document reflecting the self-reflection

The significance of Self-Assessment lies in the fact that - it provides the employee an opportunity to recapitulate, to identify his own development needs and plan for his development and to communicate to his reporting officer about his contributions, accomplishments, and reflections to enable him to view his performance in the right perspective and assess more objectively.

Steps in Self-Assessment are - employee reviews current job plan and development plan, employee receives and reviews any applicable multi-source feedback from other employees, customers or other feedback providers. For each focus area, the employee describes: what strategies were accomplished compared to planned; the performance measures results versus planned; what supervisor responsibilities were accomplished compared to planned; improvement opportunities focus area; any additional comments including any perceived barriers or extenuating circumstances to accomplishing the focus areas, strategies, performance measures, and supervisor responsibilities. Also include any relevant feedback from others. Based on the performance assessment, the employee makes a recommendation on his/her overall performance rating deserved.

Self-Assessment methods are in many forms, writing conferences; Discussion (whole-class or small groups) Weekly self-evaluations; Self-assessment checklists and inventories; Employee-supervisor interviews.

REVIEW OF LITERATURE

A review of earlier related literature is presented under three headings viz. performance evaluation, performance appraisal and self-assessment. Under each group, the reviewed articles are discussed chronologically in ascending order. Various methods of performance evaluation suitable to libraries are mentioned along with their limitations. The impact of information technology, the role of performance indicators were discussed to evaluate the library services. For performance evaluation in libraries, a set standards or guidelines are necessary. Superiors usually conduct the performance appraisal. It is understood that established standards are necessary to conduct performance appraisal in any organization. In the absence of set standards, there is no meaning to go performance appraisal, where, the self-assessment method will be the alternative to understand the issues relating to library services. In self-assessment method, the employees are attempt to understand themselves - whether they fit for the job or not.

OBJECTIVES OF THE STUDY

The main objectives of the present study are:

1. To find out the views of the library personnel on appraisal system in general and the appraisal procedure used in their libraries if any in particular.
2. To assess the professional activities and their areas of interest.
3. To understand the knowledge of the professionals on computer technology, printing and publishing technology and networking.
4. To understand the relations between professionals.
5. To understand strengths and weaknesses of professionals, and
6. To understand training needs of library professionals.

STUDY DESIGN AND METHODOLOGY

In the present study, 13 out of 17 university libraries in Andhra Pradesh (India) are covered. The four which were not covered are deemed universities and differ in some aspects with the other university libraries. The required information is gathered from a total of 215 professionals from the 13 university libraries using a carefully structured questionnaire. Out of the 215 professionals contacted only 172 have responded despite all efforts have been made for a complete coverage. The researcher visited all the universities personally to collect data from professionals. The reason for not able to get response from 43 professionals was their non-availability at the time of conducting survey or proceeded on leave. The data thus collected were analyzed by using software SPSS 12.0 version. The responses are analyzed and presented by university and also by selected background characteristics like age, sex, professional qualifications and cadre in which they are working. Suitable statistical methods are applied to draw conclusions.

OBSERVATIONS OF THE STUDY

The study is more in the form of self-appraisal to elicit information on extent of knowledge and extent of use etc., instead of whether the individual is having the knowledge or whether he is using a particular method. The information collected from respondents is recorded and presented in three-grade scale. The three grade responses were quantified by giving unit scores and the mean score computed for each of the aspect was study used to make comparison by selected background characteristics like type of university, sex, age, professional qualifications and cadre of employment.

Profile of the Respondents

Nearly 72 per cent of the respondents covered in the study are males and the remaining 28 per cent are females. Out of the 172 respondents, nearly 51 per cent are in the age group of 46 years or below. The younger age group is reported in 7 university libraries. It is interesting to note that a majority of library professionals(76 per cent) have post graduation in library and information science and higher level of educational back ground. About 53 per cent of the respondents are in cadre II which includes Library Assistants and Documentation Assistants and 26 per cent of the respondents are in cadre III which includes Technical Assistants and other professionals and 21 per cent are cadre I which includes Librarian, Deputy Librarian, Assistant Librarian and Documentation Officer.

Satisfaction of the respondents with the section they are currently working

It is obvious that 148 out of the 172 respondents are

quite satisfied with the section in which they are working at present and the remaining 24 have expressed their dissatisfaction and desire to work in other sections.

It is observed that, most of the respondents want to remain in the same section forever or for a long time is not an acceptable situation. If the staff is not made exposed to all kinds of activities in the library, it leads to a lot of dislocation in library routines in-future. Therefore, the staff should be rotated among various sections of the library, considering their interest and ability in order to improve their performance in meeting the goals of the library. In the absence of such rotation, the library will be forced to depend on an individual or a group for a particular activity, which is not advisable.

Membership in professional associations and library committees

The study reveals that, a majority of the respondents are having membership in professional associations. The association with professional bodies helps them to update their areas of knowledge through news letters, personal communications, etc., The members may develop leadership skills in their area of interest through their association with professional bodies which will encourage and increase commitment to create sharing, applying and improving their knowledge.

Usually the library committees are constituted with higher cadres of professionals like Librarian, Dy. Librarian, Assistant Librarian, Documentation Officer and the professionals of the lower cadres are not considered to be a part of library committee, for the reasons like short service, nature of job, their knowledge etc. Since the library committee is responsible to take decisions that would help the betterment of library, the knowledge of lower cadres may not be sufficient in this regard.

However, it is suggested that the lower cadre professionals should also be considered for the library committee, which will boost their commitment and responsibility towards library developmental activities.

Awareness of Performance Appraisal

The implementation of Performance Appraisal and to assess the performance of the employees is not in-practice in any of the libraries studied. It is interest to note that, most of the professionals have knowledge on performance appraisal and felt the need for performance appraisal for any award, reward, punishment, in-service training etc. Most of the respondents have expressed that, in the absence of performance appraisal, the talent and skills of the employees cannot be utilized effectively. Therefore, the respondents felt that, a kind of performance appraisal method should be used rather than depending merely on length of service for promotion, awards and rewards etc. Hence, it is suggested that, a suitable performance appraisal method should be evolved to assess the performance of the professionals to take appropriate decisions.

The professionals in higher cadres have expressed that, in the present situation, the appraisal by superior is not allowed due to administrative reasons. But majority of the employees, particularly in higher cadres felt the need for such assessment of staff at least by themselves in order to attend many of the problems that are not solved due to paucity of funds.

Knowledge and views on objectives and goals of the library

The study reveals that all most all (98 per cent) the respondents are aware of the goals and objectives of the library, which is a promising situation. If the professionals understand the goals and objectives of the library thoroughly, their commitment towards the library will be in a right direction.

It is reported that, 94 per cent of the respondents gave positive opinion regarding the extent of meeting the goals and objectives in their libraries. Since the respondents have knowledge on goals and objectives of the library, it would be easy for the management to drive the professionals towards the objectives and goals of the library. Only 27 per cent of the respondents have expressed that they have met the goals and objectives to a large extent. This situation indicate that a kind of assessment of employees is necessary in order to achieve the goals and objectives of the library by assigning right job to suitable persons in libraries, which in turn helps the improvement of information services qualitatively, and quantitatively.

Most of the respondents (83 per cent) in general reported that, the goals and objectives of the library are fulfilled beyond the stipulated targets. It is also evident that, only 16 per cent have felt that the targets as well as the goals and objectives of library are fulfilled beyond the stipulated target to a large extent. It indicates that the abilities and skills of the employees are not applied properly in the libraries studied. Therefore, suitable professionals should be placed at responsible positions considering their interest and abilities which is possible only through assessment of their performance.

A majority of the respondents (92 per cent) opined that the goals set for them are challenging enough to prove their ability in the routine work. It is suggested that, a kind of provision should be made for updating their knowledge to offer information services and products economically and efficiently.

On the other hand, a majority (91 per cent) of the respondents reported that the goals set for them are realistic and attainable. Among these, more than half (58 per cent) have expressed that the goals are realistic and attainable only to some extent. It indicates that the professionals are satisfied with the goals set for them by and large. Hence, it is suggested that the goals set for employees are to be reviewed from time to time. In such case, the assessment of performance of professionals also becomes necessary.

When sex, age, professional qualifications and cadre analyze this aspect, it is noticed that, nearly 70 per cent of the male and 65 per cent of the female respondents have reported knowledge of the goals and objectives of the library. This level of knowledge is further promising among the respondents belonging to cadre-I and among those who had higher professional qualifications.

Knowledge and perception of the Nature of Job

It is reported that, more than 78 per cent of the respondents have knowledge about their nature of work, which is a promising situation. If the staff have knowledge on their work, it would be easy to attain the stipulated targets and objectives of the library. Since most of them have knowledge on their nature of work and responsibilities, there is a need to understand their satisfaction level with the work, commitment and further interest. It is suggested that the professionals should be assessed on these lines for the improvement of libraries.

It is interesting to note that, nearly 75 per cent of the respondents have expressed that they are doing an important job or activity in libraries. Since the professionals themselves felt that they are doing an important job, it would be easy to motivate them towards achievement of the goals at a reasonable speed successfully. While motivating them with the task of their own preference, assessment of the professional is again necessary. Nearly 60 per cent of them have reported that there is a relation between their work and the work of other sections. It is necessary for all professionals to understand the relation between their work and that of other sections, in order to meet the goals set for the library. Most of the activities in the library are interrelated. Therefore, the staff should be aware of the relative importance of their work qualitatively and quantitatively. In this regard, the assessment method will definitely yield good results.

Nearly 96 per cent of the respondents are of the opinion that the jobs assigned for them should encourage initiative and originality. This is definitely a promising feature that helps in meeting the goals of the library qualitatively.

More or less the same proportion of respondents (94 per cent) expressed that the given job is clearly stated. Therefore, there is scope for the respondents to inculcate the attitude of attending the job with more commitment and dedication.

Relationship with Co-Workers

For achieving the goals and objectives of the library, a healthy relation among the professionals is one of the necessary factors. Nearly 97 per cent of the respondents have reported that they are maintaining good relations with their superiors. In such state, the libraries can achieve the goals and objectives put forth for them with ease. This kind of situation should be prevailed in all the libraries. It is interesting to note that, more than 98 per cent of the respondents have expressed that they are maintaining cordial relations with their sub-ordinates, while 97 per cent have expressed that they are maintaining, good relationship with peers. Nearly 98 per cent of the respondents felt that good teamwork and co-operation exists in their sections. Ninety eight per cent of the respondents reported that they take freedom to discuss their grievances with administration.

Discussion of these aspects reveals that the relations among professionals are promising and there is scope to improve the concept of teamwork and co-operation.

Views on Administration/Management

It is understand that, about 85 per cent of the respondents expressed that the library authority/ management protect the individual's professional interest. Out of these, 33 per cent expressed large extent and while 52 per cent expressed it is only to some extent. Therefore, the management of libraries should give importance to this aspect in order to boost the morale of professionals.

More than 98 per cent of the library professionals have reported that their immediate superiors have faith and confidence in their ability to do the work. It indicates that, the professionals have enough knowledge on the job assigned to them and they are meeting their stipulated requirements successfully. Such feeling develops needed confidence among them. Regarding the application of rules. half of the respondents have stated that, such application is average. Therefore, the library administration should develop a kind of confidence among their staff that the rules will be applied to all staff equally with no discrimination. The extent of individual's discussions about the doubts and problems related to their jobs with superiors is not promising, as more than 60 per cent are not able to approach their superiors for their problems related to the assigned job.

In order to overcome this problem, the superiors should organize meetings frequently and provide the employees an opportunity to express their problems. Another way is to encourage the subordinates to discuss their problems with superiors personally. Every superior must supervise continuously and regularly to reinforce whole part of the organization to avoid any difficulties at individual level itself and while doing so, they should not forget that, some workers get offended when their work checked. The superior should give an impression to sub-ordinates that, the reason for observing the job of the employees is for the betterment of library activities rather than a check.

Knowledge and Initiative

Awareness of the latest trends in library and information science is one of the important factors to meet the goals of the library. Nearly 94 per cent of the respondents have expressed positive in this regard. Forty five per cent have expressed moderate opinion on these areas. Therefore, there is an urgent need to encourage the staff to know about the latest developments in Library and Information Science profession.

Hence, it is suggested that the staff should be encouraged for short term and long term training or refresher courses, seminars, discussions etc. Only 27 per cent of the respondents have expressed that the available resources are enough to meet the targets given to the professionals while more than 67 per cent gave a moderate response indicating that the available resources are not up to the mark. Therefore, there is a need to review the adequacy of the available resources and infrastructure. Ninety eight per cent of the respondents have expressed that they have enough knowledge on administrative records. This situation helps the library staff to understand the problems as well as other issues that arise from time to time and to provide suitable solutions. The suggestions made to superiors by junior staff are accepted by and large. This type of situation develops congenial atmosphere and develops self-confidence among staff.

Responses regarding the implementation of suggestions made to superiors are average. In fact it is difficult and not necessary to consider all the suggestions made by the sub-ordinate, but the superiors should give an impression that the suggestions given by the subordinates are actively considered. This encourages them to apply their mind and come out with valuable suggestions some time or the other.

Superiors should also listen and take into account the opinions of their sub-ordinates; superiors must not undermine the authority of middle level employees in the eyes of their sub-ordinates.

Views on in-service training and performance

It is reported that nearly 95 per cent of the library professionals felt that in-service training is necessary for updating their knowledge, which helps them to meet the objectives of the library successfully. It is further reported that, nearly 70 per cent of the respondents were given such an opportunity through in-service training. The remaining 30 per cent of the respondents did not receive any in-service training, although they are aware of the necessity of in-service training. It is suggested that, the in-service training should be offered to all the staff at regular intervals. Nearly 54 per cent of the respondents have reported that they are deputed for training programmes outside the workplace. If the professionals were deputed to update their knowledge through in-service training elsewhere, the professionals get an opportunity to learn many things comparatively and these would help the library system.

Nearly 67 per cent of the respondents have expressed that they should be rewarded for their standard performance and punished for their sub-standard performance. It indicates the existence of a kind of competitive sprit among professionals. In such an environment, motivating the professionals towards meeting the library goals and adjusting to the latest changes becomes very easy.

There is a great change in Library and Information Science Profession after the advent of computers. The professionals are using technologies like computer technology, communication technology, storage of information and other technologies. The knowledge and operation skills in these areas are necessary to Library and Information Science Professionals. Hence, the LIS professionals should acquire technical skills, IT skills and managerial skills through in-service training programmes. The level of training programmes should be determined in accordance with the depth of the skills required in those libraries. Therefore, it is suggested that training should be a continual process in order to train the professionals with new ideas and practices through out their career.

Views on performance appraisal

Nearly 84 per cent of the respondents have felt that, there is the necessity of post appraisal developmental activities. The results of an appraisal system are effectively used in analyzing and categorizing the existing professionals in different career plateaus. These plateaus help us in undertaking different action plans required for professional's growth and development. More than 90 per cent of the respondents have felt that, potential appraisal has equal importance with Performance Appraisal. This suggests that , the professionals who are working with different nature of jobs have other potential skills which should be recorded and stored for further developmental use. This activity is known as potential appraisal. Post appraisal should be treated separately from the performance appraisal system and it's effectiveness will be determined by a number of factors, such as clarity of objectives, etc. Ninety three per cent of the respondents have reported that the performance appraisal ensures job oriented discipline in the organization. The performance appraisal method helps in job analysis, job evaluation, job description, which are key factors to motivate and encourage the professionals and their abilities successfully. All the respondents have expressed that the qualities like sincerity, honesty, commitment, initiative, etc. should be considered in the performance appraisal method. It indicates that, the job responsibilities of employees and the other qualities of professionals are two sides of the same coin. Therefore, these two areas are to be taken into account in performance appraisal.

Awareness of information technology and views on automation

More than 80 per cent of the respondents are aware of Information Technology and nearly 97 per cent are aware of library automation and house keeping activities. A significant proportion of respondents (93 per cent) have expressed their interest in acquiring knowledge on library automation from time to time. It is evident that, all the respondents have realized the importance of computer technology and its use in library operations. Since the respondents have positive attitude towards library automation and willing to learn the latest developments, it is not difficult to adopt the information technologies and reach the goals of the library with the available manpower and resources.

The impact of computer technology on libraries is significant and therefore, the awareness, knowledge, skills etc., on computer technology is necessary for library professionals. This technology helps the professionals in creating database for their collections and makes them available to users within the library as well as outside the library through networks. This technology has to be applied in four ways in libraries:

1. Library Automation;
2. Information storage and retrieval ;
3. Office automation; and
4. Resource sharing.

Ability to use computer and communication technologies

Regarding the use of computer and communication technologies, more than 71 per cent of the respondents have reported that they know the library software and database management of the library. Nearly 47 per cent of the respondents have reported that they have the ability to interact with library software packages for library housekeeping operations which means, they can attend to the problems of the software at least to a minimum extent instead of waiting for the system-administrator in the event of any problem. More than 70 per cent of the respondents have reported that, they have sufficient ability and skills to use electronic resources. It is a known fact that, the electronic resources are increasing in libraries, which have rich information and requires specialized skills to make use of them. Seventy two per cent of the respondents have reported that, they have knowledge in communication technology in Electronic Environment. Communication of information is very important and the professionals should have thorough knowledge in communication technology. With this knowledge, the professionals can transfer the information as well as receive and modify the information according to the requirements of the users.

Extent of use of computer printing technology

With regard to the use of computer and printing technology, 25 per cent of the respondents have reported knowledge on computer and printing technology to a large extent and 46 per cent had it to some extent. It indicates that, the professionals' knowledge and skills on computer and printing technology is not promising in University Libraries. In fact, the professionals in University Libraries should have a reasonable knowledge of these, to make use of the Printers, Desk Top Publishing, Page Makers, Electronic Publishing, LCD,VDU etc., Computers are also used for making reports and statements in libraries by the lower level staff. To satisfy the administration and user community, a variety of statements and reports have to be generated and it requires the skills of printing technology. Therefore, it is suggested that, the management should encourage the professionals in these libraries to learn the printing and publishing skills by conducting short-term training programmes preferably at their work place.

Knowledge and abilities to use network facilities

A majority of the respondents (86 per cent) have reported that their library is in a network. Out of these respondents, more than 66 per cent have reported that they have the capacity to transfer and download information through networks. It is a fact that, for several reasons, libraries are moving towards network environment. Since the library professionals are reported to have the required skills such as storage of information, management of information, dissemination of information etc., the benefits of networks could be exploited to the maximum extent. It is necessary to impart such training to all the library professionals for making effective use of networks.

It is observed that, nearly 85 per cent of the respondents are desirous of knowing the procedure for processing and supply of information through networks. In fact, it is an appealing feature which shows the interest of the professionals to go for latest technologies of networks for information handling and processing. Seventy six per cent of the respondents have reported that they know about University Grants Commission (UGC) Infonet. The Inflibnet is offering a good number of e-Journals on various disciplines to University Libraries. If the professionals have the capacity to use the facility available at UGC-Infonet, it definitely helps in satisfying the potential researchers with recent literature.

Knowledge on general procedure related to services

Almost all the respondents (99 per cent) have knowledge of the procedures followed for acquisition. Acquisition of a variety of materials is one of the important activities in any library. Different methods and procedures are followed for acquisition of books, electronic sources etc., It means that, all the respondents have the capacity to work in acquisition section. Nearly 96 per cent have reported that they have knowledge on accession register, which is an important record in libraries. The reason for lack of this knowledge among the remaining 4 per cent is that, they are not getting an opportunity to work in the acquisition section. About 97 per cent of respondents have enough knowledge on the procedures of circulation activities. In these days, most of the libraries are automating their circulation activities. The respondents have reported knowledge of traditional as well as modern methods of charging and discharging. In such a situation, the libraries can go for automation in circulation section and can develop a model for other libraries.

Knowledge on classification and cataloguing

Knowledge organization or library classification is one of the important activities in libraries. It is reported that, all the respondents have excellent knowledge on classification schemes used and cataloguing procedures followed in their libraries. The proportion of respondents, having knowledge of the latest developments in classification and cataloguing is also significant. Therefore, the implementation of latest edition of classification schemes and revised editions of cataloguing codes can be considered and initiated.

Knowledge of computer applications

Nearly 78 per cent of the respondents have knowledge regarding computer applications in acquisition section. Rest of the libraries are going for library automation by developing their own package or adopting commercial packages and it is observed that some of the University Libraries have already using a software package for various activities in libraries. If the professionals have basic knowledge of computer applications, Data Base Management etc., it would be possible to attend the quires like the list of books ordered by date wise, publisher wise, author wise and so on. With this facility, the user queries can be attended successfully. The level of knowledge of computer applications in circulation section, serial control and office management among the respondents is fairly good. Therefore, the library can make use of the skills possessed by these professionals in various sections for achieving the goals of the library as well as to advance technically and technologically also.

When the responses are quantified by using unit scores for each of the aspects and a final Total Score is computed, it is observed that, for almost all the aspects, the maximum and minimum mean total scores are recorded in the cadre groups. From the Correlation Co-efficient computed between mean scores and background characteristics of the professionals, it is noticed that the cadre of the professional, type of university, professional qualification and age group are having some influence on the responses to questions put under the 15 aspects including the total score of the study. The influence is also noticed to be in the same order of characteristics given above. In general, the observations made through the analysis are in the expected direction.

SUGGESTIONS

1. Rotation of professionals between different sections is necessary to avoid the dependency for a particular work by an individual or group.
2. The professionals should be encouraged to become members of professional bodies where they get an opportunity to exchange their ideas with other professionals working elsewhere.
3. Suitable Performance Appraisal method should be evolved to assess the performance of professionals and also to assign right job to right person.
4. Suitable training facilities be made available for updating their knowledge to offer information services and products economically and efficiently.
5. The professionals should know the latest

developments in Library and Information Science field.

6. The professionals should be encouraged to attend short term and long term training programmes, seminars, discussions etc.,
7. The professionals in supervisory cadres should appear that they are considering suggestions made by the sub-ordinates.
8. A kind of Post Appraisal method is also necessary.
9. While doing the assessment, the factors like sincerity, honesty, commitment, initiative etc., should be taken into account.
10. The professional staff should be aware of Computer Technology, Communication Technology and Network Technology and related aspects.
11. The professional staff should have reasonable printing and publishing skills in order to generate reports and statements according to the requirements.
12. The professional staff should be encouraged to attend workshops on library classification and cataloguing.
13. Standards for Academic Libraries be developed keeping in view of latest developments like information technology.

The Performance Appraisal is not being practiced in any of the libraries studied. It is also evident from review of literature. This concept is not applied in Indian Academic Library System. Still the Performance Appraisal concept is needed in academic libraries in one form or another for the following reasons;

1. Impact of Information Technology;

2. Human Resource;
3. Financial Constraints.

The development of Information Technology influencing the library activities particularly the information storage, processing and dissemination. To get the benefit of the Information Technology in libraries, the capacity of professionals should equally be understood. In most of the libraries, the recruitment process is almost stop. In such a situation, the library has to make use of the available Human Resources to satisfy the requirements of the users. In addition, the parent institutions are coming forward to meet the budgetary requirements of the libraries. Instead, the libraries are advised to develop their own mechanism to over come the problems. This problem can be successfully attended by implementing the facilities of Information Technology with the available professionals. Therefore, a kind of review, assessment and appraisal of professionals in libraries is become important and necessary.

Bibliography

Andhra Pradesh, State Council of Higher Education: *Profile of Higher Education, Andhra Pradesh*. Hyderabad, A.P.S.C.H.E., 2003.

Abbott, Andrew: Professionalism and the Future of Librarianship. *Library Trends*, 46(3), 1998, pp.430-443.

Aggarwal, J.C: *Landmarks in the history of Modern Indian Education*. Delhi, Vikas, 2002.

Aggarwal, Y.P: *Statistical Methods*, 2nd ed. New Delhi, Sterling, 1988.

Aina, J.O: Impact of Automation on the Performance of Library Staff in University Libraries in Nigeria. *Herald of Library Science*, 47 (1-2), 2002.

Airasian, Peter W: *Class Room Assessment*, 2nd Ed. New York, McGraw-Hill, 1994, p.436.

Ali, Amjad: University Libraries in the Current Perspective. *University News*, 39(48), 2001, pp.10-14.

Amrik Singh and Sharma, G.D. Ed: *Higher Education in India - The Institutional Context*. Delhi, Konark, 1989.

Anand, C.M and Sen, B.K: Manpower Development for Computer Applications to Library and Information Activities Role of INSDOC. *IASLIC Bulletin*, 36(4), 1991, pp.157-169.

Kakatiya University (Warangal): *Annual Report 2001-2002.*

Kakatiya University Press, 2002, pp.32-34.

Arun Monappa and Mirza and Saiyadain: *Personnel Management*, 2nd Ed. New Delhi, Tata McGraw-Hill, 2002.

Aschbacher, Pamela E: Writing for Assessment Programs. *Practical Assessment, Research and Evaluation*, 1(3). http://PARE online.net/getvn.asp?v?1 & n=3.

Ashok Babu, T: Modern Information Technologies, their Impact on Library Services. *Journal of Information, Library and Society*, 2(3-4), 1998, pp.12-15.

Ashrat, Tariq: New Information Environment: A Challenge for Librarianship. *University News*, 41(19), 2003, pp.9-15.

Association of University Teachers, Professional Accreditation of University Teaching. *AIU Bulletin* (Supplement) January,1996.

Baker, J: *Causes and Failures in Performance Appraisal and Supervision*. New York, Quorum, 1988.

Baston, Caro: The Concept of Formative Assessment, *Practical Assessment, Research and Evaluation*, 8(9)

Bayles, M.D: *Professional Ethics*, 2nd Ed. Belmont CA, Wordsworth, 1989

Besterfield, Dale H. et al.: *Total Quality Management*, 3rd Ed. New Delhi, Pearson Education, 2004.

Bhagoliwala, T.N: *Personnel Management and Industrial Relations*. Agra, Sahitya Bhavan, 1989.

Blumer, Herben: Preface in *Professionalization*, New Delhi, PHI, 1991.

Chopra, H.S.: *Information Marketing*. New Delhi, Rawat, 1996.

Chopra, R.: *Dictionary of Management*. 1st Ed. New Delhi

Anmol, 1990, pp.269.

Choudhury, N.G.: *Effective Management*. New Delhi, Orient Longman, 1988.

Cohen, L.R.: Performance Evaluation. *Library Trends*, 38(1), 1989.

Cohen, Lucy R.: Conducting Performance Evaluations. *Library Trends*, 38(1), 1989, pp.40-52.

Crawford, John: Reviewing a Programme of Evaluation in an Academic Library: the Case of Glasgow Caledonian University. *Performance Measurement* and Metrics, Vol.4(3), 2003, pp.113-121.

Dale, Ernest and L.C. Michelon: Modern Management Methods. Auckland, United Kingdom, Penguin, 1986.

Dessler, Gary: Human Resource Management, 7th Ed. New Delhi, Prentice-Hall of India, 1999.

Dharma Vira Aggarwal: Manpower Planning, Selection Training and Development. New Delhi, Deep and Deep, 1999.

Drucker, Peter F: *Management: Tasks, Responsibilities and Practice*. New Delhi, Allied, 1975.

Dwivedi, R.S: *Managing Human Resources: Personnel Management*. New Delhi, Galgotia, 1997.

Eldred Smith: Academic Status for College and University Librarian – Problems and Prospects. *CRL* (Jan 1970) pp.7-13.

Fisher, Maritin: *Performance Appraisal*. London, Kogan Page, 1995.

Good, S.P. and Sharma, C.L: *Outstanding Studies in University Librarianship*. Jaipur, RBSA Publishers, 1991.

Gopinath, M.A and Meera: Informatics and its use in Library Management as an area of specialization. *Library Science with a Slant to Documentation and Information Studies*, 28(3), 1991, pp.109-113.

Gopinath, M.A: "Humanizing Library and Information Services: Role of the Library Profession". *Library Science with a Slant to Documentation and Information Studies*, 29(4), 1992.

Gupta, K. Dinesh: "Quality Management in Library and Information Services". *ILA Bulletin*, 36(2), 2000, pp.52-55

Gupta, K. Dinesh: Quality .Management in Library and Information Services - Is Ranganathan Revisited?. *ILA Bulletin*, 36(2), 2000, pp.52-55.

Haimann, Theo: *Management: Theory and Practice*, 2nd Ed. New Delhi, S. Chand & Co., 1976.

Sri Krishna Devaraya University (Ananthapur): Sri Krishna Devaraya University Colleges, Anantapur Hand Book, 2004. Ananthapur, SKDU Press, 2004.

Hannabuss, Stuart: "Library Performance and Evaluation". *Aslib Information*, 17(2), 1989, pp.43-44.

Henderson, R.: *Performance Appraisal: Theory and Practice*. New Delhi, PHI, 1980.

Hilton, Robert C: Performance Evaluation of Library Personnel. *Special Libraries*, 69(11), 1978, pp.429-434.

http:// www. mazemaster.on.ca.

http:// www.hull.ac.uk/ctls/educlib/edulib.html.

http://staff web.library.north westerm.edu/assembly/pesa.html.

http://www.lboro.ac.uk/library/objectives.html

Hughes, G.C: "The Information Age". *Asian Libraries*, 1(1),

1991, pp.29-32.

Ifidon, Sam E: "The evaluation of Performance". *Libri*, 36(3), 1986, pp.224-239.

Dr. B.R Ambedkar Open University Library (Hyderabad): *Information Brochure*. Hyderabad, Dr. B.R.Ambedkar Open University, 2004.

Insko, C.A: *Theories of Attitude Change*. New York, Appleton Century-Crofts, 1967.

Issac, K.A: *Professional Development of Libraries*. New Delhi, Ess Ess Publications, 1991.

Ives, J. David: "Staff Empowerment and Library Improvement through Networking". *Journal of Education for Library and Information Science*, 36(1), 1995, pp.47-51.

Jagga Rao and Das, R.P.: "HRM Lapses in University Administration". *University News*, 39(2), 2001, pp.1-4.

Jordon, P: *Staff Management in Library and Information Work*, 1st Ed. Mumbai, Jaico, 1996.

Kaul, P.N: Role of Information Services in Modern World. *Herald of Library Science*. 18(1-2), 1979, pp.9-18

King, Geraldine, B.: "Performance Appraisal in the automated environment". *Journal of Library Administration*, 13(1-2), 1990, pp.195-205.

Kumar, P.S.G.: "Library Manpower Development: a Case Study of Nagpur University LIS Department". *Journal of the Delhi Library Association*, 25(2-3), 1986, pp.88-89.

Lantz, B.: "Staff Training for Information Technology". *Journal of Academic Librarianship*, 2(1), 1987, pp.44-64.

Leysen, J.M and Black, W.K: "Peer Review in Carnegie

Research Libraries". *College and Research Libraries,* 59(6), 1998, pp.512-22.

Linn, Robert L.: "Assessment and Accountability Practical Assessment". *Research and Evaluation,* 7(11).

Mahapatra, P: *The Computers in Library Services.* Calcutta, The World Press, 1985.

Mahapatro, M and Ramesh, D.B: *Information Technology Applications in Libraries: A Text book for Beginners,* 1st Ed. Bhubaneswar, ReproPrint, 2004.

Malaisamy, T.K: Information Technology in Library Management and Education. *IASLIC Bulletin,* 43(1), 1998, pp.27-31.

Mamoria, C.B and S.V. Gankar: *Personnel Management,* 23rd Ed. New Delhi, Himalaya, 2003.

Martin, M.S: The Changing Library Environment. *Library Trends,* 42, 1994, pp.476-486.

Mason, Richard O: "What is an Information Professional?". *Journal of Education for Library and Information Science,* 31(2), 1990, p.122.

Masoom Raza, M and Anita Gupta: Job Satisfaction and Job Anxiety among Library Professional Employees Working in Delhi: University Library System. *IASLIC Bulletin,* 45(3), 2000, pp.129-134.

McGuire, W.J.L: Nature of Attitude and Attitude Change. In G.Lindzey and E.Aronson(Eds.) *Hand Book of Social Psychology.* 2nd Ed. Reading Mass, Addison-Wesley, 1968.

Mittal, R.L.: *Library Administration - Theory and Practice.* Simla, Himachal Pradesh University Press, 1978.

Mohanty Jagannath: *Current Trends in Higher Education.* New Delhi, Deep & Deep, 2000.

Mohsin, S.M: *Attitude Concept, Formation and Change.* New Delhi, Wiley Eastern, 1990

Monga, M.L: *Management of Performance Appraisal.* Mumbai, Himalaya, 1997.

Nelavigi, Savitha, M: Performance Evaluation of Library Professionals: Need and Criteria. *SRELS Journal of Information Management*, 40(1), 2003, pp.23-29.

Odini, Cephon: The Management of Change in a Library Science. *Library Review*, 39(4), 1989, pp.8-20.

Osif, B.A. and Harwood, R.L: Performance Appraisal. *Library Administration and Management*, 10(3), 1996, pp.176-81.

Ostrom, T.M: The Relationship between the Effective, Behavioral Cognitive Components of Attitude. *Journal of Experimental Social Psychology*, 5 (12-30), 1969.

Patkar, V.N: Information Technology Adoption by Libraries: Opportunities and Barriers. *Information Studies*, 6(2), 2000, pp.125-138.

Philip Kotler: *Marketing Management*, 11th Ed. New Delhi, Pearson, 2005.

Potti Sreeramulu Telugu University: *Potti Sreeramulu Telugu University Library - A Profile.* Hyderabad, Telugu Bhavan Complex, 2002.

Prakash, Jaya A. and Ramanaiah: Management of Change for Quality Improvement in Library and Information Centres. *University News*, 39(46), 2001, pp.11-14.

Prasad, Z.M: *Principles and Practice of Management*, 6th Ed. New Delhi, S. Chand & Co., 2001.

Praveen Kumar, Kumbargoudar: Application of Artificial Intelligence Techniques to Library and Information Science. *University News*, 37(49), 1999, pp.20-26.

Prodhan, Sribatscs: Benchmarking: Its Need and Applications in Libraries. *University News*, 36(36), 1998, pp.11-13.

Sri Padmavati Mahila Viswa Vidyalayam (Tirupati): *Prospectus of Sri Padmavati Mahila Viswa Vidyalayam, Tirupati*. Tirupati, Sri Padmavati Mahila Viswa Vidyalayam, 2003.

Raina, Roshan: Total Quality Management in Library and Information Services. *University News*, 1995.

Raju, J.S: Information handling as a Profession-Current Trends and Emerging Opportunities. *International Information Communication and Education*, 12(2), 1993, pp.221-6.

Ranganathan, S.R: *Library Administration*. Bangalore, Sarada Ranganathan Endowment, 1989

Rao, T.V and Pareek Udia: Performance Appraisal and Review. *Operating Manual*, New Delhi, Learning System, 1978.

Rao, T.V: 360 *Degree Feedback and Performance Management System*. New Delhi, Excel, 2003

Rao, T.V: *Appraising and Developing Managerial Performance*. New Delhi, Excel Books, 1999.

Rao, T.V.: *Human Resource Development*. New Delhi, Sage, 2000.

Rao, T.V: *Performance Management and Appraisal System*, 1st Ed. New Delhi, Sage, 2004.

Rao, T.V: *Re-designing Performance Appraisal System*. New Delhi, Tata McGraw Hill, 1990.

Rao, V.S.P. and Narayana: *Principles and Practice of Management*, 1st Ed. New Delhi, Konark, 1987.

Roeber, Edward D: *Guidelines for the Development and Management of Performance Assessments*. 5(7), 1998.

Sahai, Shrinath: *Academic Library System*. New Delhi, Allied, 1990.

Saiyadain, M.S: *Human Resources Management*, 3rd Ed. New Delhi, Tata McGraw Hill, 1988.

Sansaawal, D.N: Technology and Higher Education. *University News*, 38 (46), 2000, pp.1-6.

Saroj, Pandey: Managing Quality through Teacher Appraisal. *University News*, 36(27), 1998, pp.1-4.

Schuman, H. and Johnson, M.P: Attitudes and Behaviour. *Annual Review of Sociology*, 2(161-207), 1976.

Sen, Aloke, K: *Human Resources: Planning and Development (Public Sector Perspective)*, 1st Ed. New Delhi, Asian Books, 2003.

Singh, Mahavir and Gautam, J.N: Motivation and Job involvement - A Study. *Library Herald*, 32 (3-4), 1995, pp.156-165.

Singh, Mahavir and J.N. Gautam: Motivation and Job involvement – A Study. *Library Herald*, 32(3-4), 1995, pp.157-160.

Smith, P.C and Kendal, L.M: Retranstation of Expectations: An Approach to the Construction of Unambiguous Anchor for Rating Scales. *Journal Applied Psychology*, Vol.31, 1996, pp.838-88.

Souvenir, 47th All India Library Conference–2001, University Library, Kakatiya University, Waramga, Andhra Pradesh, 2001.

Sridhar, M.S: Skill Requirements of Library Professionals in the Electronic Environment of Twenty First Century. *Information Technology in Libraries: A Text book for*

Beginners, 2004, pp.597-605.

Subba Rao, P: *Essentials of Human Resource Management and Industrial Relations: Text Cases and Games.* Mumbai, Himalaya, 1999.

Tedd, Lucy, A: *An Introduction to Computer Based Library System.* 2nd Ed. Vol.3, New York, John Wiley, 1984, p.92.

Tejomurthy, A: *Studies in Academic Librarianship.* Jaipur, Printer, 1987.

Thornton, Steve: Two Years of Impact Assessments. *Performance Measurement and Metrics,* 1(3), 2000, pp.141-156.

Trivedi, R.S: Performance Appraisal of Teachers. *University News,* 30 (20), 1992, pp.10-12.

University Grants Commission: *University and College Libraries - Report of the Library Committee.* New Delhi, University Grants Commission, 1965.

University Newsletter, A Nagarjuna University Publications, Nagarjuna Nagar, Andhra Pradesh, July-Sep 2002.

Varalakshmi, R.S.R: Measurement of College Library Performance: An Evaluative Study with Standards. *International Information and Library Review,* No.35, 2003, pp.19-36.

Varalakshmi, R.S.R: Professional Challenges: Need for Attitudinal Changes among Librarian. *University News,* 37(11), 1999, pp.12-14.

Vegan, R: New Dimensions in Management of Academic Libraries. *University News,* New Delhi, 38(14), 2000, pp.4-9.

Vengan, R: New Dimensions in the Management of Academic Libraries. *University News,* 38(14), 2000, pp.4-9.

Venkataraman, C.S and Srivastav, A.D: *Personnel Management and Human Resources*. New Delhi, Tata McGraw-Hill, 1997.

Viswanathan, C.G: *University Libraries of India – Principles and Policies*. New Delhi, Concept, 1990.

www. Engineering studies.com/info/JNTU.htm.22k.

www. prefmtg.com/terms.htm

www.atz.org/Resources/Glossary.asp

www.question mark.com/UK/glossary.html

WWW.Wcer.Wisc.eder/archive/cl./flag/start/primer 2.html.

Xavier, P. Francis: Time Management: Personnel Management. *University News*, 35(29), 1997.

Index

❑❑❑